THE PLOT TO
CHANGE AMERICA

THE PLOT TO CHANGE AMERICA

How Identity Politics Is
Dividing the Land of the Free

MIKE GONZALEZ

Encounter
BOOKS

New York • London

First American edition published in 2020 by Encounter Books,
an activity of Encounter for Culture and Education, Inc.,
a nonprofit, tax-exempt corporation.
Encounter Books website address: www.encounterbooks.com

Manufactured in the United States and printed on
acid-free paper. The paper used in this publication meets
the minimum requirements of ANSI/NISO Z39.48-1992
(R 1997) (*Permanence of Paper*).

FIRST AMERICAN EDITION

LIBRARY OF CONGRESS CATALOGING-IN-PUBLICATION DATA

Names: Gonzalez, Mike, 1960– author.
Title: The plot to change America : how identity politics is dividing the
land of the free / by Mike Gonzalez.
Identifiers: LCCN 2019058983 (print) | LCCN 2019058984 (ebook)
ISBN 9781641771009 (cloth) | ISBN 9781641771016 (ebook)
Subjects: LCSH: Identity politics—United States. | United States—Social
conditions—1960–1980 | United States—Social conditions—1980–
Social change—United States.
Classification: LCC HN65 .G595 2019 (print) | LCC HN65 (ebook)
DDC 306.0973—dc23
LC record available at https://lccn.loc.gov/2019058983
LC ebook record available at https://lccn.loc.gov/2019058984

To Jack, Saskia, and Rafe

Contents

Introduction

Identity politics is all around us. Whether you know it or not, we are all bathing in it. Some Americans have embraced it gladly, while others have simply become inured to it and no longer bat an eyelid. Many others, however, have begun to take notice, and to them something does not seem right.

If you are one of the latter, you raise an eyebrow when the principal at your daughter's school repeats the incantation "diversity is our strength!" and you hear that some subjects, even math, are taught differently depending on a student's race. You think of Orwell—"War Is Peace," "Freedom Is Slavery." But you understand why parents don't put up a fuss. Who wants to get on the wrong side of the principal by explaining to her that, in fact, we can observe in the laws of physics, and in the social sciences, that it is unity that forges strength? Who wants to tell her that two plus two always equals four no matter what your race is? Likewise, at the office, when the head of HR asks you to place a sign on your desk that reads, "I'm an ally!" you stifle the urge to wisecrack, "Why? Are we at war?" It's the head of HR, after all. Again, you understand why so many of your colleagues put the darn sign on their desk, and you refrain from asking about rumors that another session is afoot to uncover employees' subconscious bias.

Back at home, when the talking head on TV spends the first ten minutes of airtime discussing all the identity groups that the newly elected dogcatcher belongs to, you want to snap back, "Who cares? Can she catch strays?" Only crazy people talk to the TV, however. But you do talk back when the next news item is about a father who has lost custody of his seven-year-old son because he disagrees with his estranged wife, who wants the boy to "transition" into a girl. Later that evening, when your own son, who is applying to college, announces he will identify as Hispanic because your mother's father was born in Monterrey, your first reaction is to tell him, "but I never even met Grampa Ortiz." On second thought, it might get Jimmy into Cornell, so you repress the unease you feel about gaming the system. You also feel relieved that, if he's no longer considered white, at least he won't be made to feel at fault for everything. At the same time, it will sting your neighbor deeply when he finds out that his small company did not get the city contract. He couldn't produce a narrative of oppression, and someone else got the contract through a set-aside program. His mother's father was born in Salerno, and after immigrating was repeatedly beat up by rough Irish kids in Boston. But that doesn't do your neighbor any good, since Italians are not one of the designated oppressed minorities.

Or say you're an immigrant from Peru's port of Callao. You came to New York in the 1970s, settling in Queens with dreams of becoming American and one day having American children, the same as other Americans. Soon after your arrival, however, you heard people on TV saying that you were now a third thing, a *Hispanic*, and you should be proud of belonging to this category. Joining the American mainstream was an unattainable goal, said these loud people, and you shouldn't aspire to it, anyway. America is a racist place, they went on, and if you wanted to have a measure of success, you had to join this massive new ethnic collective. All this disturbed you somehow, even if you could not articulate why. Decades later, it dawns on you that you had been enlisted into a struggle to overturn the very country and system that had attracted you to emigrate in the first place, and you are not happy about this.

In all these small and large ways, identity politics has become the operating system of our national hardware. As with war, even if you are not interested in it, identity politics is interested in you.

This Book

But what is identity politics, anyway? In a Twitter exchange on this question with *Vox* Media reporter Jane Coaston last year, I took a stab at defining the term: "I mean the deliberate creation of pan-ethnic and other identity groups; the idea that members of this panoply of collectives should get compensatory justice; the culture of victimhood all of this engenders." Twitter's character limits force us to cram complicated ideas into pithy epigrams, and in my tweet I tried to concisely present the main elements of what has become an ideology of our times. The purpose of this book is to explain how and why these elements came together, who was behind the ideology's rise, and what we can do about it.

Many theories have been put forward to explain how this ideology was suddenly sprung on America. They cover the gamut, from the demise of the family, to the erosion of social capital in many working-class neighborhoods, to the absence of a unifying enemy following America's victory in the Cold War.[1] What follows in this book is a more-or-less-chronological account of the rise of identity politics, put in the context of the doctrines and philosophies that fed into it, and discussion of its impact on the American system and the threat it poses to the liberties that sustain the American way of life. We have identity politics today because our government has created ethnic and sexual categories whose members have been instilled with resentments against the country and its system and given real financial benefits for nursing their grievances. Insisting on group grievances thereby perpetuates the identity groups. If we stop this vicious cycle, we may be able to free ourselves from the grip of identity politics.

The book traces the origins of identity politics to the late 1960s and 1970s, when the white establishment panicked over the black riots then tearing up parts of northern cities. This panic led to two main outcomes. First, members of the establishment offered "temporary" racial benefits to pacify Northern blacks, who had seen fewer advances than their Southern counterparts during the civil rights era. Second, they accepted the assertion by leftist activists claiming to mediate on behalf of other groups that there was an analogy to be made between the suffering of blacks and the experiences of Americans of Mexican, Chinese, Puerto Rican, Japanese, Filipino, and other descents. This analogy, which was also extended to women as a group, was drawn over and over. It was, of course, dishonest and deceitful: the experience of black Americans was in fact unique. Nevertheless this way of thinking led in time to such absurdities as immigrants fresh off the boat receiving "compensatory justice" for the real and imagined suffering of their ancestors. Racial preferences also never went away, but more than half a century later have become a fixture of American life, and keep being expanded. As this book further demonstrates, activists of those earlier decades sought to move the country away from its limited-government traditions inherited from the Anglo-Scottish Enlightenment toward the centralized state planning drawn from the Continental Kantian, Hegelian, and Marxian worldviews.

Stated plainly, my goal is to change how the nation thinks about identity politics and identity groups. We do not have to accept these categories, the discourses of "privilege" and "victimhood," or politically loaded (and recent) terms such as "minorities," "diversity," and "persons of color." Rather, I seek to snap the country out of its identity trance by exposing the actors, their actions, how they came up with these terms, and the theories that led us to this juncture. The identity collectives have done nothing to alleviate the very real racial discrimination and social injustice that continues to exist in America—nor were they intended to do so—but have only exacerbated them. As we will see in the chapters to follow, many of the actors who first sought to transform America through identity politics in the 1960s believed that Americans (whether Mexican Americans, European ethnics, or WASPS—the only exception perhaps being northern blacks) were too contented and too confident in the ownership of their fate, and that such complacency got in the way of revolutionary transformation.

The book is divided into two parts. The four chapters of part 1 describe how the main ethnic and sexual categories were created. In part 2, chapters 5, 6, and 7 explain the ideological basis for such category creation; chapter 8 concludes the book by offering policy and political solutions for ending identity politics. Although the book does tell a comprehensive tale, with cross-references to topics and personalities in other chapters, each chapter can also stand alone, and the reader pressed for time can pick and choose which to read.

Identity politics did not become our cultural and increasingly corporate and legal operating system by chance. It took concerted effort to insinuate this worldview into our lives, hence my emphasis in the concluding chapter on the hard work needed to undo it. To succeed, we must first understand identity politics' genesis and purpose. And if we fail, we will live out Reagan's warning of one day having to explain to our grandchildren how liberty was lost.

The Threat of Identity Politics

And what if we do get stuck with identity politics? The best-case scenario would be the implementation in America of corporatism, a system under which interest groups control the state and settle their intergroup disputes through constant negotiations. Though it may sound benign, this least bad outcome would be inimical to the liberties traditionally associated with the American way of life.

The more likely, and much worse, outcome would be the extinguishing of our freedoms. A particularly dangerous component of identity politics is the coercive diversity to which we must all pay lip service today. This is decidedly *not* the inclusive melting-pot idea that Americans come from many different lands but are united in a common cause. In fact, our children are now taught that this ideal is abhorrent. The new diversity is its opposite: it is the idea that America is divided into semiautonomous, formal, and cohesive subgroups that have distinct outlooks, aspirations, privileges, and rights. Every classroom, factory floor, and corporate or government office must reflect the proportion of certain groups—racial, ethnic, sexual— in the nation as a whole, and if that does not happen organically, then the people in charge must take positive, that is, compulsory, action to ensure that it does. The only way to attain the right mix is by choosing some over others on the basis of race, sex, or sexual orientation. This new America ceases to pursue the aspirational standard of equality set by the founders, a standard the nation long failed to live up to but that made possible the achievements of Lincoln and Martin Luther King. America becomes instead something closer to the Ottoman Empire, under which each confessional or ethnic community (the Armenians, the Arabs, the Jews, etc.) abided by its own laws, with independent courts, or millets. The idea that a multiethnic

America has common purposes, epitomized by the motto *E Pluribus Unum*—suggested in 1776 to the Continental Congress by the Swiss-born American patriot Pierre Eugene du Simitiere, and meaning "out of many, one"—decomposes into multiculturalism, *de uno, multis*. American millets to follow.

This is the hidden, and ugly, truth behind the programmatic incantations about diversity from the principal at your daughter's school. One problem is that, while compensatory justice may sound reasonable and moral, this supposed remedy violates some of America's most cherished principles, such as equal treatment under the law, the right to private property, freedom of speech, and many others. "Social justice," for example, requires the redistribution of resources to members of identity groups simply because of their membership in these groups. When diversity of race becomes the lodestar by which we must all navigate our lives, diversity of views ceases to exist: if we must all pay homage to the diversity of identity politics, then dissent disappears. Another example is the suppression of speech that the gatekeepers of identity politics label as hateful. Hate speech is in the eye of the beholder, not to mention that the First Amendment makes no exception for whatever might be subjectively defined as such; the British viewed the ideas of the Patriots of 1776 as hateful, as did the Southern segregationists view the ideals of the civil rights movement.

What we are facing, as I suggested in the tweet mentioned above, is the division of society into subnational groups along identities that can be based on race, ethnicity, sex, sexual orientation, gender identity, and even disability status. What matters here is the ability to claim oppression. Only one narrow group is not allowed to claim it: heterosexual, able-bodied, white males. Anyone with these characteristics is the enemy: because he has unfair "privilege" as a member of a "dominant" group, he has to stop speaking and atone for the imputed wrongs of his ancestors. (Like Emmanuel Goldstein in Orwell's *1984*, he exists to be hated.) His only option is to become an "ally" of the victims his kind has supposedly oppressed. Indeed, at the height of the hysteria over the nomination of Brett Kavanaugh as a justice of the US Supreme Court, Senator Mazie Hirono of Hawaii sputtered on TV: "I just want to say to the men in this country: Just shut up and step up!"

Although the white male, especially the white male Christian, is constantly said to be privileged, he is in fact habitually ridiculed in entertainment, the news, and academia, and is at a *dis*advantage when it comes to the division of spoils. Any narrative that purportedly advances white males' well-being—what professors of grievance studies call "the hegemonic narrative"—must be crushed and replaced with the counternarrative. The speed with which it has become acceptable to demand that all members of a supposed group—never mind that it's ridiculous to lump all white men into a single, homogeneous group—permanently don sackcloth and ashes is bewildering. Identity as a member of any other group, however, confers a claim to victimhood, which has been elevated above individual accomplishment as the wellspring of self-worth and recognition.

There is also an obverse side to this process that can be even more pernicious, and it goes completely unnoticed. It never dawns on the purveyors of these notions that their efforts could have the opposite effect of what they say they intend. By ascribing all these supposed privileges to the white, Christian, heterosexual male, the purveyors of identity politics are endowing him with almost superhuman qualities. To insist that all others are disfavored victims is to mentally subjugate them.

Self-image and self-esteem are powerful motivators, affecting our chances of success or failure. To be told that someone who "looks like you" has built-in structural advantages can have the unintended consequence of inducing the type of self-confidence that builds on itself; to be told that someone who "looks like you" faces structural disadvantages can instill self-doubt and encourage you to nourish grievances. Consider the matter this way: what the purveyors of identity politics are pushing is a new version of noblesse oblige. This version is disfigured, shorn of its volitional and virtuous aspects, but it is still the case that the burdens of noblesse oblige can fall only on those of a noble caste. Conversely, to feel a victim can only be demoralizing. Nobody can rescind the natural instinct that victims are pitiable. This can never be the path to equality.

In fact, equality has become almost a dirty word: the goal of social justice warriors isn't equality but the more ambiguous concept of "equity." The woke millennial male who asserts that "someone who looks like me" should behave with humility makes an (often unwarranted) assumption about what others think of him based on his looks; this expectation has been drilled into him by ideologues who, ironically, wanted to take him down a peg or two. Likewise, those who go around in search of racial or sexual slights are setting themselves up for a lifetime of grief, much if not most of it self-inflicted. In exchange for the benefits they receive for being one of the "oppressed"—the university admissions, the city contracts, and so on—they are trading in individual agency, pride, and success. If ever there was a Faustian bargain, this is it. We are all living in this victimhood culture today. This is the way our world is organized.

This is not to say that all activists' motives were impure—no doubt some sought to alleviate the effects of discrimination. But whatever the intentions of some, many others from the start intended to divide the country into groups as a strategy to change America completely. In academia, the philosophical movement known as critical theory tries to replace the white, Western, patriarchal hegemony with a counterhegemony (your college student son or daughter may very well be immersed in such talk as you read this), using scorched-earth tactics to destroy everything in its path. Whatever good intentions once existed among those applying critical theory in various disciplines have since morphed into a full-frontal attack on the Enlightenment tradition of liberal democracy. (The intellectual roots of this attack are explored in chapter 5.) Hence, it is no exaggeration to call this book *The Plot to Change America*.

If you are one of those people who is already alarmed by all these developments, who seethes when you hear the words "cultural appropriation" and bristles at the mention of "subconscious bias," this book is for you. It will confirm that your alarm is justified, but it will also give you a granular understanding of the process that got us into this mess and offer a way out. If you are just starting to question all these developments, and whether you call yourself conservative or liberal, Democrat, Republican, or independent, this book is for you, too. It pulls back the curtain on identity politics, explaining the myths that keep it in place and its consequences for our society.

A Liberal Crusade, Too

Many of identity politics' biggest critics are old-style liberals—academics and writers like Steven Pinker, Helen Pluckrose, Andrew Sullivan, Claire Lehmann, and Dave Rubin. Chapter 7 examines some of their critiques. They may want more government spending and eschew the social conservatism of movement conservatives, but they grasp the importance of the liberties and rights that are being crushed. The fight against identity politics, it is important to note, has nothing to do with conservatism or Donald Trump, despite what those who want to maintain the status quo pretend. In 2018, Pinker, an evolutionary psychologist who teaches at Harvard and who could never be called a conservative, told the *Weekly Standard*, the now-defunct conservative magazine:

> Identity politics is the syndrome in which people's beliefs and interests are assumed to be determined by their membership in groups, particularly their sex, race, sexual orientation, and disability status. Its signature is the tic of preceding a statement with "As a," as if that bore on the cogency of what was to follow. Identity politics originated with the fact that members of certain groups really were disadvantaged by their group membership, which forged them into a coalition with common interests: Jews really did have a reason to form the Anti-Defamation League.
>
> But when it spreads beyond the target of combatting discrimination and oppression, it is an enemy of reason and Enlightenment values, including, ironically, the pursuit of justice for oppressed groups. For one thing, reason depends on there being an objective reality and universal standards of logic.[2]

As Uri Harris wrote in *Quillette* in 2019, most of the thinkers now characterized as belonging to the emerging online group known as the "Intellectual Dark Web" (IDW) are pro-abortion, favor policies that curb gun rights, support same-sex marriage, and support policies to address man-made climate change. In other words, they are left-of-center liberals. What brings them together is an understanding that identity politics threatens their values, too. The IDW, Harris writes, "includes many people who don't think of themselves as being on the right, but who nevertheless find common ground with conservatives in opposition to the 'new' left, with its focus on identity and structural oppression."[3]

If you are, then, a liberal who is starting to wonder where all of this is going, you will want to know how it all began. This book explains how myths about identity politics are designed to conceal coercive means to transform America from a culture that values the work ethic and individualism to one that stresses group privileges, as individual natural rights are swept away in a headlong rush to collectivism.

This book is not all gloom and doom, however: it shows that reversing course can be done. America does not need to be transformed; there is always room for improvement, of course, but reforms must be achieved while conserving the core elements that have given Americans historically unprecedented levels of liberty and prosperity. There is a way out, and the time is ripe for taking it. More than at any other time since the country started heading down this path in the 1960s and 1970s, Americans are beginning to sense that something is wrong. Without being too wonky, this book explains how the plot to change America can be defeated.

The Myths of Identity Politics

To achieve that end, the most urgent tasks are to expose myths, reveal what really has happened, explain why it is urgent to change course, and offer a strategy to do so. Though we should not fool ourselves into thinking it will be easy to eliminate identity politics, we should not overthink it, either. Identity politics relies on the creation of groups, and then on giving people incentives to adhere to them. If we eliminate group making and the enticements, we can get rid of identity politics. Explaining all this is this book's main goal.

The first myth to expose is that identity politics is a grassroots movement. The fact is that, from the beginning, it has been—and continues to be—an elite project. For too long, we have accepted the fairy tale that America grew organically into the nation gripped by victimhood and identitarian division that it is today, that it is all the result of legitimate demands by minorities for recognition or restitution for past wrongs. Another myth is that identity politics responds to the demographic shifts this country has undergone since the 1965 Immigration Act, which ended the national origins quota system that had served as the basis of immigration law since the 1920s. A third myth is that fighting identity politics is not only depraved but futile, because by 2040 America will be a minority-majority country, anyway. None of these things are true, as is demonstrated throughout the book, especially in chapter 6 on demography.

Popular belief in these myths, and a general lack of awareness of how we came to be where we are, helps identity politics preserve itself. Most Americans have a basic sense of fairness, and so it has been relatively easy to persuade them to support what appear to be legitimate demands for recognition and restitution. But the purveyors of identity politics have taken advantage of that sense of fairness, allowing them to perpetuate the myths that this book reexamines.

Among the myths to debunk, none is more pernicious than the recognition and restitution canard. Pan-ethnic umbrella groups such as "Hispanics" and "Asians" were created by political activists, intellectuals, philanthropists, and their allies in the bureaucracy, not by the man on the street. In fact, the elites encountered pushback from the rank and file as they sought to implement their blueprint, as is demonstrated in chapters 1 to 4. The individual Mexican American or Chinese American certainly had barriers to overcome, and met them often enough. But they believed they could remedy their plight through individual action and improvement. They were aspirational. The activists using groups as the building blocks of identity politics—the hardware to the software of ideology about hegemony, victims, and whiteness—had set out to strip them of such bourgeois notions.

The activists' project took time, money, and effort, and even then it was not easy. This is where philanthropy money was of so much help. As we will see in chapter 1, as late as 1970 a seminal Ford Foundation–funded megastudy conducted by UCLA researchers revealed that Mexican Americans still had no consciousness of themselves as a "minority" and still less of being victims of racial discrimination. That study was an important step toward casting "Mexican American" as a national minority category, a process that, according to the researchers, struck most people, especially Mexican Americans themselves, as a novel idea.

To the chagrin of the UCLA researchers, even among those Mexican Americans who had experienced discrimination they were unable to find much resentment. In fact, respondents to the survey said they had agency—they owned their own failures, which their experience told them were remediable through individual actions, not group mobilization. Theirs was an ethos of self-reliance, personal responsibility, and independence—values that Americans of all ethnicities cherished back then, and that many still do, but that are anathema to the activists and intellectuals. This book analyzes how these values have been purposely eroded.

The goal of the activists was simple: they sought to create voting blocs that would elect politicians who would then transform the country. To facilitate resentment—always useful as a bonding agent of solidarity for groups in the process of being created—the organizers deliberately recast America's idiosyncratic resistance to foreign interference exclusively in terms of racial animus. The activists racialized everything. Terms such as "minority," "person of color," and "privilege" were introduced, freighted with new meanings, in the effort to promote the sense of grievance that is so important to identity politics.

Mexican Americans, whose conversion into a racial group in the 1960s and 1970s presaged what would later be applied to all immigrants from Latin America, the Caribbean, and Iberia—which together comprise the synthetic pan-ethnic group known today as "Hispanics"—offer a textbook case of the top-down approach of identity politics. Because abstracting them into a racial group was such a foundational step in the creation of identity politics, their example is examined in depth in the first chapter of this book.

Mexican Americans began to be consolidated into a voting bloc in earnest by the organizing guru Saul Alinsky, who started the effort during the 1948 presidential campaign of Henry Wallace and the 1949 Los Angeles City Council election of Ed Roybal. Alinsky's groups trained men like Herman Gallegos, Julian Samora, and Ernesto Galarza, who in the 1960s became Chicano movement intellectuals and used Ford Foundation money to found the ethnic special-interest organization La Raza.

La Raza's founders were surprisingly successful in analogizing the unique experience of black Americans to other groups. The term *la raza*, literally "the race," by itself epitomized this racialization process. Ford Foundation director of public affairs Paul Ylvisaker was specific on this point. When he handed the UCLA researchers in 1966 the then goodly sum of $647,999 for a deep survey of Mexican Americans in the Southwest, one of the things he asked them to find out was in what respect these people's experience was comparable to that of blacks. In another example of this explicit linkage, we have Spanish-language ballots today because the Mexican American Legal Defense and Educational Fund (MALDEF)—also established by the Ford Foundation—was able to convince Congress in 1975 that English-only ballots were the equivalent of Jim Crow poll taxes. As Peter Skerry observes in his 1993 book, *Mexican Americans: The Ambivalent Minority*, the idea was "that, like blacks, Mexican Americans comprise a racial minority group. This abstraction poses no problems for the ideologically oriented Chicano activists who see the world in such terms."[4]

The creation of an Asian identity group was spearheaded by Chinese American and Japanese American Marxists who were indoctrinated by the Black Panther movement, as we will see in chapter 2. Yuji Ichioka, a radical Marxist student at Berkeley who in 1966 coined the term "Asian American," went on to found the Asian American Political Alliance, an organization philosophically influenced by the works of Chairman Mao and the Black Panthers. Little wonder, then, that half a century later Chinese Americans would be kept out of elite schools by an affirmative-action system that smacks of aspects of the Cultural Revolution. Chapter 2 traces the history of a group even more incongruous than Hispanics (as it includes people with ancestry in

China, Korea, Japan, the Philippines, India, Pakistan, Indonesia, Laos, etc.) and explains how it may be this group that helps to end identity politics.

President Barack Obama in 2016 tried to create yet one more pan-ethnic category, for people with ancestry in the Middle East and North Africa (MENA). The author can take some credit for helping, along with others, to thwart this misguided effort, as discussed in chapter 3. There, I quote transcripts of a 2015 meeting at the Census Bureau, at which activists plot in real time to entice Americans to adhere to the would-be MENA category with affirmative action and other race-conscious benefits. This leaves no doubt that, to the activists, identity politics is simply about political power and economic benefits.

Chapter 4 explains how 1960s feminists influenced by the work of early Marxists, particularly Marx's colleague Friedrich Engels, extended the analogy to the real plight of black Americans to women. Because it is one of the main battlefields today, chapter 4 also analyzes groups based on sex, sexual orientation, and gender identity. Two constituencies of identity politics, feminists and trans people, are now pitted against each other in a faceoff that will probably prove the axiom that whenever conflicts arise between identity groups (as they inevitably will), the disagreement will be adjudicated in the manner that most favors leftist ends. The issue of sexual orientation and gender identity, known as SOGI, is also spilling into the international realm, especially at the United Nations, and shows the global implications of identity politics.

Part II of the book will delve into the origins of and reasons behind identity politics. Those involved in this cultural project were at the very top of society in terms of money, education, and political power. Ylvisaker, though little known today, was one such figure; he saw philanthropy as "the passing gear of social change," and he was right. By the early 1960s, Ylvisaker, from his perch at the Ford Foundation, had begun to wonder whether Mexican Americans could be organized into what he called a "united front."[5] This is a communist concept from the earliest days of the Soviet Union that took hold in Maoist China. Another important figure, discussed in chapter 6, is McGeorge Bundy, who served as national security advisor in the Kennedy and Johnson administrations before becoming president of the Ford Foundation in 1966. Faced with the race riots that convulsed America at that time, members of the establishment panicked. Bundy's response was to put Ylvisaker's program on steroids, having decided that the only way out of racial chaos was to offer racial preferences on a temporary basis. But this dispensation became permanent.

Chapter 6 debunks the myth that group identities such as "Hispanic" or "Asian" respond to the demographic changes that have taken place in America since immigration law was changed in 1965. This idea must be discredited if we are to defeat identity politics. The seminal UCLA study, for example, commissioned in 1966 and published in 1970, surveyed a population that had been in the Southwest for decades, in many individual cases for centuries. In 1974, the Census Bureau (where a lot of the group-making mischief is hatched), created the first National Advisory Committee on Race; in 1977 the Office of Management and Budget mandated the use of the Hispanic category. The point is that all these things happened before the 1965 Immigration Act had any effect. The new law had not yet made a dent on demography in 1966, 1974, or 1977. In fact, in 1974 the percentage of the foreign-born was probably at its lowest in US history, around 4.6 percent, one-third of what it is today or was in the last decade of the nineteenth century or the first decade of the twentieth. America has always been multiethnic, and after 1965 the nation could have benefited from the melting-pot approach just as much as it did when earlier groups of immigrants arrived, had the activists not militated against such an option.

The doleful role of the Census Bureau's national advisory committees (NACs) in the establishment of identity politics, and the way radical organizations have used them to insinuate themselves into the policy-making process, is discussed in chapter 8, on solutions. The topic is covered there because eliminating the NACs is an important step toward finally ridding society of identity politics.

You may have heard it said America has embraced the idea that "demography is destiny"—or, to paraphrase the subtitle of *Dr. Strangelove*, how society learned to stop worrying and love identity politics. This leads us to a third myth: that America will soon become a minority-majority country. This notion is something that, once implanted in people's minds, can act as a self-fulfilling prophesy. It must be combatted on several philosophical grounds.

First, this is racialized thinking and must be rejected as such. The idea that America is composed of racial groups negotiating with each other in never-ending rounds of power politics corrodes the concept of individual liberty. We are not now and should never become a country like Lebanon, for example, where the Maronites, Sunnis, Shiites, and Druze have constitutionally reserved government offices. Second, this future will obtain only if we continue to organize society in such a way that it is forced to follow the strictures of ethnic grouping.

Our leaders undertake this societal structuring through a carrot-and-stick approach. First we force Americans to divide themselves into ethnic groups through the decennial census and other such means; then we imbue them with grievances about what white, heterosexual, Christian men have done to their particular group; and then we tempt them into identifying with such groups in perpetuity through a system of entitlements like affirmative action, set-asides in contracts, racial gerrymandering, and so on. This prevents the nation from following the more normal approach, the one that has always obtained, which has been the process of ethnic attrition. It also prevents the gathering of tribes into a nation, the progression that the Israeli philosopher Yoram Hazony describes as the precondition for nation building.[6]

"Ethnic attrition" is a term used by demographers to describe the process whereby descendants of immigrants cease to identify with the ethnic group of their immigrant forebears, usually because of intermarriage. For example, a man with one Mexican grandmother, married to a woman with a Korean grandfather, is highly unlikely to think of himself as Mexican American, just as his wife is unlikely to think of herself as Korean American; nor will either have any feeling of marginalization. Unless, that is, the man is told repeatedly that he is Hispanic, a member of an oppressed group, who should feel resentment of and hatred for the white majority, and who is entitled to real financial benefits because of his group membership.

The Ideological Component

The activists, in other words, knew what they were doing when they elevated victimhood as a source of self-worth, and declared that victims were entitled to "compensatory justice." Because it is important for the reader to grasp the origin of these ideas, chapter 5 exposes identity politics' Marxist foundations. We should not shrink from calling these ideas what they are for fear of sounding paranoid. The Progressives, whose writings and social analysis laid the foundations for the edifice of identity politics, were attracted to socialism; the critical theorists of the Frankfurt School (prominent among them Herbert Marcuse), on whose body of work identity politics is based, were Marxists; and the postmodernists, based in Paris, were likewise sympathetic to Marxism. Many communists were involved in the effort to organize what would later be called minorities and in the philanthropic halls of the Ford Foundation. Identity politics, with its secularism, power politics, and urge to destroy what it views as cultural hegemony, is fundamentally a Marxist concept.

Communists were indeed involved in the campaigns of Roybal and Wallace, and to say so is hardly a controversial statement. Mario T. García writes that "the Communists recruited adherents and admirers" among Mexican laborers because of their defense of the "rights of Mexican workers."[7] Alinsky himself never bothered to deny it, telling *Playboy* in 1972, shortly before his death, "Anybody who tells you he was active in progressive causes in those days and never worked with the Reds is a goddamn liar."[8] The most overt communists were sidelined. These politicians and activists also sought the backing of the Catholic Church and other respected moderate institutions that could provide cover. It is entirely legitimate to ask whether the communists who participated were acting on behalf of Moscow or out of a real desire to obtain social justice according to their lights. It is timely, too, in view of Vladimir Putin's continued attempts today to exacerbate our social fissures. It at least bears remembering that the Communist Party in the twentieth century was not in the least an independent actor, but a wholly owned subsidiary of the Soviet Union.

An important reason why grievances proliferate today is, in fact,

the Marxism that became the ideological fashion among intellectuals of the twentieth century. To their great chagrin, the Marxists
realized that a satisfied workingman, one who aspired to better his
life and gain further comforts through his own hard work, would
never overthrow the American system. A pivotal figure for American
Marxists was the Italian communist leader Antonio Gramsci. During
his imprisonment by the Italian fascists in the 1930s, Gramsci jotted
down a transformative epiphany he had once had: Marx had promised eighty years earlier that the working class would overthrow the
bourgeoisie, but the working class had been astonishingly bad at
achieving revolution. Gramsci, and later others, particularly Herbert
Marcuse, the German-born American social theorist of the Frankfurt
School, agreed that it was nearly impossible to instill into the proletariat the consciousness of grievances that would lead to the mass
organization necessary for revolution. Like the Mexican Americans
the UCLA researchers encountered, people remained too stubbornly
aspirational. Campaigns of indoctrination would need to be deep-
ened and expanded, and perhaps economic conditions should not
be used as the basis for instilling resentment. People can aspire to
change their economic situation, after all. What they cannot change
is their race or sex. (No, they really can't.)

Gramsci observed that the rank and file would resist at first, and
would concentrate on their own problems rather than their "ties of
solidarity" with their fellow workers. That is why a "consciousness-
raising" campaign was needed. As Marcuse argued decades later,
no one can be free who does not first understand he is not free. The
workingman, however, had no interest in such self-realization. "They
find their soul in their automobile, hi-fi set, split-level home, kitchen
equipment," said a despairing Marcuse when faced with the same
aspirational striving that has so discombobulated successive waves of
leftist thinkers and activists.[9] The vanguard of the revolution, he added,
would therefore have to come from "the substratum of the outcasts and
outsiders, the exploited and the persecuted of other races and other
colors"—an oracle-like insight of identity politics.[10]

To convince people that they were outcasts required grievance-
mongering. That effort was so successful that it led to something new

in America. Whereas social scientists have long recognized that there are societies with a "culture of honor" and others with a "culture of dignity," in 2014 sociologists Bradley Campbell and Jason Manning identified a third culture present in America, which they call the "culture of victimhood."[11] As we will see in chapter 7, the victimhood paradigm is predicated on a collectivist understanding of society, rather than the individualist striving and voluntary civil associations that Alexis de Tocqueville identified as the hallmark of America.

Victimhood has become a key aspect of our lives, not least in federal law. The 1976 legislation that outlines what a Hispanic is—the only such racial law in US history—pins the definition not on race or language but on victimization. The law states that "a large number of Americans of Spanish origin or descent suffer from racial, social, economic and political discrimination and are denied the basic opportunities they deserve as American citizens." Victimization also extended to the federal bureaucracy, as discussed in chapters 6 and 7. The historian John Skrentny dates the federalization of victimhood culture to the Equal Employment Opportunity Commission's first EEO-1 form, sent out in 1966 to companies nationwide requesting them to furnish data on "Negro, Oriental, American Indian, and Spanish-surnamed" employees. "Being listed on the EEO-1 was a crucial prerequisite for benefiting from a difference-conscious justice," he notes.[12]

Several decades later, the status of victimhood is on a hamster wheel. New and more heinous forms of exclusion must therefore be constantly discovered; with Jim Crow long behind us, "structural discrimination" and "implicit bias" must be found instead.

Still, Americans throughout their history had refused to rally to militant leftist causes. What finally convinced some to follow the siren song of radical organizing? Chapter 8 explains that the answer is a common one: money. Lyndon Johnson decided in the mid-1960s that the government was going to spend lots of it on social programs, and in the Great Society activists saw a pot of gold. While some funding outlays, such as welfare, were color-blind entitlements, others, such as contracting, housing, and hiring, were often race-conscious. The activists quickly persuaded Americans that it was in their economic self-interest to organize around radical race-based political ideologies.

Other benefits, such as affirmative action in university admissions and electoral redistricting, helped as well.

The radicals understood how government benefits and funding could be used to radicalize the masses. "Whereas America's poor have not been moved in any number by radical political ideologies, they have sometimes been moved by their economic interest,"[13] Frances Fox Piven and Richard A. Cloward wrote in 1966. You can almost sense the excitement of the authors as the Great Society spigots were being opened.

The vectors for grievance mongering would be identity groups with various claims on fabricated victimhood, loosely based on ethnic, racial, sexual, and even disability statuses. Groups such as "Hispanics," "Asians," and later LGBT (and the many more letters that keep being added), would be the Marcusian "substratum," the new activist vanguard.

But there was a fundamental problem with equating the experiences of Mexican Americans, women, gays, and so on to the suffering of blacks. It ignored that, as Justice Thurgood Marshall argued in his dissent from *University of California v. Bakke*, "[t]he experiences of Negroes in America has been different in kind, not just in degree, from that of any other ethnic group."[14]

It is for this reason that this book does not have a chapter dedicated to African Americans. The point of identity politics was to create a raft of groups under the pretense that their situation resembled the real black–white divide in this country, that their condition was a version of the real suffering of blacks under Jim Crow, and before that, in slavery. That is how we get the folly of immigrants who have willingly come to America being entitled to the same special rights and preferences as black Americans. This book asserts that this confection of groups was meant as an instrument to transform America, both by people who genuinely, though mistakenly, sought in racial separation a way out of the race riots of the 1960s, and by others who wanted to make America take a turn toward socialism. They both reversed, indeed betrayed, the promise of a color-blind society that was the emblem of the civil rights movement. Blacks did not need to be confected as a group, however. There is no evidence that racial set-asides have helped the condition of black Americans, and if we compare cultural indicators such as out-of-wedlock birth rates now and in the 1960s, it is clear that reverse racism has hurt. But blacks have undeniably been the "objects of collective discrimination," to use Louis Wirth's 1945 definition of minorities.

How Visigoths Got Their Name

Is the synthetic nature of "Hispanic," "Asian," "LGBT," and so on, something that preordains the ultimate failure of these categories' appeal, and thus of identity politics? We should not underestimate the saliency that these group identities have now gained. One theory about the origin of the Visigoths, for example, is that they were made up of different types of barbarians who developed "fictive kinship" merely because the Roman Empire thought of them as a collective and gave them the name of Visigoths, or western Goths. The Visigoths themselves then "invent the notion that they all come from one place and one ancestor," says Paul Freedman in a Yale University lecture. "This process of sort of fictitious ethnic invention is called 'ethnogenesis.' Ethnogenesis means the birth of an ethnicity, rather than some biological fact that you could confirm with DNA." This question of who forms a real group, Freedman adds, is "important as a real thing," but "just because something is false it does not necessarily lack historical importance."[15]

So, yes, our problems are daunting. Yet there are reasons to be optimistic. As Samuel Huntington wrote, societies are "capable of postponing their demise by halting and reversing the processes of decline and renewing their vitality and identity." Evidence of a shift in this country since 2016 suggests that America still has the opportunity to reverse the damage of the preceding three decades. It has dawned on many people that what has taken place has not worked out. Asian Americans, for example, many of whom are being kept out of elite universities despite their achievements, are beginning to realize that the culture of victimhood is punishing them for their very success.

The final chapter sets out how average Americans, and the policy makers they elect to represent them, can start to reverse course.

The key is to eliminate the economic enticements of adhering to group identities, which in many instances have been fabricated for the express purpose of dividing us into factions. Society must decide to withdraw the inducements to group making—to shut down the casinos of identity politics. But to create the conditions for such an American national awakening, the entire process of identity politics must be exposed, its processes and purposes understood. Only then can we move forward and begin to heal. I hope with this book to contribute to this healing, so you can tell the principal at your daughter's school to stuff it and fear no consequences.

PART I

AND ACTIVISTS
CREATED GROUPS

★ ★ ★

CHAPTER 1

★ ★ ★

Hispanics Are Birthed

In the early 1950s, the esteemed University of Texas at Austin social scientist George I. Sánchez wrote to a young scholar to warn him that a pan-ethnic identity group for Americans with Latin American roots made no sense. The professor did not mince words: "For gosh sakes, don't characterize the Spanish-American with what is obviously true of the human race, and then imply, by commission or omission, that his characteristics are peculiarly his and, of course, radically different from those of the 'Anglos'!" He enumerated further objections: "We insist that 'Latin American' ('Spanish-American,' 'Mexican-American,' etc.) has no precise meaning nor does the term connote generalized cultural attributes.... We say that, for convenience, all non-Latins are to be called 'Anglos' (Germans, Italians, Jews, Catholics, Baptists, hill-billies, Bostonians, poor whites, Texans, Minnesotans, ad infinitum) have a precisely defined common culture whose features can be correlated with the non-existent (or, at best, undefined) features of the Latin 'culture.'!!!!"[1]

The recipient of this letter was Julian Samora. What had occasioned Sánchez's letter was a paper by Samora on a Colorado health-care program for "Spanish Americans." As quoted by Benjamin Francis-Fallon, Sánchez went on: "The time orientation of a 'poor white' is no different from that of a poor Negro or of a poor Spanish. Neither can provide for the future; each *has* to live for the present; after laboring for 14 hours a day, none of them has the energy or interest or curiosity to go to PTA's or to Association meetings. You wouldn't either, nor would I—nor would Abraham Lincoln!"[2] Sánchez belonged to that generation of Mexican Americans that still believed that individual effort would lead to prosperity and assimilation. As Francis-Fallon puts it: "Material improvements in jobs, housing, and schools would not only allow them to live better but would reveal their fundamental similarity with other Americans." Sánchez's concerns were with obstacles to individual improvement.[3]

Sánchez criticized the notion that Mexicans were a race and even more vehemently rejected the attempt to create a pan-ethnic group out of people with origins in various Spanish-speaking countries. Not only did this not make sense to him, but it stood in the way of the emphasis on individual agency. In an earlier letter to Samora, Sánchez urged him to consider that "the characteristics that distinguish the Spanish-speaking group in any part of the United States are much less ethnic than they are socio-economic." He also sent Samora a review he had written of a book about Spanish-speaking Americans, in which, as Francis-Fallon notes, "Sánchez cast doubt on the entire concept of such a book. It 'takes a veritable shotgun wedding to make Puerto Ricans, Spanish-Mexicans, and Filipinos appear to be culturally homogeneous,' he wrote."[4]

Sánchez remained constant in this view. A decade later, in 1963, after the influx of Cubans escaping Fidel Castro's communist takeover of the island nation, he wrote, Spanish-speaking Americans "are just too many different peoples to be adequately covered under one umbrella. While they could be called, loosely, 'Americans who speak Spanish' they would have to be treated in separate categories—for, by way of illustration, though a Cuban in Florida and a Mexican in Laredo both speak Spanish, they really have little else in common (even though both may be aliens or citizens, or a combination)."[5]

Historical Fault Line

Samora, however, persisted in his belief that a collectivity was needed. Both men are towering figures in the history of the Mexican American evolution in the twentieth century, and this early clash of views represents an ideological divide of historic proportions. In Sánchez, we see the emphasis on individual agency and the strong belief in the goal of becoming part of the American mainstream; in Samora, we see the emerging rejection of this view in favor of a collectivist, ethnic identity–based category to lift a "subjugated" people out of their plight. This category would need official and legal recognition by the federal government. Samora became a leader for members of the new generation.

The Census Bureau in 2018 put the number of Mexican Americans at close to thirty-seven million, or just over 11 percent of the US population. Mexican Americans, as the earliest sizable group of Spanish-speaking people to live in the United States, form the nucleus of the group that came to be called Hispanic, and any analysis of this group must therefore start with them. The creation of "Hispanics," moreover, was an early cornerstone of the identity politics edifice, which is all the more reason to begin at the beginning.

The Hispanic collective was created, to put it simply, to give the leaders of then-emerging Mexican American–identity organizations a measure of political clout and federal funding. Many of the activists and elites who conjured up the collective were, indeed, transparent about this. Before Antonio Gramsci made his observations about the inability of the proletariat to overthrow an existing system, Marxists had thought that the members of the working class would rise up. Their analysis was color-blind; the proletariat was an economic class made up of all races. The problem, as Gramsci, and later Herbert Marcuse, came to see it, was that too many proletarians reasoned like Sánchez and believed in their ability to improve their individual lot; they believed that personal striving would allow them in time to overcome barriers and join the mainstream.

Samora was deaf to Sánchez but attuned to Gramsci and Marcuse. Recognized today as the founder of Hispanic ethnic studies, Samora in 1967 cofounded an ethnic identity organization, the Southwest Council of La Raza, which went national in 1973, changing its name to the National Council of La Raza. La Raza was devoted to that "shotgun wedding" that Sánchez had warned about, and for the past half century it has been at the forefront of the effort to implant identity politics in the educational system, corporate America, and government. It continues this work under its new name, UnidosUS. Its original goal was precisely to eliminate the "false consciousness" that Gramsci had derided: the belief in individual agency. To the followers of Gramsci, assimilation was the height of false consciousness.

Samora used key positions he held to make Mexican Americans a racial group apart from the mainstream. He and his colleagues in this project then did the same with the larger group, Hispanics. They persuaded wealthy donors and federal officials to regard Hispanics, whether individuals whose ancestors had arrived in the United States a century ago or had themselves arrived one year earlier, as an oppressed group that could succeed only by acting as a racial collective. In the process, they altered the American social order, perhaps permanently. In addition to his role as La Raza leader, he was also appointed to the Census Bureau's first Advisory Committee on the Spanish Origin Population for the 1980 Census, the first census to include the pan-ethnic categories, and held top positions in universities. From these lofty perches in nonprofit advocacy, the academy, and the federal bureaucracy, he wielded great authority.

Samora's personal experience with discrimination had a great impact on his thinking, something with which we can't help but empathize. "I tried to be equal to, and as good as, the Anglos. I wanted to make as much money, speak as well, and have all the goodies as the dominant society. But no matter what I did, I was always a 'Mexican,'" he once said, as quoted by his daughter, Carmen Samora.[6] He had struggled with abject poverty, fatherlessness, and intense discrimination while growing up in Colorado. An episode that must have particularly stung occurred while he was in college, when he ran for class president. His own roommate voted against him, telling Samora he could not bring himself to vote for a Mexican.

Seen another way, however, his personal story also proves that Mexican Americans could indeed surmount barriers through individual striving. Samora earned a PhD in sociology and anthropology at a major university, Washington University in St. Louis. He later founded the Mexican American Graduate Studies program at the University of

Notre Dame. This last achievement came courtesy of a grant from the Ford Foundation, which in the late 1960s was already in the midst of a spending spree aimed at bolstering what the foundation was calling "group identity." Chapter 6 delves further into this endeavor, but suffice it to say here that Samora's founding of the program at Notre Dame represents a personal victory over adversity by a man who grew up in poverty and suffered from discrimination.

It is worth noting that George Sánchez also faced discrimination. After lobbying to improve the education of New Mexico's rural, poor, Spanish-speaking population, which put him at odds with the governor, he and his family required police protection, and Sánchez started carrying a gun. At one point he found a pipe bomb outside their home.[7] Sánchez and Samora may have had the experience of discrimination in common, but they took sharply different approaches to how to overcome it and to questions of ethnicity.

Samora drank deeply from the well of German philosophies brought over during and after World War II. The language of "dominant" and "subservient," or "subordinate," groups, integral to critical theory and the Frankfurt School (covered in more detail in chapter 5) pervades Samora's academic work. His dissertation, titled "Minority Leadership in a Bi-Cultural Community," quotes the German-born American social psychologist Kurt Lewin, who was associated with the Frankfurt School.[8]

Samora's thesis can in fact be seen as a classic of the critical theory genre. The very first "problem" that Samora sets out is that Mexican Americans (the "subordinate group") have no chance of succeeding if the standards of success are defined by American society (the "dominant system"). As with all critical writing, his thesis and other writings can be abstruse. Here's one example: "In situations of dominant–subordinate relationships where the goals of the subordinate group are largely goals to be achieved within the dominant system, the in-group cohesion of the subordinate group will be considered inadequate by members of the subordinate system." Creating a race out of people of many backgrounds became for Samora and others of the same mindset the way to break out of this dominant system. The decision to turn Mexican Americans into a racial minority produced the first artificial but legal identity group, and thus one of the first building blocks of identity politics.

As Peter Skerry observes, "Mexican-Americans emerge in California as not just any interest group, but—in keeping with the dynamics of our new American political system—as one organized around an idea. That is that, like blacks, Mexican Americans comprise a racial minority group. This abstraction poses no problems for the ideologically oriented Chicano activists who see the world in such terms." This racialization, Skerry adds, "is highly useful to elite-network insiders who are in need of some cogent category that subsumes the disparate population they aspire to represent. Yet, this race idea is somewhat at odds with the experience of Mexican-Americans, over half of whom designate themselves racially as 'white,' and the overwhelming majority of whom draw sharp distinctions between themselves and blacks."[9]

That many Mexican Americans saw themselves as white was a problem for activists and elites. Indeed, the federal government counted them as white on the decennial US census and for legal purposes. When the census of 1930, in an exception to general practice, classified Mexican Americans as a race of their own, Mexican American leaders protested bitterly, and officials reverted back to the white classification in the 1940 census. The leading Mexican American organization at the time, the then pro-assimilationist League of United Latin American Citizens (LULAC), complained that declassifying Mexicans as white had been an attempt to "discriminate between the Mexicans themselves and other members of the white race, when in truth and fact we are not only a part and parcel but as well the sum and substance of the white race.... Jim Crow did not apply to us."[10] In 1947, in *Mendez v. Westminster*, a case concerning the segregation of Mexican American students in remedial schools in Orange County, California, both sides, and the court, agreed that Mexican Americans were classified as white.(The judge in his ruling wrote, "It is conceded by all parties that there is no question of race discrimination in this action."[11]) What the district was accused of doing was using Spanish-speaking as a proxy for segregating darker-skinned Mexican Americans while admitting lighter-skinned ones.[12]

Mexican Americans inhabited a racial space not unlike that of American Jews. Both were classified as white, yet both faced discrimination and some segregation. To this day, Mexican Americans and other Hispanics are technically not a race. On the census, "Hispanic" is treated as an "ethnicity." The Obama administration tried to revise the 2020 census form by amalgamating the census question on whether a person is "Hispanic" with a question about biological race, but the Trump administration didn't support the change. To what extent Hispanics are now considered a race by their fellow Americans is open to question. It is obvious to me, at least, that for reasons I explain in this chapter and subsequent ones, many Americans now dimly view Hispanics as something of a race apart from whites but that this process of racialization is not yet complete. Social scientists define racialization as "the extension of racial meaning to a previously unclassified relationship, social practice or group."[13] That process is well under way but can still be stopped. What is important for those who want to stop identity politics is to recognize that racialization is a main goal of the Left.

The process of making all Mexican Americans into victimized "people of color" (POC) came at a price. As Cristina Mora observes in her study *Making Hispanics*, it required that Mexican Americans "[accept] a disadvantaged minority status,"[14] with no possibility of ever escaping minority status. For the elites and activists such as Samora who desired this racialization, the process was not easy and is still not complete. But they had a powerful ally in the media and the entertainment worlds, who liked the idea of another sort of POC. "Journalists tend to accept uncritically the racial minority interpretation of the Mexican-American experience offered by advocates and activists,"[15] wrote Skerry in the 1990s, an observation that indubitably holds today. Philip Gleason surmises, aptly in my view, that the expression "people of color" came into vogue because it makes acceptable in the popular mind the status and benefits accorded to "designated minorities," which are distinguishable by "racially linked phenotypical features."[16] That runs into trouble with Mexican Americans and others designated as Hispanic who don't look different from non-Hispanic Americans— think Marco Rubio or the Boston Red Sox's David "Papi" Ortiz—or other "whites" who can be phenotypically identifiable, for example, some Italians and Jews. Nevertheless, the exigencies of group making required that what's obvious to the eye be ignored, if the entire group was to be deemed POC.

But, as Mora puts it, with emphasis, *"It did not have to happen."*[17] Absent the conflation of ideology, the economic benefits granted to members of some groups, and the emergence of determined individuals in powerful positions, Mexican Americans would not have been abstracted into a racial minority, let alone form the nucleus of a larger pan-ethnic group. By extension, we might not have identity politics today. There was a roadmap in America that showed a different path, and Mexican Americans seemed eager to follow it.

The People of the Southwest

After the 1846–48 Mexican-American War, the "common" school system, which had been so successful in teaching civics and patriotism, along with the three Rs, to the children of immigrants in the Northeast, was brought west in an attempt to turn the former citizens of Mexico into English-speaking Americans. The state of Texas alone "established a permanent system of common public schools in 1854 with the Common School Law," according to a study by the National Park Service. With the goal of assimilating not just the children of Mexican immigrants but also those of German immigrants, the law then was amended in 1856 and 1858 to stipulate that "no school shall be entitled to the [monetary] benefits of this act unless the English language is principally taught therein."[18]

This is not to say that relations between the different peoples who soon found themselves living side by side were always excellent, but then neither was that the case in Manhattan in the 1600s, nor in Louisiana and Florida in the early 1800s, nor anywhere else. As late as the 1820s, some 160 years after their absorption, the Dutch of New York still lived with some separation from their English neighbors. Some politicians believed that Mexicans, after their absorption, could be assimilated, but others were skeptical. The *New York Sun* editorialized in 1847 that the American mission in the Southwest would be to "liberate and ennoble, not to enslave and debase."[19] That year Lewis Cass, senator from Michigan, voiced the opinion that the Mexican population would soon "identify itself with ours."[20] By contrast, John C. Calhoun, senator from South Carolina, always reliable to say something nasty, wondered, "Can we incorporate a people so dissimilar to us in every respect?"[21] It is generally the case that today's purveyors of identity politics sound eerily familiar to our worst race-obsessed politicos and thinkers of the nineteenth century. How different is what Calhoun said, for example, from what activist José Ángel Gutiérrez was to write more than a century later, in his mission statement for the Mexican Youth Organization: "We will not try to assimilate into this gringo society, nor will we encourage anyone else to do so."[22] Indeed, we can well imagine Calhoun agreeing that even the subject of mathematics must be taught differently to Mexican American students than to others, something that (as discussed in chapter 8) today's champions of pedagogies such as "culturally responsive teaching" advocate.[23]

Then again, comments as bilious as Calhoun's were made of the thirty thousand or so free inhabitants of the Louisiana Territory, a people of French and Spanish ancestry. Some Yankees feared that the Roman Catholicism of these new additions would prevent them from becoming "good Americans" and from being able to understand and practice republican government. Pennsylvania congressman John Lucas averred that "it could not be said that a people thus inured to despotism were prepared on a sudden to receive the principles of our government."[24] New York congressman Samuel Mitchill stated that the Louisianans would have to undergo an "apprenticeship to liberty; they are to be taught the lessons of freedom; and by degrees they are to be raised to the enjoyment and practice of independence." In this manner, Mitchill told the House, the Louisianans would have to be assimilated before they could be allowed to have any impact on American politics. He continued, "There will be no alien influence thereby introduced into our councils."[25] The future president John Quincy Adams spoke for many New England intellectuals when he despaired that the Louisiana Purchase would introduce "a colonial system of government."[26] The critics were wrong, and the Cajun today are indistinguishable from any other Americans.

We have good sources on which to base a belief that Mexican Americans were similarly on their way toward assimilation: Mexican Americans themselves. Even a modern liberal proponent of ethnic pride and separation, David G. Gutiérrez, writes that by the 1920s various segments of Mexican American society had accepted "the reality of their permanent incorporation into American society. The basic tenet of this perspective was that Mexican Americans were in fact Americans and therefore should make every effort to assimilate into the American social and cultural mainstream."[27]

This desire to be immersed into the great American melting pot led many Mexican Americans and the organizations they formed to be suspicious of continued immigration, which was high from the 1890s on and continued to be high right through the Great Depression. Between 1880 and 1920, the Mexican-born population grew from 68,000 to 478,000. Mexican Americans quite rightly sensed that the fear and sometimes contempt the immigrant attracts would stick also to those who had been here for generations. According to Gutiérrez, Mexican Americans came to the "conclusion that the needs and interests of American citizens simply had to take precedence over the problems faced by the growing Mexican immigrant population."[28]

Two organizations were particularly attached to assimilation: The League of United Latin American Citizens (LULAC), created in 1929 and which grew to have eighty chapters in several states by the early 1940s, and the Mexican American Movement (MAM), established in 1938. A MAM editorial in *The Mexican Voice* in 1940 declared: "If you desire to remain here, if your future is here, you must become a citizen, an American." A LULAC editorial struck the same chord in 1948: "The American citizen of Mexican ancestry is weak because he is a minority citizen. Discrimination will pursue him until he blends with the majority group in this country enough to lose his present identity."[29]

Continued immigration made this process harder. Gutiérrez quotes George Sánchez of the University of Texas telling the *New York Times* in 1951 that illegal immigration in large numbers could transform "the Spanish-speaking peoples of the Southwest from an ethnic group that might be assimilated with reasonable facility into what I call a culturally indigestible peninsula of Mexico."[30] But as noted at the start of this chapter, the 1950s saw the beginning of the end of assimilationist sentiments. Community organizers, union leaders, socialists, and communists who had toiled for years to little avail to ensure the persistence of separatist enclaves or even internal colonies of unassimilable Mexican Americans, grew from strength to strength through the 1940s and 1950s until they achieved complete victory in the 1970s and 1980s.

California Dreamin'

Skerry was on the mark in identifying both the "elite-network insiders" as the beneficiaries of the process of racialization and California as the birthplace of the evolution that culminated in it. In the late 1940s the goal of identity creation in the Golden State was votes. Two elections—the 1948 presidential campaign of Henry Wallace, who had served as Franklin D. Roosevelt's second vice president and who spoke Spanish, and the 1949 campaign for the Los Angeles City Council of Edward R. Roybal—proved to be the starting point for organizing Mexican Americans.

It was there that Ernesto Galarza and Herman Gallegos, who went on to cofound La Raza with Samora, met most of the key activists and earned their political spurs by learning community organizing from the best in the business. In the words of activist and UC Berkeley scholar Kenneth C. Burt, these two elections were "a turning point in American politics."[31] Both Roybal and Wallace attracted strong support from radical elements, including communists and community organizers who saw the Mexican American as a potential source of political power, if only he could be organized around feelings of racial grievances. (This matter is treated at greater length in chapter 5.)

Among the groups that were formed during that time, the most influential was the Community Service Organization (CSO), which was financed by the radical community organizer Saul Alinsky and supervised by his top lieutenant, Fred Ross. The CSO became the crucible of all the changes that were to come. What the CSO wanted was votes: making Mexican Americans into a unified voting bloc was the first step to racialization and official categories. As Carmen Samora wrote, "The CSO effectively politicized the community of Mexican immigrants and Mexican-Americans in Los Angeles after WWII."[32] Cross-fertilization between the Wallace and Roybal campaigns was strong. Roybal became president of the CSO after losing his first council election in 1947. Wallace came to Lincoln Heights stadium in Los Angeles, where he addressed a massive audience of ten thousand Mexican Americans in Spanish.

Alinsky and Ross (dubbed "Red Ross" by critics) thought that Mexican Americans had the potential to deliver votes but were appalled by how disorganized they were. Laura Westhoff quotes from Ross's report to Alinsky's Industrial Areas Foundation, in which he says Mexican Americans lacked "civic organization that could provide a base for people to work on their own problems and to cooperate with other groups that shared similar goals." According to Westhoff, civil rights organizations across the country, including Ross's supervisors in the California Federation for Civic Unity, the American Council on Race Relations, and Alinsky's IAF, agreed with Ross and "viewed Mexican Americans as lacking the means to build bridges to other organizations."[33]

The organizing muscle Ross and the others brought to bear paid dividends, however. The CSO, by then headed by Roybal, registered fifteen thousand new voters for the Wallace campaign, especially in places like the Boyle Heights neighborhood of Los Angeles, which "was a cauldron of leftist political activity, residents radicalized by events in their home countries (including the Mexican Revolution and the Russian Revolution) and by the upsurge in political and labor activism during the Great Depression," writes Burt. "This spectrum included various shades of New Deal liberals, as well as Communists, Socialists, Trotskyists, Wobblies and radicals too independent to follow any party line."[34] Mexican Americans were finally beginning to forge ethnic coalitions that could deliver reliable votes for leftist causes.

Though votes, and not racial identity, were the earlier goal, one led to the other. Within a decade, there emerged in LA what the sociologists Edward Telles and Vilma Ortiz describe as "an explicitly nonwhite racial identity...which provided fertile ground for progressive political activism, including the Chicano movement."[35] And what was sparked in LA didn't stay in LA but shook the entire country. These tremors soon extended throughout the Southwest and then expanded northward. Roybal himself did yeoman's work in the cause of identity politics and other leftist endeavors. In 1950, barely one year after being elected to the LA City Council, he cast the sole council vote opposing an ordinance that required communists to register with the police department. In 1962, he was elected to the US House of Representatives, where he served for three decades representing Boyle Heights. In 1967, he wrote the first federal bilingual education bill, and in 1976 he founded the Congressional Hispanic Caucus, which is an arm of the Democratic Party that denies membership to Republicans. That same year, Roybal also founded the National Association of Latino Elected and Appointed Officials (NALEO), a key leftist ethnic advocacy organization with a seat on the Census Bureau's National Advisory Committee on Race and Ethnicity, a pulpit from which NALEO calls for perpetuating the Hispanic identity in the US census.

But it was something else he did in 1976 that secured Roybal his place in the identity politics pantheon: he sponsored Public Law 94-311, a remarkable piece of legislation that identifies what a "Hispanic" is and why this designation has to be created. The law maintains that "a large number of Americans of Spanish origin or descent suffer from racial, social, economic, and political discrimination and are denied the basic opportunities they deserve as American citizens and which should enable them to begin to lift themselves out of the poverty they now endure." Therefore, what Hispanics had in common was neither ethnicity, race, nor language, but being victims of discrimination. Victimhood was the bonding agent. The objective of the legislation was to "implement an affirmative action program within the Bureau of the Census for employment of personnel of Spanish origin or descent."[36] As Ruben Rumbaut puts it, it was "the first and only law in U.S. history that defines a specific ethnic group and mandates the collection, analysis, and publication of data for that group."[37]

As a historical footnote, in 2014, President Obama posthumously awarded Roybal the Presidential Medal of Freedom, the nation's highest civilian honor.

Organizing Goes National

To continue the organizing they had begun in Los Angeles three years earlier, in 1952 Ross and Alinsky hired a young Herman Gallegos (who, as has been noted, went on to cofound La Raza). Gallegos became president of the East San Jose CSO chapter, whose first vice president was none other than Cesar Chavez. Soon to become the country's best known Mexican American farm-labor organizer, Chavez was another Alinsky disciple.

Alinsky, indeed, appears to have been the nerve center of the network of men and women who would go on to play leading roles in first racializing Mexican Americans, then creating the Hispanic category, and thus erecting the identity politics edifice. Chavez's trade union coleader Dolores Huerta, a Fidel Castro sympathizer, told an interviewer in 1995 that "Fred Ross brought Ernesto Galarza around to every CSO chapter, and then we were supposed to organize farmworkers for Ernesto Galarza."[38] As quoted by Carmen Samora, Gallegos heard about Galarza from "Ross and Alinsky because they knew about Ernie and the work he was doing with the farm workers' struggles. Along the way we connected.... Gallegos was building valuable leadership skills and contributing to the training of other leaders."[39]

Soon, Gallegos began to work for the Youth Opportunity Center, a Ford Foundation–funded jobs training program in the black ghetto of San Francisco's Hunter's Point. It was there that he met the foundation's national affairs director, Paul Ylvisaker, an energetic Minnesotan and son of a Lutheran minister. It was a fateful meeting in the annals of identity politics. Influenced by the philosophy of Immanuel Kant, Ylvisaker had taught at Princeton, Yale, and Harvard, where he was the dean of the Graduate School of Education, a hotbed of liberal activism. He personified, in other words, the high-minded, well-funded, ideological activism that was about to transform so many American institutions.

Carmen Samora writes that Gallegos related his first encounter with Ylvisaker this way: "Paul asked, 'What was a Mexican-American doing working in essentially a program for blacks?' I replied, 'Ford does not fund programs to help Mexican-Americans.'" This was how

Gallegos began to lobby Ford to support Mexican American projects. It was not long before Ylvisaker asked Gallegos, Galarza, and Julian Samora—all of whom had been working together with Alinsky in a Rosenberg Foundation–funded project—to undertake a comprehensive regional assessment of Mexican Americans for the Ford Foundation. "Ford recognized that little was known from a policy formation standpoint about a significant population of Americans," writes Ms. Samora. Ford then contracted with Samora, Galarza, and Gallegos "to conduct a study of Mexican-Americans in the Southwest. Ylvisaker asked for a completed evaluation in six months' time."[40] The problem of disorganization that Alinsky and the others had noticed in Los Angeles in 1949 was uppermost on Ylvisaker's mind a decade and a half later. One of the things he wanted to know, as noted in the introduction, was whether Mexican Americans could be organized into what he called a "united front."

Their work together led in turn to a massive 1970 Ford Foundation–funded study that played a seminal role in the racialization of Mexican Americans, culminating in the creation of La Raza and the Mexican American Legal Defense and Educational Front (MALDEF), and the creation of a Hispanic identity. The study, authored by UCLA researchers Leo Grebler, Joan Moore, and Ralph Guzman, was based on interviews with 1,550 residents of Los Angeles and San Antonio. It was provocatively titled *The Mexican-American People: The Nation's Second Largest Minority*, deliberately using the word "minority" even before the people in question had accepted the definition. As sociologist Vilma Ortiz told the *Los Angeles Times* in 1999, thirty years after the study was published, "Up to that point, the discussion had been about African Americans and whites. This brought to light a whole other population that had really been ignored."[41] The study played a formative role in creating a consciousness of minority status among Mexican Americans, and analogizing their experience to the unique history of African Americans.

The study brought together all the different disciplines that were converging on the mission of casting Mexican Americans as a victimized minority—academics, activists, politicians, and the deep-pocketed foundations. It did not just provide information—laying the groundwork for the organizing work that lay ahead—it was itself an important promoter of the idea that Mexican Americans constituted a minority, one that was racial, whose grievances raised it (or lowered it, depending on one's view) to the category of victimhood, and therefore entitled it to certain benefits. The leaders of new ethnic affinity organizations then sprouting up were starting to grasp the importance of the concept. "Their spokesmen were beginning to recognize that the 'national minority' definition would ease rather than aggravate the group's problems.... The concrete gains that would result from a joint classification with other disadvantaged national minorities were increasingly seen as more than offsetting a possible loss," wrote the researchers.[42]

There was one problem: Many if not most of the Mexican Americans they surveyed did not think their experience should be analogized to that of African Americans. Grebler, Moore, and Guzman were quite open about this fact:

> Prejudice has been a loaded topic of conversation in any Mexican-American community. Indeed, merely calling Mexican-Americans a "minority" and implying that the population is the victim of prejudice and discrimination has caused irritation among many who prefer to believe themselves indistinguishable white Americans.... There are light-skinned Mexican-Americans who have never experienced the faintest discrimination in public facilities, and many with ambiguous surnames have also escaped the experiences of the more conspicuous members of the group. Finally, there is the inescapable fact that...even comparatively dark-skinned Mexicans...could get service even in the most discriminatory parts of Texas a generation or two ago.[43]

The experiences of Mexican Americans, so different from that of blacks in the South or even parts of the North, had produced "a long and bitter controversy among middle-class Mexican-Americans about defining the ethnic group as disadvantaged by any other criterion than individual failures. The recurring evidence that well-groomed and well-spoken Mexican-Americans can receive normal treatment has continuously undermined either group or individual definition of the situation as one entailing discrimination."[44]

It is incumbent on us at this point to pause to take in what exactly the Ford Foundation–funded UCLA researchers are lamenting. Their own survey had discovered that Mexican Americans' lived experiences showed them that they weren't passive victims of invidious, structural discrimination, much less racial animus. They felt they had agency, and they owned their own failures, which—their experience told them—were remediable through individual actions (such as dressing and speaking well), not group mobilization. Their traits were "achieved," or acquired through their individual actions, not "ascribed," or permanent and set at birth.

Make no mistake about it, Mexican Americans did encounter discrimination. In parts of South Texas, it could be pervasive at times. After a far-fetched conspiracy called the Plan of San Diego was discovered in 1915—it called for blacks and Indians to join Mexican Americans in killing all male Anglos over the age of sixteen, in an effort to take back the lands lost by Mexico in 1848—Texas Rangers and vigilante groups launched attacks on Mexican Americans. Estimates of the number killed vary.[45] There were also many Anglo deaths. The events took place within the context of the chaos of the Mexican Revolution and bloody raids into US territory by bandits like Pancho Villa.

Here again, however, the reaction by Mexican Americans is instructive. President Wilson sent the US Army to establish order on the border, and instead of continuing the Rangers' lawlessness, "the Army went out of their way to guarantee the safety of Tejanos (Mexican-Americans) and Mexicanos trying to return to their homes in Texas," writes Ralph Edward Morales.[46] As a result, many Mexican Americans developed a high regard for the US military, and the experience sparked patriotic feelings. When the United States entered World War I, many joined the military to prove their value as Americans. One of them was José de la Luz Sáenz, who later founded the staunchly patriotic LULAC and who told his friends that "Tejano service in the military was vital in showing the devotion to the United States."[47] Paradoxically, the Plan of San Diego contributed much to the American patriotism of Mexican Americans.

Their ethos was, then, one of self-reliance, personal responsibility, and independence. But such virtues were anathema to the activists and academics steeped in Marxism and critical theory and undermined the community organizers' mission. The UCLA researchers intended for their study not to encourage individual aspiration and pride but to subvert it: it was the "collective definition of the Mexican Americans as a minority" that was paramount.[48]

In their introduction to the 777-page study, the researchers freely acknowledge the tension between detached scholarly work and politicking, and they make clear that the very nature of their work had transformed their pursuit into activism: yes, "the scholar's preoccupation with rules of evidence, broad abstractions, alternative interpretations, and cautious conclusions are definitely not those of the ethnic activist." They then admit that "this problem became immediately apparent at the beginning of our research. Our first exploratory interviews with Mexican Americans throughout the Southwest in 1964 suggested that we were defining the Mexican-American population in a particular way—as a national minority. To a leadership involved in local and regional quarrels, this was a novel interpretation. Our definition (tentative at the time) seemed threatening to many leaders." In other words, the researchers were trying to impose a category on Mexican Americans that the Mexican Americans themselves resisted. In the conclusion they make their project crystal clear: the "classification of an ethnic group as a collective entity serves the limited purposes of enabling one to see the group's problems in the perspective of the problems of other groups.... Thus, we have shown that Mexican Americans share with Negroes the disadvantages of poverty, economic insecurity, and discrimination."[49]

To be sure, the same thing could have been said in the late 1960s of the Scots-Irish in Appalachia or the Irish Catholics in South Boston, and many other groups. As the UCLA researchers found, the experience of Mexican Americans was that even those with dark complexions, and thus most visibly susceptible to prejudice, could achieve success even in the most benighted parts of Texas. This was most definitely not the case with African Americans in the South, who faced inescapable and degrading legal discrimination on a daily basis.

It was, moreover, this comparison that large majorities of the hundreds of respondents surveyed by the study firmly rejected. As the study itself states, the respondents emphasized "the distinctiveness of Mexican Americans" and "the difference in the problems faced by the two groups."[50] It is easy to understand, then, the mix of optimism and realism in the UCLA report: "Mexican Americans will probably increasingly come to view themselves as a minority with rectifiable grievances. However, they are not yet easy to merge with the other large minorities in political coalition."[51]

That work still lay ahead. But the equating of Mexican Americans to blacks was key to organizing ethnic bloc coalitions and to extending the status of victimhood. The study quoted the social scientists Lloyd Warner and Leo Srole as stating that the final stage of assimilation required "the dissolution of ethnic solidarity as members became absorbed in the larger system." But the UCLA authors made clear that their preferred model for Mexican Americans was "intra-ethnic diversity and the process creating such differentiation"—in other words, Samora's Frankfurt School–influenced rejection of assimilation.[52]

The UCLA study was a milestone. It represented the Ford Foundation's first major foray into group creation, from which it later expanded to "Hispanics." (The reasons the foundation went in that direction are looked at more closely in chapter 6.) The 1970 study, then, laid the foundations for the group making that was to come. But it wasn't the only dividend paid by the work that Galarza, Samora, and Gallegos did together for the Foundation. They also convinced it to pony up $10 million so they could found the Southwest Council of La Raza (later the National Council of La Raza, and known today as UnidosUS).

Whereas the seminal role of the UCLA study is unfamiliar to many, La Raza's track record is well known and does not need to be plumbed to great depths here. Less well known is that it, too, lacked grassroots support and faced opposition from Mexican Americans and their elected representatives. The thoroughly liberal Rep. Henry González of Texas, for example, took to the floor of the House of Representatives in April 1969 to denounce the foundation for creating "a very grave problem" in his district:

I cannot accept the belief that racism in reverse is the answer for racism and discrimination. As deeply as I must respect the intentions of the Foundation, I must at the same time say that where it aimed to produce unity, it has so far created disunity. The Ford Foundation believed that the greatest need of this particular minority group [Mexican Americans] was to have some kind of effective national organization.... This good desire may have rested on a false assumption; namely that such a disparate group could, any more than our black brothers or our white "Anglo" brothers, be brought under one large tent.[53]

González was pointing out a problem that has existed with La Raza and other such bodies from the start: they are top-down organizations with little input from the grassroots. They have "weak community ties," as Skerry says, but they win policy fights because they partake in "a process of specialization and professionalization by which politics become more and more an insiders' game." The racial identities they have intimidated the Census Bureau into adopting are "highly useful to elite-network insiders who are in need of some cogent category that subsumes the disparate population they aspire to represent."[54] The only problem is, these categories do no good to the people themselves, or to the nation.

González observed that, "not long after the Southwest Council of La Raza opened for business, it gave $110,000 to the Mexican-American Unity Council of San Antonio; this group was apparently invented for the purpose of receiving the grant," which "has not given any assistance that I know of to bring anybody together" and existed only to "promote the rather odd and I might say generally unaccepted and unpopular views of its directors."[55] On another occasion, speaking generally on ethnic solidarity, González rejected it as a "new racism [that] demands an allegiance to race above all else." In an early instance of "cancel culture," González was pilloried for saying these things. The Texas organizer José Ángel Gutiérrez accused González of the worst of all crimes, holding "gringo tendencies," what later critical theorists would call "false consciousness." Gutiérrez argued that Chicanos should become "a culturally separate people from the gringo."[56]

What Gutiérrez intended to do in the United States was made abundantly clear in April 1975, when he led a delegation of his Raza Unida party to Cuba, at the invitation of communist dictator Fidel Castro. At a news conference after his return, he said that the Cuban Revolution was alleviating the problems of poverty and racism on the island that Mexican Americans experienced in Texas. A reporter said, "You are going to be asked sometime that if you like socialism so much, why don't you and all the other Mexicans go to Cuba," to which Gutiérrez replied, "Because we are going to make a Cuba over here."[57]

In time, the social scientists, the Chicano activists, the political operatives, and the bottomless barrel that was the Ford Foundation overwhelmed members of the old guard like Sánchez, who thought in terms of individuals improving their economic lot and assimilating, as well leaders of the older groups that preached American patriotism, like LULAC. An ethnic-based, transnational group that demanded compensatory justice based on victimhood began to take form. "Even if many Mexican Americans refused to accept a Chicano identity, much less the ethnic separatism espoused by the militants, the actions of the Chicano activists undoubtedly convinced at least some government officials that the militants' grievances warranted attention," writes David Gutiérrez.[58] The Chicano activists that emerged from the academic cauldron of the 1960s in fact hounded their elders. Mora writes that they humiliated members of LULAC and other patriotic groups as "sellouts for emphasizing assimilation and a connection to Spain." In this way, "Chicanos drew a clear line between Mexican Americans and the descendants of European migration. For Chicanos, Mexican Americans constituted a '*raza*,' a distinct racial minority that had been persecuted...."[59]

In 1971 a Texas district court ruled, in *Cisneros v. Corpus Christi Independent School District*, that Mexican Americans constituted an "identifiable ethnic minority class sufficient to bring them within the protection of *Brown [v. Board of Education]*."[60] From this point on, Mexican Americans were phenotypically distinct before the law, and thus victims with a claim on compensatory justice. The process had taken a quarter century. Just twenty-four years earlier, in California (and a scant six years before *Brown* finally ended "separate but equal" in education), the premises held in *Mendez v. Westminster* pointed in the opposite direction.

The Hispanic Expansion

Another problem soon dawned on Mexican American leaders trying to do ethnic category formation. Mexican Americans may have constituted the lion's share of the American population with origins in Latin America (which is even more true today), but being mostly limited to the Southwest kept them from getting sufficient national attention at a time when attention from Washington—because of the rise of racial preferences—was taking on enhanced importance. So the Hispanic pan-ethnicity had to be created.

Militants from La Raza, MALDEF, and other organizations thus began to put pressure on the Census Bureau to create a Hispanic identity for the 1980 census. The term "Hispanic" itself was suggested by Grace Flores-Hughes, who worked at the Department of Health, Education and Welfare (HEW) in the mid-1970s.[61] The idea was "to persuade them to classify 'Hispanics' as distinct from whites." Recategorizing Mexican Americans and lumping them together with Cuban Americans and Puerto Ricans under a "Hispanic American" umbrella was needed because "this would best convey their national minority group status."[62] La Raza executive director Raul Yzaguirre wrote that the census should reject impartial national origin questions it had used for decades ("Where were you born?"; "Where were your parents born?"; "What language do you speak at home?"). As Mora points out, "It is one thing to classify the population and another to count it." Yzaguirre himself both saw the matter clearly and was transparent about it, writing, "There is a difference between a minority group and a national origin group—a difference recognized in terms of national economic and social policies as well as a lengthy, broad ranging legal history relative to civil and minority rights."[63] MALDEF's Vilma Martinez was even more to the point, telling the *New York Times* in 1978, "We are trying to get our just share of political influence and federal funds."[64]

And then there was Rep. Roybal's 1976 legislation, mentioned above. It was the clearest indication that what brought together such disparate people under one ethnic umbrella—and is today in fact perceived as one race, despite all the differences among those said to belong to it—was not race, culture, or language but victimhood. Victim status made it clear "that they deserve respect and assistance," as Manning and Campbell note.[65]

All of this happened before the Immigration and Naturalization Act of 1965, also known as the Hart-Celler Act, had any impact on the nation's demography, so one thing that cannot be argued is that changes in the population required a new category. Census Bureau figures show that in 1970 the foreign-born amounted to 4.7 percent of the entire population, probably an all-time low in American history. In 1850, when the number of foreign-born residents was about to start a sixty-year rise (with some dips along the way), the proportion was 9.7 percent.

Even then, there was pushback. Mexican American militants did not want to be placed in the same group with Cubans because, as Mora points out, the latter had a "higher educational and class status." Cuban Americans themselves resisted group formation. "It did not help that some Chicano and Puerto Rican nationalists had begun to incorporate Cuban revolutionary symbols, such as the images of Che Guevara and the writings of Fidel Castro," in their organizational materials. "Under these circumstances, it was hard for [La Raza] to justify the establishment of Cuban American affiliates to either potential Cuban American networks or to its own Mexican American and Puerto Rican constituency." La Raza had to wait for a Cuban American group that would accept "a disadvantaged minority status."[66] In time, a Cuban group was hoodwinked into getting in under the ethnic umbrella.

There was some resistance from the bureaucracy. Census officials were ambivalent, holding the view that "persons of Latin American descent were quite diverse and would eventually assimilate and identify as white," writes Mora. The census was already doing a good job counting people objectively, said bureau officials, who fought back against the pressure to establish a new category. Mora quotes Conrad Taeuber, associate director of the 1970 census, arguing with

Robert Gnaizda, MALDEF's attorney, during Taeuber's deposition in a suit filed by MALDEF to prevent the bureau from releasing data on Mexican Americans garnered in the 1970 census (which MALDEF contended was flawed): "I'm not sure what you mean by Mexican Americans. Let me tell you what we have. We will have in the [census] report…the number of persons born in Mexico who are living in the U.S. and California. We will have the number of persons born in the U.S. who have a parent born in Mexico. We will have this figure, the Spanish-language population, and we will have the number of persons who reported Mexican in response to the question of origin. That's who we have."[67]

Some people were prescient, fearing from the start that creating a large pan-ethnic group to encompass all these Americans would in fact be divisive. During a House Appropriations Committee debate in in 1969 on a bill to fund an expanded Interagency Committee on Mexican American Affairs (IMAA), Representative Daniel Flood, Democrat of Pennsylvania, asked the IMAA director, "Are you forming a bloc? Are we financing the formation of a bloc?"[68] A bloc was exactly what was being formed.

Eventually the bureaucracy threw in the towel. In 1977, after many rounds of meetings between bureaucrats and the leaders of La Raza and MALDEF, the Office of Management and Budget standardized the categories of "white, black, Hispanic, Asian and American Indian and Alaska native." Its Statistical Policy Directive No. 15 stated: "the categories specified above will be used by all agencies in either the separate or combined format for civil rights compliance reporting and equal employment reporting for both the public and private sectors and for all levels of government."[69] Three years later, the Census Bureau duly took the most decisive step toward creating today's identity politics: it asked Americans to carve themselves up along ethnoracial lines.

But across the country the rank and file has continued to resist the "Hispanic" label. As recently as 2015, the results of a Pew Research survey revealed that less than a quarter of the "Hispanic" population called itself that.[70] Asked what "nationality label" they used, 50 percent of respondents said they used their country of origin, 23 percent said

American, and 23 percent said Hispanic or Latino. The trend, in fact, shows "American" as growing at the expense of the other two labels.

The writer Tom Wolfe, always at his best in chronicling social change, from 1960s radicalism to the rise of the banking class in New York in the 1980s, took humorous note of this phenomenon in his 2012 novel set in Miami, *Back to Blood*. The narrator voices the thoughts of the hero, Cuban American cop Nestor Camacho, on the way the "Anglos" (a word that seems *"off"* to him) had "divided the world up into four colors": "They lumped all Latinos together as brown!—when here in Miami, in any case, most Latinos, or a huge percentage, a lot anyway, were as white as any Anglo." He goes on: "*Latino*—there was something *off* about that word, too. It existed only in the United States. Also *Hispanic*. Who the hell else called people Hispanics?"[71] The latest iteration, "Latinx," created by the superwoke as a response to the supposed male dominance of the Spanish language—the term is "more than a middle finger to the patriarchy," a *Salon* writer helpfully explains, "it's a word that demands inclusion"[72]—is very unlikely to gain traction in any New York bodega or Miami coffee stand.

That 23 percent of those surveyed by Pew would come to accept the Hispanic/Latino bureaucratic labels is still astonishing, however. Government labeling is a powerful force. Mora offers the best explanation as to why so many people inside and outside the synthetic "Hispanic" grouping have come to believe that it is a real classification with a basis in culture and even race: "A sort of collective amnesia sets in as organizations begin to refer to the new category's long history and develop narratives about the rich cultural basis of the classification. By then, the category is completely institutionalized, and the new classification is, like other classifications, assumed to have existed."[73]

Many institutions willingly participated in the creation of this collective amnesia, at the lead of which was Spanish-language media. The Spanish language was the one indisputable shared factor (Brazilians and Portuguese and the small number of speakers of Indian languages who are monolinguals being the exceptions). TV and other media benefit from endowing their audiences with an identity, which helps them to inculcate loyalty. But for the idea that all newly minted Hispanics were victims of American oppression to take hold required something else again: the triumph of the concept, deeply ingrained in Samora's thinking, that society is made up of "dominant" and "subordinate" groups vying with each other in power politics. The idea of America as a melting pot in which new citizens gained a sense of joint mission had to be squelched. This process was replicated with other groups, starting with "Asian Americans," as we will see in the following chapter.

CHAPTER 2

★ ★ ★

The Asian Paradox

Yuji Ichioka, the Berkeley graduate student who coined the term "Asian Americans" in 1966, was a man with a radical Marxist worldview. He founded the first ethnic affinity organization for people from the Asian continent, the Asian American Political Alliance (AAPA), a body that bore the mark of the violent Black Panther movement as well as Maoist thinking and practice, including Mao's use of the Red Guards to transform society during the Cultural Revolution. The AAPA's materials often quoted the works of Chairman Mao and other communist leaders. But Ichioka and the AAPA were not alone among the pioneers of Asian identity to draw inspiration from communist ideas. Many other militants who sought to create a pan-ethnic Asian collective in the 1960s were hard-core Marxists directly indoctrinated by Black Panther leaders. One group, also enthralled by Mao, called itself the Red Guard Party. While Mao was attempting to erase the inheritance of five thousand years of Chinese tradition in mainland China, the racial categories being confected in America were aiming to reverse the "hegemonic narrative" of American history. These ideas were in the air during the middle of the last century—here, in Asia, and everywhere.

It is not happenstance that half a century later, the numbers of admitted students of Chinese (and other Asian) descent are being restricted by elite colleges employing an affirmative-action system that shares the same ideological roots as the "five black categories" and the "five red categories" of Mao's Cultural Revolution. The pariah black categories in China included landlords and rich farmers considered enemies of the revolution; the favored red ones included poor farmers and workers. Today, in America, university admissions departments are assigning certain applicants to a pariah category. "We were treated a certain way not because of anything we did, but because of government categories we were born into," a Chinese immigrant who settled in Connecticut told me in an interview, with bitterness in her voice, adding, "Now we have come to America and are presented with government categories again."[1] At the root of such ideas is a conception of the world as a place divided between dominant and subordinate groups, where language and traditions are not organic developments that reflect natural reality and carry meaning but instruments of the powerful that a well-indoctrinated revolutionary vanguard can change by fiat. At Yale, at Harvard, at specialized high schools in New York City, in the middle schools of Montgomery County, Maryland—indeed throughout the country, Asians have now joined whites in the new Maoist debtors' category and are expected to pay for the supposed oppression of others.

For all these reasons, Asian Americans, particularly the category's largest and most restless component, Chinese Americans, could be the group that brings down the system of racial preferences known as affirmative action. And because racial preferences are one of its gateway drugs, their actions could start to unravel identity politics. As Wesley Yang, writing in *Tablet* in 2018, put it, the "defection of Chinese-Americans from the Asian-American coalition doesn't just threaten the Asian-American political project. It also threatens the entire system of racial patronage, in which America is organized into four racial collectives—white, black, Hispanic, and Asian, with the three non-white groups allied together to defend the interests of minorities amidst white hegemony."[2]

In one of several ironies, the Chinese Americans who may bring down this system by proving many of its tenets wrong started to arrive in great numbers after immigration law was changed in 1965, and after Ichioka first conceived of the Asian American collective. Designating people of such disparate origins as Chinese, Hmong,

Japanese, Filipino, Korean, Laotian, Cambodian, and so on as one large, official category followed the same rationale as the creation of the Hispanic category: a basis on which to demand restitution for supposed past wrongs. (Americans with origins in South Asian countries such as India and Pakistan joined the Asian American category later.) There is a glaring problem, however. The overwhelming majority of Asian Americans today are themselves immigrants who came after 1965 or their descendants. Because there were so few Asian immigrants in America prior to 1965, few of the post-1965 immigrants married Asians already here for many generations. This sets them apart from the experience of Mexican Americans, among whom immigrants and their children often do marry Mexican Americans whose roots in America date back to the 1700s.

The result is that the vast majority of "Asian Americans" today never experienced any sort of legal segregation in the United States, nor have any of their ancestors. There are no family recollections of legally being forced to go to the back of the bus, or being denied service at a lunch counter, or being refused naturalization or the right to marry outside their race. In a manner reminiscent of Cristina Mora's "collective amnesia" with regard to Hispanics, memories of discrimination must be manufactured out of the historical experience of others and then scripted into the minds of young Asians, an indoctrination that starts during K–12 education and is reinforced at the university level by professors like Ichioka, who went on to teach for many years at UCLA. Thus, Asian American students today must be indoctrinated with feelings of victimhood by being drilled on the evils of the Chinese Exclusion Act of 1882, which forbade Chinese immigration or naturalization for those who were here for nearly a century; the 1907 "Gentlemen's Agreement" with Japan, which did the same for Japanese albeit in a more face-saving way; California's Alien Land Law of 1913, which prevented Asians from buying land; and the Japanese internment camps of the 1940s.

Revolutionary Birth

This mental programming that ethnic affinity groups, whether national ones such as Asian Americans Advancing Justice, or smaller, local ones at the campus level, promote to today's Asian Americans echoes an earlier form of indoctrination into hatred of America, its economic system, and small-government traditions as practiced by the Black Panthers in the 1960s. The Panther militants saw the potential to form a revolutionary vanguard in San Francisco's Chinatown and began to train a group of Chinese Americans in Marxist ideology and violent activism. Chinese Americans had indeed experienced legal discrimination, and yet, as with Mexican Americans, a pro-American, pro-assimilationist organization had risen among them. The Panther-trained Chinese American activists, using the same tactics as their Chicano movement counterparts, accused the assimilationists of being sell-outs who practiced "a strategy of white acceptance,"[3] thereby preserving the hegemonic narrative, and eventually ran them off of the field.

These Chinese American activists, the Red Guards, then used the same strategy as their Chicano counterparts to achieve the same goal: they equated their experience to the suffering of black Americans to facilitate the creation of a pan-Asian identity and category. According to the historian Daryl J. Maeda, "The Red Guards adopted the Black Panthers' language and style—two key elements of the Panther mystique—as a political statement that underlined their espousal of the Panthers' racial politics. Thus, they inserted Asian Americans into a racial paradigm, arguing that Asian Americans constituted a racialized bloc subject to the same racism that afflicted blacks." For Asian Americans, "adopting and adapting the ideology of Black Power... enabled them to construct Asian American identity as a new subjectivity that rejected assimilation and consolidated multiple Asian ethnicities under the rubric of race."[4] As with Mexican Americans, the formula had another desired result: it stifled the natural evolution toward assimilation to the norms of the country.

The Panther influence was direct. The Red Guard Party recruited from the Legitimate Ways (known as Leway) community agency in San Francisco, and that's where the black activists found them. "The Panthers used the radical core of Leway to build a revolutionary organization and invited them to weekly study sessions on revolutionary theory" in the Bay Area, Maeda writes. "This core group returned to

Leway armed with an ideological framework derived from reading Mao Tse-Tung, Frantz Fanon, Che Guevara, and Fidel Castro, and began recruiting members."[5] Some of the members of the Red Guard Party even consciously mimicked the dress, language patterns, and habits of the black ghetto. Maeda quotes the writer and Bay Area native Frank Chin, who told interviewer Studs Terkel that in the 1960s, "a bunch of us [Asian Americans] began to appropriate 'blackness.' We'd wear the clothes, we'd affect the walk and began to talk black. We'd call ourselves 'Bro' and began talking Southern."[6]

The Asian American movement borrowed heavily from the black liberation movement, especially its increasingly anti-integrationist and separatist tendencies, but it also layered on top of that Third World decolonialization ideas and opposition to the Vietnam War. Whereas the transnational dimension of Chicano activism was a mere consequence of the effort to put the American of Mexican origin and the Mexican national into one racial box, and the inter-racial coalition that took hold in LA's Boyle Heights in the late 1940s emerged only because Alinsky and Ross put real effort into it, "the Asian American movement was fundamentally committed to the ideologies of interracialism and internationalism," writes Maeda in *Rethinking the Asian American Movement*. From the start, too, he argues, the movement "sought to achieve radical social change by building interracial coalitions and transnational solidarities. Coalitional politics was not simply a by-product or late addition to the movement, but rather was foundational to its understanding of the United States as a capitalistic and imperialistic system that exploited people of color both within and outside its borders." The push to put all Asians into a collective was, at its root, a deeply ideo-logical Marxist effort. Maeda credits the movement with "ideological fearlessness," "boldly [calling] for a revolution that would end U.S. racism, imperialism, and capitalism."[7]

Ichioka himself was an active member of the protest movement at Berkeley, notably marching to demand the release of Black Panther extremist Huey Newton from prison while on trial for killing a police officer in 1968, and whom Ichioka referred to as a "political prisoner." He also marched in support of the United Farm Workers, led by

Alinsky disciple Cesar Chavez. His AAPA, according to Maeda, "frequently quoted Communist Chinese leaders, especially Mao Zedong, but also figures such as Chou En-Lai."[8] Its activism in Third World Liberation protests aside, the AAPA was pivotal in creating the Asian collective. The rationale was to create a large group that could change American society. In an interview years later, Ichioka said: "There were so many Asians out there in the political demonstrations, but we had no effectiveness. Everyone was lost in the larger rally. We figured that if we rallied behind our own banner, behind an Asian American banner, we would have an effect on the larger public. We could extend the influence beyond ourselves, to other Asian-Americans."[9]

Ichioka's method for creating a pan-Asian collective (meaning, really, East Asian at that time, since people from the Indian subcontinent had not yet started immigrating in large numbers) was novel. He and his fellow activist wife, Emma Gee, started combing through the roster of the Peace and Freedom Party, a far-left party that was formed in California and then spread to other states, for Asian-sounding names. They invited as many people as they could find to attend a meeting, and out of it emerged AAPA. It was the first time the term "Asian American" had been used and that any known group was formed out of this pan-ethnicity. A list of demands included in a document called "Understanding AAPA" all started with the words, "We Asian Americans" to underline this emphasis on pan-ethnicity. A typical demand read, "We Asian Americans refuse to cooperate with the White Racism in this society which exploits us as well as other Third World people, and affirm the right of Self-Determination."[10] From Berkeley, AAPA quickly spread to other California campuses, and soon pan-Asian groups were being formed on East Coast campuses, including Columbia and Yale, where students themselves taught a course on the Asian American experience[11]—one reason why New Haven is often thought of as the place where Asian pan-ethnicity was born.

One of AAPA's members was Manila-born Lillian Fabros, a Berkeley undergraduate studying comparative literature. She had been arrested in 1967 for disturbing the peace while trying to disrupt the activities of the US Army Induction Center in Oakland and given a ten-day prison sentence.[12] Fabros was also a member of the Third World Liberation Front, another militant organization that brought together black, Asian, and Latin American students at Berkeley. Her zeal for radicalism and group making was soon put to good use by the federal government. As was the case with Julian Samora, Fabros was crucial in transforming what had been at first a campus-based pan-ethnic identity into a rigid category ratified by the US census. She was named by the Census Bureau to be a founding member of its Advisory Committee on the Asian and Pacific Americans Population for the 1980 census, the first to have the Asian category. Later in life, she became a program manager for Los Angeles County and continued to attend radical get-togethers at Berkeley to celebrate the success of the AAPA's earlier efforts.

AAPA's foundational place in history is assured not only because of the creation of the Asian American collective but also because of its contribution to the establishment of Asian American Studies as an area within the Department of Ethnic Studies created at Berkeley in 1969. Ethnic studies departments are another mainstay of identity politics. (As we will see in a later chapter, Angela Davis calls these departments "the intellectual arms of the revolution.") The AAPA accomplished this by holding a strike on campus. The following year, the AAPA activists decided to take their mission off campus, and the organization mutated into the Asian Community Center, which inculcated radical ideas through movies and literature extolling Maoist China.[13] That same year, Ichioka became associate director of the new UCLA Asian American study center, a post he held until his death in 2002 and which he used to influence thousands of young minds. He devoted most of his research to the history of Japanese Americans and socialism, and played a significant, and in this instance laudable, role in winning reparations for Japanese Americans who had been interned during the Second World War through his testimony before a congressional committee in 1981. Reparations eventually came to pass with the Civil Liberties Act of 1988, with surviving former internees receiving $20,000.

Political Considerations

Asian Americans vote in large numbers for Democratic candidates and support liberal causes. This might lead one to conclude that Asian American activist groups, having swept people into the category, succeeded in indoctrinating them into left-wing ideology. But underneath the general voting patterns is the fact that the numbers of Chinese Americans and Indian Americans who vote are small. They are mostly still sitting on the fence, waiting to see which ideology best suits their circumstances.

We can sense this current ambivalence in the tension among Chinese Americans over racial preferences, and in the behavior of today's Asian Americans. Far from adopting the ways of the radicals of the 1960s, the new generation of Chinese and Indian Americans (again, the vast majority of whom are immigrants or the children of immigrants who arrived after 1965) have willingly assimilated. Chinese and Indian Americans at high levels of educational and professional achievement are no different, in terms of study and work habits, speech patterns, and so on, from elite Americans of any race or ethnic background. But today's assimilation into current elite habits can cut both ways. Another layer of irony is added by the fact that today's Chinese and Indian Americans who support systems of racial preferences (in higher education and hiring) and other progressive policies may actually be appropriating the views of their woke, white, elite counterparts, who engage in what Reihan Salam, writing in the *Atlantic*, calls "white-bashing." In this way they can demonstrate that they have cracked the code of America's class strata, in which low-class whites are the losers in the racial spoils system. As Salam observes, "in some instances, white-bashing can actually serve as a means of ascent, especially for Asian Americans. Embracing the culture of upper-class self-flagellation can spur avowedly enlightened whites to eagerly cheer on their Asian American comrades who show (abstract, faceless, numberless) lower-white people what for."[14]

There are signs that the political momentum may be on the right, as Chinese Americans and Indian Americans rebel against universities and school systems, from Boston and New York to Los Angeles and

San Francisco, that use affirmative action to keep their children out. Indeed, we could be witnessing what the *Wall Street Journal* columnist William McGurn calls an Asian American "awakening" against the realities of racial preferences. McGurn, who spent many years in Hong Kong, where I first met him, writes that, in one of many ironies when it comes to progressives, it is they who have "poked a sleeping giant."[15] The enthusiastic reception that some fifty thousand Indian Americans gave President Trump and India's prime minister Narendra Modi at the "Howdy, Modi" rally in Houston in September 2019 caught many on the Left by surprise.[16]

Such a rally reminds us of the demographic changes that have taken place among the people denominated "Asian Americans." Prior to the changes in immigration law in 1965, Japanese Americans represented 53 percent of the then-small Asian American population. Most had living memories of internment, or their parents did; thus many still felt deep resentment, and with good reason. These two traits combined in a powerful mix: because of their superior numbers and the outright Marxism of some of their militants—Ichioka being the prime example—Japanese Americans played a role in the creation of the Asian group akin to that of Mexican Americans with Hispanics. They were an early engine, supplying the ideology and the leaders. The big difference is that, whereas Mexican Americans have if anything grown in proportion and overall numbers, Japanese Americans have retreated in terms of share of the Asian population: once the leading component, they are now sixth, behind people with origins in China, India, the Philippines, Vietnam, and Korea, in that order. Simply put, fewer people in stable and prosperous Japan saw a reason to immigrate to the United States after 1965, while people from all those other nations did.

In 1930, for example, the population of Japanese origin was nearly twice as large as the then-negligible population of Chinese origin (138,834 to 74,954), and many more times as large as the population of Indian and Filipino origin (there were only 3,130 "Hindus" then—a far cry from Houston 2019).[17] The situation was completely reversed by 2017, at which point the 1965 immigration law had taken full effect.[18] By then, Japanese Americans, including those of partial origin, amounted to only 6.5 percent of the Asian American population, while ethnic Chinese Americans amounted to 23 percent of that population, Indian Americans 20 percent, and Filipinos 18 percent. Japanese Americans, therefore, are much more likely to have been born in the United States, with a rate of 76 percent native birth,[19] compared to 37 percent for Chinese Americans and 31 percent for Indian Americans. Japanese Americans are not only the oldest, they also have the highest rate of marriage outside their national origin group. By the third generation, the out-marriage rate of Japanese Americans reaches more than 60 percent—which means that this oldest and most politically liberal of all the components of the Asian category is, paradoxically, in many ways the most integrated and the least Asian.

The case of reparations for those Japanese Americans who were interned reminds us that—radical politics, Third World decolonialization, and Maoism aside—the concoction of the Asian American pan-ethnicity has also been a spoils system. The idea that group rights would be the conduit for compensatory justice was there from the start. In the case of interned Japanese Americans, one can argue the need for compensation for a grave wrong. What is completely absurd is reparations for people who are fresh off the boat. The unique experience of Indian Americans makes that clear.

Indian Americans Become POC

People from the Indian subcontinent have been classified in a variety of ways by American courts, the census, and other surveys, sometimes as Hindus, as we have seen, and sometimes as black or white. Some courts, as Taunya Lovell Banks notes, have considered high-caste Indians and Parsees (descendants of Persian Zoroastrians who have lived in India for centuries) to be white; in a 1910 case allowing the naturalization of a "'dark-skinned' Afghani born in India," the court made references to the petitioner's "'blue veins' that shone through those parts of his body not exposed to the sun."[20] Indians themselves have also made appeals based on race. In 1923, Akhay Kumar Mozumdar petitioned to be allowed to become a citizen, stating: "I am a high-caste Hindu of pure blood belonging to . . . the warrior or ruling caste.... The high caste Hindus always consider themselves to be members of the Aryan race."[21] By the census of 1970, three-quarters of South Asians (Indians, Pakistanis, Bangladeshis, etc.) were being classified as white. However, following the OMB's 1977 Policy Directive No. 15 (discussed in chapter 1), Indian American organizations successfully lobbied the US government to stop putting them in the white category and instead to include them in the Asian pan-ethnicity being created for the 1980 census.

The reason? As Yen Le Espiritu, then chair of the Ethnic Studies department at the University of California, San Diego, put it, "affirmative action programs have produced a material incentive for Asian Americans to organize along pan-Asian lines."[22] In other words, the same reason as everyone else's: to cleave to an identity, even one that's made up. The Indian American organizations recognized this, and they too wanted a piece of the pie. In a 1975 statement to the US Civil Rights Commission in 1975, the Association of Indians in America (AIA) makes this clear:

> The language of the Civil Rights Act clearly intends to protect those individuals who might be disadvantaged on the basis of appearance. It is undeniable that Indians are different in appearance; they are equally dark skinned as other non-white individuals and are, therefore, subject to the same prejudices.... While it is commonly believed that the majority of Indians working in this country are well-educated and employed in jobs of a professional nature, their profiles are not at all unlike those of Korean and Japanese immigrants.[23]

Not only did the census reclassify Indians, Pakistanis, and others as "Asians," but, crucially, the Small Business Administration found them to be a "socially disadvantaged minority group" and thus eligible for set-aside contracts. It didn't hurt that Manoranjan Dutta, the president of AIA between 1974 and 1977, was also a founding member of the Census Advisory Committee of Asian and Pacific Americans Populations for the 1980 census. The year was, as we have seen and will see again in this book, the start of the agency capture by advocacy groups that has become almost complete in the second decade of this century. Ann Morning, a member of the Census Bureau's NAC on race and ethnicity, writes approvingly that "the group was able to impose its choice on the state—which otherwise would have continued its practice of designating South Asians as white—rather than the other way round."[24]

But there was another reason why the Asian category was a good place to park Americans of Indian, Pakistani, Sri Lankan, and other descent. As Morning as many other experts concede, Indian Americans had an abiding fear of being mistaken for, and of being classified as, either black or Hispanic. "Although this fear betrays bigotry," Morning acknowledges, "it is not necessarily unfounded."[25] In other words, America is to blame for having a racist nature.

Viewed in this way, advocacy organizations such as the AIA were trying to have their cake and eat it, too. They wanted the group rights and benefits that came with being classified as a minority, without the lowly social status of being considered a member of an undesirable group. This win-win especially pleased the upper-caste Indian immigrants who, like Mozumdar in 1923, were zealous about keeping their upper-class self-regard. Thus, Indian Americans, members of a group with the highest educational attainment and highest median household income in America today ($114,261, as compared to a national median figure for all groups of $57,652) are able to get minority set-asides because they are thought "to suffer the same prejudices" as, say, black Americans.[26] We should pause to consider what this says about the incentives that affirmative action provides for identity politics. Any mention of "white privilege" is, at this point, a farce. On paper, Indian Americans had whiteness, which they—or at least the leaders of their organizations, a very different thing to be sure—traded in for affirmative-action benefits.

It is here, however, in the America of the twenty-first century, that the story turns tragic, at least for the children of Americans of Chinese, Korean, and Indian heritage. People of Asian descent account for only 6.7 percent of America's population. Yet this small population stands out for its high levels of success. In America, parents of Asian origin have modeled success that their children have striven to match or exceed as high achievers. Expecting their achievements to gain them access to highly selective US colleges and universities, thus paving the way for professional success, they have discovered that the very fact of their high achievement has put them at a disadvantage. Their parents' success was built on their own efforts and cultural habits; it did not come not from government benefits. (If it had, then other people counted today as disadvantaged racial minorities would be enjoying similar success, which, sadly, is not the case.) Given that the Asian American category contains so many disparate elements—reflecting the fact that Asians account for nearly half of the world population—it would be useful at this point to do a deeper dive into its makeup.

Disaggregating the Collective

The leaders of organizations such as the AAPA and AIA wanted the Asian American category created, of that there is no doubt. But do the people so designated even accept the huge pan-ethnic collective, any more than "Hispanics" accept that label? The indications are that the answer is a resounding no. According to a 2012 Pew Research study, "the Asian-American label itself doesn't hold much sway with Asian Americans": 62 percent describe themselves by their country of origin, just 19 percent describe themselves as Asian American, and 14 percent just call themselves American.[27] When they marry, Asian Americans tend to do so within their national-origin group, and when they marry out, they tend to marry whites, not other Asians. As Wesley Yang observes, "All races are, to varying degrees, artificial constructs. The 'Asian-American' identity is an artificial construct that scarcely anyone claims. . . . Such a confected identity, imposed from above by political entrepreneurs and the government, does not mean anything coherent to the vast majority of those to whom it ostensibly applies."[28]

The statistics alone tell a story of a very disparate group. One particular area where the Asian American category is of little or no use for policy formation is business activity. At least one regression analysis (albeit now an aging one, done after the 1990 census) shows that "Korean Americans stood at the very top of all groups surveyed, Laotian Americans at the very bottom, Chinese and Japanese

Americans at the mean." As Samuel Leiter and William Leiter note, "these statistics show that treating Asian Americans as a single category is 'clearly overinclusive.'" Similarly, within the "Hispanic-American" category, "Cubans stood well above the mean in business formation, Central and Mexican Americans considerably below it."[29] These differences are important in light of the fact that Cuban and Korean Americans are given the same Small Business Administration set-aside considerations as Laotian and Mexican Americans.

Further statistics may explain why the label "Asian American," so important to ideologues like Ichioka, is rejected by the people themselves. If we look at median household income, Indian Americans, as mentioned above, are in the highest bracket ($114,261), well above that of, to take three examples, Hmong Americans ($81,080), Japanese Americans ($80,763), and Bangladeshi Americans ($57,606).[30]

If we look at the percentage of American-born Japanese Americans, at 73 percent, are the most established "Asian" population. By comparison, 37 percent of Chinese Americans were born in the United States, and this population is young, with about half being under eighteen. Just 31 percent of Indian Americans are American-born, two-thirds of whom are under eighteen.[31] This is exactly what one would expect from a new population.

A look at these numbers helps explain voting patterns that have befuddled observers. Some 77 percent of Asian Americans are estimated to have voted for Democrats in the 2018 election, a higher rate than Hispanics. But when we look closer, we see that both Chinese and Indian Americans remain largely unengaged, or rather, they are still sitting on the political fence. Also, of the 63 percent of Chinese Americans who were born overseas, only 58 percent are American citizens and therefore eligible to vote. Overall (pooling both foreign- and native-born), just 54 percent are eligible to vote. Of these, just 48 percent are registered to vote, and 41 percent actually vote (that is, 41 percent of the 54 percent eligible).[32] A small percentage, in other words.

Now, let's look at the Indian-origin population. Half of the 69 percent who are foreign-born are citizens, and 66 percent of the American-born population are under the age of eighteen and therefore nonvoting. Of the voting-eligible population, just 68 percent are registered, and 62 percent actually vote. This means that, though fewer are eligible to vote than those of Chinese origin, those who are, are much more politically engaged.

It is also important to note that the educational level of both Indian and Chinese Americans is among the highest in the country. For Chinese-origin residents, 27 percent have at least a bachelor's degree and another 27 percent have a graduate degree. For Indian-origin residents, 32 percent have at least a bachelor's degree and another 40 percent have a graduate degree. By comparison, only 17 percent of Mexican Americans have a bachelor's, and the figure sinks to only 7 percent among Mexican immigrants. The education success story of Chinese Americans (and Indian Americans to a lesser degree) has down sides, however. That they are experiencing discrimination in admissions to elite universities, which claim to be maintaining "diversity" in their student bodies, has exposed them to the harsh reality of racial preferences (which might be winning them over to the conservative fight against those preferences). And then there is this problem: the high numbers that do go to top colleges, whether or not the school they attend was their first or second or tenth choice—means that this very young population is being indoctrinated into the leftist ideas that permeate the academy.

The strong economic indicators of Indian, Chinese, and Korean Americans are reflected in, and strongly correlated with, cultural indicators such as high rates of marriage, low rates of divorce, and low rates of out-of-wedlock births. Combing through Centers for Disease Control and National Institutes of Health statistics, we find big differences between "Asians" and other groups (though data on specific country of origins for Asians, which would have been far more useful, is unsurprisingly scant).

In terms of family formation, statistics from 2015 showed that nearly nine out of ten Asian American women had married by their early forties (a slightly higher number than among whites), as had more than eight out of ten Hispanic women, with the number for black women about six out of ten. Asian women had the lowest divorce rate, followed by foreign-born Hispanic women. Black women divorced at three times the rate of Asian women, and white women at twice the rate.[33] Asian American women also had by far the lowest rate of out-of-wedlock births, 11.7 percent, compared to 28.2 percent for white women, 51.8 percent for Hispanic women, 68.2 percent for American Indian women, and 69.4 percent for black women.[34]

With stable families often comes a greater emphasis on education. From the National Center for Education Statistics we find, for example, that Asian kids do 60 percent more hours of homework per week (an average of 10.3 hours) than white (6.8), Hispanic (6.4), and black (2.3) kids.[35] As one might expect, hours of homework correlate with dropout rates. Asian Americans ages sixteen to twenty-four have by far the lowest dropout rate in the country, at 2.1 percent, compared to 4.3 percent for whites, 6.5 percent for blacks, 8.2 percent for Hispanics, and 10.1 percent for American Indians/Alaska Natives. A breakdown reveals that the top six (in terms of population numbers in the US) Asian groups (Chinese, Indian, Filipino, Korean, Vietnamese, and Japanese) have pretty much the same rate, with Vietnamese Americans showing the highest dropout rate (3 percent) and Korean Americans the lowest (1 percent). Among Hispanics the variation is wider: Guatemalans have a 27 percent dropout rate while Colombians only 3 percent.[36]

Strong family formation, low rates of divorce and out-of-wedlock births, children who get their schoolwork done, extremely low dropout rates—what Washington think tanks from Brookings to the Heritage Foundation call "the success sequence"—go a long way toward explaining the high earnings and general prosperity enjoyed by Americans of Indian, Chinese, and Korean origin. These practices appear to have enabled "those individuals who might be disadvantaged on the basis of appearance"—in the words of the AIA petition in 1974—to overcome such roadblocks. Not just overcome, but succeed wildly, as we see with these numbers.

What this means for Asian Americans is captured by a blogger for *Medium* who goes by the nom de plume of "Akemi." A *Yonsei*, or fourth-generation Japanese American, she acknowledges not only that she does not face legal discrimination, but also, with a certain ennui, that her generation does not have to work as hard as her parents did. Her UCLA-educated father, she writes, "got his MBA and eventually became the CIO of a large software company." In a blog that sounds more like a complaint than an expression of gratitude, she writes:

> My parents moved to Yorba Linda, a mostly white suburb of Orange County that was also one of the richest cities in the entire country. And that's where I spent my adolescence. Think white picket fences and identical looking rows of two-story homes, perfectly paved streets and even an artificial lake. Think stay-at-home moms overly active in their children's PTA. In Yorba Linda, *"the Land of Gracious Living,"* all my classmates in my honors and AP classes were white or Asian and upper-middle class. On the weeknights, my dad helped me with my Calculus homework and in the summer, I went to horseback riding and science discovery camps....When I think about it now, it's fairly ironic that my community's struggle and success resulted in me being too privileged to be able to conceptualize the oppression my family faced as anything other than abstract and far-away, but that's what happened. And that's the reality of the vast majority of fourth generation Japanese Americans like me.[37]

So, where did Akemi discover "oppression," then? "If I hadn't gone to college and made friends from different ethnicities and socio-economic classes and learned there that systemic racism is still a very real thing, I would still be just as complacent and clueless to this day."

From Fighting the System to Fighting the School System

School, especially college, is the place where Asian Americans are taught to nourish grievances that their own lived experiences (to use a phrase of the Left) have not given them. That is not to say that Asian Americans don't experience occasional person-to-person discrimination. They do, as the blogger Akemi herself writes and as many Asians have told me. The Connecticut resident I quoted earlier tells me she's been told "go back to your country," even though she's a proud and successful American citizen. But it is also a fact that Asian Americans do not encounter legally sanctioned discrimination, and whatever social barriers they do encounter clearly do not hold them back. Their habits and virtues have given them the picket-fence house in America's many Yorba Lindas.

This leads us to another paradox. The very same elite schools that would indoctrinate these young people into the view that America is a racist society are now acting in a racist manner to these same Asian Americans. Research that has come to light since a group of Asian American students, Students for Fair Admissions (SFFA), sued Harvard University in 2017, demonstrates that these applicants are discriminated against when they apply to Harvard and other elite universities, entry to which is an important rung on the ladder of success in this country. The data, moreover, is strong that this discrimination against Asian American applicants is due to the very diversity goals and group rights that moved such organizations as the AIA to petition for inclusion into the Asian collective in the first place. Elite colleges are limiting the number of Asian American applicants granted admission—who, if objective criteria such as academic achievements, test scores, and extracurricular activities were to be considered alone, would be deserving of acceptance letters—because they are Asian. Admissions boards have noticed the success of these students, but they're looking for other minority students in the name of diversity.

In a sinister way, Chinese Americans and Indian Americans who have surmounted sporadic personal racism are met with the return of the truly institutional kind. Rather than try to lift up students being left behind—by, for example, sharing and encouraging best practices—the higher-education establishment has opted to penalize Asian Americans. Indeed, central, though implicit, to today's discrimination by universities is the idea that Asians are too focused on success, forcing their children to do too many hours of homework and join too many clubs. It was similar envy over the success of Japanese and Chinese immigrants in the nineteenth century that led to quotas to keep them out in the 1880s, when white Californians thought they "worked too hard." Jealousy of the farming success of Japanese Americans, many of whom "had become very successful at raising fruits and vegetables in soil that most people had considered infertile," also paved the way for their internment during World War II.[38]

The *Harvard Law Review*, to its credit, explained in 2017 how the university came to engage in discrimination against Asian American applicants. The essay "The Harvard Plan That Failed Asian Americans," like much of the literature surrounding the Harvard case, cites a study that showed that "in order to be admitted to certain selective institutions, Asian applicants needed to score—on the 1600 point scale of the 'old SAT'—140 points higher than whites, 270 points higher than Hispanics, and 450 points higher than African Americans if other factors are held equal."[39] A separate study by Duke professor Peter Arcidiacono, cited in the Harvard case, comes with a model that showed that an Asian American applicant with a 25 percent chance of admission would see his chances rise to 35 percent if he were white, 75 percent if Hispanic, and 95 percent if black.[40]

If objective academic criteria such as grade-point averages and SAT scores were the sole consideration in the admissions process, the proportion of Asian American students admitted to Harvard would rise from 18.7 percent to 43.4 percent, according to Harvard's own internal reports, which came to light in the suit. Even when factoring in "legacy" admissions and athletic recruitment (which takes place even though Harvard and the other Ivies do not give out athletic scholarships), the proportion of Asian American students would almost double to 31.4 percent. The estimates, incidentally, were issued in 2013 by Harvard's own Office of Institutional Research, which had conducted an internal probe that came to light only because of the suit.

How does Harvard manipulate its admissions review to keep down the number of Asian American admissions? In a motion for summary judgment filed in district court in Boston on June 15, 2018, SFFA accused Harvard of using the "personal rating" to hit Asian Americans with a "statistically significant" penalty. "After reviewing six years of admissions data, Duke Professor Peter Arcidiacono (SFFA's expert) found overwhelming evidence that Harvard's admissions process disproportionately harms Asian-American applicants." According to Arcidiacono, the plaintiff's memorandum explains, the university manipulates the "personal rating" criterion in its admissions process. The motion charged that "Harvard's admissions officials assign Asian Americans the lowest score of any racial group on the personal rating—a 'subjective' assessment of such traits as whether the student has a 'positive personality' and 'others like to be around him or her,' has 'character traits' such as 'likability...helpfulness, courage, [and] kindness,' is an 'attractive person to be with,' is 'widely respected,' is a 'good person,' and has good 'human qualities.'"[41]

As an aside, Harvard did not have to reinvent the wheel here. As the SFFA motion made clear, what is being done to Asian Americans is more or less what Harvard did in the 1920s to Jewish applicants, members of another group whose hard work, tendency to have stable families, and high value placed on educational success put their children in good stead. In the 1920s, Harvard president Abbott Lowell wanted to limit the number of Jews at the university but realized that imposing a quota "would trigger opposition and resistance." Therefore, he adopted a version of the subjective personality assessments being used today with Asian American applicants, giving his admissions committee "authority to refuse admittance to persons who possess qualities described with more or less distinctness and believed to be characteristics of the Jews."[42]

In the case of Jews, the Harvard of the 1920s obviously considered them social inferiors. Today, is the case of Asian Americans very different? A dean of admissions at MIT was stunningly candid, if thoughtlessly bigoted, when she described an Asian American applicant as "yet another textureless math grind."[43] As I wrote in a 2018 column: "Small wonder that Chinese-American parents and their children are organizing and storming state legislatures and public school hearings to protest any move they think will perpetuate this system. They're wisely ignoring the pleas of their purported leaders at ethnic affinity organizations, which have completely bought into the racial spoils system produced by racial preferences."[44] The predicament of Asian American families has got everything journalists profess to like, and the fact that you are not reading more stories about this is a sad commentary on the press.

The Boston district court deciding the Harvard case ruled on October 1, 2019, that Harvard's plan did not violate the constitutional rights of the plaintiffs. Judge Allison Burroughs admitted that members of other groups, namely blacks and Hispanics, were given an advantage over Asians, but she said that Harvard did not do this intentionally. However, by relying on the "temporary solution" argument— "[a] race-conscious admissions program allows Harvard to achieve a level of robust diversity that would not otherwise be possible, at least at this time"[45]—the judge leaves open the possibility that, if the Supreme Court reviews the decision, the justices may ask themselves just how much longer the can should be kicked down the road.

Of course, what happens in Cambridge radiates to the rest of the country. In New York City, Asian American parents are fighting attempts by the far-left mayor Bill de Blasio to break up nine selective public high schools that are jewels in the city's tarnished crown. Why? Because they have too many Asian students. No, seriously.

To get into these schools a student must take the highly competitive Specialized High School Admissions Test (SHSAT), a rigorous exam of a student's aptitude in math and English. This makes admissions, needless to say, color-blind and meritocratic. For all the reasons described already in this chapter, in 2019, Asian Americans accounted for 51 percent of the offers of admission by the schools, exactly the same ratio as the year before. Whites accounted for 28.5 percent, a slight uptick from the year before. The problem for de Blasio and the city's other leftist leaders is that blacks accounted for 4 percent of offers and Hispanics for 6.6 percent. In the city's public schools, black and Hispanic students together total 66 percent of the student population, while Asians represent 16 percent.[46] Pretty much since the day they took office, de Blasio and his school chancellor, Richard Carranza, have been targeting the schools by trying essentially to scrap the SHSAT. But in March 2019, when news broke that one of the schools, Stuyvesant High, had accepted just seven black students for the following school year, the story once again went into overdrive. In an indignant tweet, Rep. Alexandria Ocasio-Cortez, the Left's darling, wrote, "68% of all NYC public school students are Black or Latino. To only have 7 Black students accepted into Stuyvesant (a *public* high school) tells us that this is a system failure." Carranza put out a statement that read: "We're also once again confronted by an unacceptable status quo at our specialized high schools. We need to eliminate the single test for specialized high school admissions now."[47]

If Carranza, de Blasio, and Ocasio-Cortez want to change the system, they should look for ways to encourage all families to focus on education as successfully as are the city's Asian Americans. Often from impoverished immigrant families, Asian Americans account for 31 percent of the test takers, around double their proportion of the city's public schools.[48] Non-Hispanic white kids represent 18 percent of test takers, compared to 15 percent of the public school population. Some 24 percent of test takers were designated as Latino, though they are 40 percent of the public school population. Some 20 percent of test takers were black, six percentage points under their overall number. The composition of the Latino and Asian categories is another factor to consider. Population breakdown figures for the city show that 60 percent of its Hispanics are Puerto Rican or Dominican, 23 percent Central American, and 14 percent Mexican. Among the Asians, 48 percent are Chinese, 19 percent are Indian, and almost 8 percent are Korean. Thus, some three-quarters of Asians in the city comprise groups that statistics show have high cultural indicators, including placing a high premium on education, whereas this is not true of the Hispanic groups. But encouraging some city populations doing less well in school than Asians to adopt habits that have helped Asians attain educational success is not an option that has occurred to city leaders.

In another example of the Asian American awakening that McGurn highlighted, parents of Chinese, Indian, and Korean origin filed an antidiscrimination suit in December 2018 charging that de Blasio's plan disproportionately hurt Asian American students. One of the parent plaintiffs, Yi Fang Chen, has the typical profile. She emigrated to Brooklyn from China in her teens with basically no English. As she told the *Wall Street Journal*, her father was a construction worker and her mother a seamstress. Chen, who earned a PhD from Stanford and became a data scientist, was not going to let de Blasio get in the way of her two children's ambitions. "I feel like everyone deserves equal opportunity. This is what this country is for, not equal outcomes," she said.[49]

The same situation has developed in Montgomery County, Maryland, a leafy suburban area outside Washington, DC, with a public school system to which the capital's bureaucrats and lobbyists send their children. Again, moved by the "too many Asians" syndrome, the woke school district administrators decided in 2016 to make changes to the admission policy for the middle school magnet program that resulted in a sharp decline in Asian American admissions. As reported in my article for *National Review*, for the 2016–17 school year, the drop was 23 percent, and for 2017–18, 20 percent, while "the numbers for whites, Hispanics, and blacks went up." Just as in New York, the mostly Chinese American parents raised a ruckus, and this time the US Department of Education's Office of Civil Rights said it would investigate the matter. The evidence strongly indicated "that the effort was…an attempt at 'race norming,' which is unfair and illegal." Race norming refers to "adjusting outcomes to account for the race or ethnicity of an applicant. In selecting people for school admission or employment, the selector would not admit, say, the top 5 percent of all candidates, but the top 5 percent in each racial silo…." Congress outlawed the practice in 1991."[50]

The district changed the magnet-school admissions process because of "recommendations included in a 2016 report commissioned by the school system from the…consulting agency Metis Associates. The report noted that the system 'experienced significant increases in the number and diversity of students over the past 20 years.'" As I noted in my article, the school superintendent had said that "the county had 'created structural and systemic barriers that have prevented some of our students from full participation in an instructional program that meets their needs and pushes them to excel.'"[51] But the county had done no such thing. It was the habits and practices and cultural mores of families in the district that had led to their children's demonstrable success or lack thereof.

To take one well-known example of student success, Indian American kids have won every Scripps National Spelling Bee since 2008, except for 2019, when there was a tie among eight children, seven of whom were Indian American. As anthropologist Shalini Shankar wrote in the *Los Angeles Times*, these children come from "a culture invested in competitive spelling and parental investment in a child's educational success."[52] But rather than make the case that other groups could benefit from adopting these practices, the leaders of the mostly leftist Asian American affinity organizations decry what they call "the myth of the model minority." In so doing they have abandoned Asian Americans. Asian Americans Advancing Justice–Asian Law Caucus (AAJC), for example, wants to disaggregate the Asian group to show that there are smaller country-of-origin groups that do not as well in terms of education and income, such as Cambodians, Laotians, and the Hmong. Wesley Yang pokes fun at this further contradiction:

> *We have poor people too!* the activists insist. *See?* We're not a model minority after all. In other words, the Asian-American leadership petitioned the government to cease treating them as the single group that they are not and never were. They aggregated the group into a fictitious identity in the first place (and still purport to represent the interests of 20 million Americans of Asian descent) so as to maximize the numbers they could claim to represent on paper. They then resorted to disaggregating what they had themselves aggregated, so as to have a claim to represent disadvantaged minorities who need civil-rights leaders.[53]

The AAJC leadership is despised by many of the Asian parents who are organizing to fight educational discrimination. That won't matter so much to these activists, however, who are much more dependent on their (white) liberal donors than on the people they claim to represent. They are, too, prime examples of the elite network insiders discussed in the previous chapter; the Ford Foundation alone has given AAJC $30 million between 2006 and 2019.[54] While leaders of traditional ethnic organizations have typically strived to show their members in a good light, AAJC ironically pushes back against any idea that Asian Americans constitute a model minority, using its social media platforms to fight the idea of Asian success. In one instance, the organization promoted a *New York Times* op-ed by a Harvard student, a leader in the university's Asian American Women Association, that stated, "The model minority is yet another myth of meritocracy that reinforces racial hierarchy and shrouds discrimination. It's time to acknowledge the truth: the model minority does not exist."[55] Another opinion piece the group promoted, by Kat Chow, then with NPR, was titled "'Model Minority' Myth Used as a Racial Wedge Between Asians and Blacks."[56]

What caused Chow's ire was a *New York Magazine* column by Andrew Sullivan, in which he observed that, despite

> brutal oppression, racial hatred, and open discrimination over the years…today, Asian-Americans are among the most prosperous, well-educated, and successful ethnic groups in America. What gives? It couldn't possibly be that they maintained solid two-parent family structures, had social networks that looked after one another, placed enormous emphasis on education and hard work, and thereby turned false, negative stereotypes into true, positive ones, could it? It couldn't be that all whites are not racists or that the American dream still lives?[57]

Time was when ethnic affinity organizations would have paid good money for messages that presented the group in a good light. The vast majority of people who applaud the success of Asian Americans would like to see blacks, whites, and everyone else emulate them—most people want to see not one group pitted against another but everyone lifted up. The activist affinity groups get things exactly backward.

That the activists at AAJC reject the image of Asians as model citizens tells you all you need to know about what interests they defend. They are not working in the interest of the members of the Asian American category—if they were, they would embrace the model-minority idea; they are working, rather, to change society. The problem for them and the Left in general (and it is a big one) is the following: Asian Americans have succeeded in precisely the way that Gramsci, Marcuse, and Ichioka despised, through individual action, striving, and aspirational effort. They have succeeded not by copying the Red Guard radicals of the 1960s. Their success gives the lie to all the leftist theories about how supposedly "subordinate" people succeed in America. More than any other group, they shred the notion that it was the immigrants who came in after 1965 who demanded the categorizing of races and ethnicity. With them, it was exactly the opposite.

The radicalized children of pre-1965 immigrants mimicked the ways of black militants and sought mass mobilization, but that did nothing for the Chinese and Indians who immigrated in the 1960s and thereafter, whose lives demonstrated the value of individual action. And yet the illusion of collectivism and group making persists. President Obama, as we will see in the next chapter, tried in his last days in office to confect yet one more marginalized category out of a group of Americans who have already succeeded.

CHAPTER 3

★ ★ ★

Don't Be So MENA

Linda Sarsour is no stranger to controversy. A Palestinian American activist, she is well known as a race-baiting, anti-Israel provocateur who supports sharia law and the virulently anti-Semitic Nation of Islam led by Louis Farrakhan. In a 2011 tweet (later deleted) attacking the human rights campaigner Ayaan Hirsi Ali, along with another activist, for denouncing the practice of female genital mutilation, Sarsour said, "I wish I could take their vaginas away—they don't deserve to be women." Later, as a founder of the Women's March in protest of the election of Donald Trump, she attacked Jewish members of the organization's leadership who supported Israel's right to exist; the Women's March later cut ties with her over charges of anti-Semitism. And yet, in 2015, despite Sarsour's intolerant extremism, which was well in evidence at that point, the Census Bureau invited her to its bunker-like headquarters in Maryland, tapping her to share her "expertise" and give advice on the fabrication of yet one more ethnic category, for those from the Middle East and North Africa. Referred to by the acronym MENA (rhymes with Tina), this category was to encompass all American residents, citizens and noncitizens alike, from the region also designated as MENA: the countries in that vast expanse from Morocco to Iran, and from Turkey to the Sahara Desert, which separates North Africa from black Africa. In other words, a pretty big patch of real estate, comparable to the geographies where "Asian Americans" and "Hispanics" hail from, and just about as heterogeneous. Indeed, comparisons with the creation of the Hispanic pan-ethnicity were made time and again at the 2015 Census Bureau meeting.

One year after this auspicious meeting at the Census Bureau headquarters, an interagency task force formed by President Obama's Office of Management and Budget finally pushed the idea out into the open. The task force made its proposal to add MENA to the 2020 census just two months before the November 2016 presidential election, with the comment period set to end on October 31. Another part of the proposal was to "formalize Hispanic/Latino as a racial category rather than…an ethnic category of people of any race."[1] Hispanics would thus join other races in a new category that would be labeled not "races" but, well, "categories." This vague label would also be applied to MENA, together with whites, blacks, and so on. The overall impact would have been to help perpetuate the Hispanic identity by giving it, however ambiguously, the same weight as race. The OMB notice sought to downplay the significance of the proposals by calling them a "limited revision" needed to improve data collection.[2] Clearly, the Obamaites fully expected a Clinton administration to bless the entire project. Then history got in the way.

If transparency is of any value, then it was indeed fortuitous that the bureau included Sarsour in its session. She was not the only participant who made clear what MENA—an idea that has been kicking around for decades—was all about, but she was one of the most outspoken. John Fonte, of the Hudson Institute, a colleague of mine in the Washington think-tank world who also looks into these issues, found a video recording of the entire census forum and contacted me. He and I watched it and realized that we had discovered a gold mine. I had a Heritage intern transcribe the hours of discussion.[3] We discovered along the way that Sarsour and the others had a pretty powerful audience. On hand were John Thompson, then the Obama-appointed director of the Census Bureau, and Roberto Ramirez, the chief of the Census Bureau's Ethnicity and Ancestry Statistics Branch, who moderated the session. The change that the activists were advocating was nothing less than overturning a racial scheme that had existed for over a century.

Since 1909, and to this day, the US government has categorized Arabs as white, in the census and all official surveys, in the courts, and so on. For any who may scoff at this notion, let's remember the long list of Americans who are partly or wholly of Arab descent: Purdue University president and former Indiana governor Mitch Daniels; former California congressman Darryl Issa, who had the distinction of being the wealthiest member of Congress; Florida congresswoman and former secretary of health and human services Donna Shalala; famed former football quarterback Doug Flutie; the political Sununu family of New Hampshire (father John H., the state's former governor and chief of staff to George H. W. Bush; son John E., former US senator; and son Christopher, current governor); Apple founder Steve Jobs; and actor Tony Shalhoub. The list could go on, but the reader gets the picture. These are not marginalized people whose ancestry got in the way of their success, or who were in need of a mobilization movement to help them. Arab Americans have a higher median income than their fellow Americans.[4]

To take another group, Americans of Iranian (or Persian) descent have been incredibly successful. Many are professionals who emigrated around the time of the fall of the shah, in 1979, or their descendants; in 2005 Iranian Americans' per capita average incomes were estimated to be 50 percent higher than that of the rest of the population.[5] Overall, there are 2.5 million persons of Arab or Persian origin in America (just 0.5 percent of the country's total).[6] Of these, the largest groups by far are those of Lebanese and Iranian descent (each roughly 30 percent of the total); Egyptians (many of them Coptic Christians, like Dina Powell, a top security advisor to George W. Bush) are the third-largest group, at around 12 percent of the total. If we add to that 222,593 Americans of Turkish origin, the MENA population is approximately 2.25 million.

In trying to invent a category for these Americans, the Census Bureau was at least being transparent when it asked for the "expertise" of Sarsour, whose *métier* is activism and organizing. Like Lillian Fabros, whom we met in the previous chapter, and Julian Samora, whom we met in the first, she's another racial hustler maneuvering for power. Sarsour, in fact, understands this so well that she once quipped in a YouTube video, "When I wasn't wearing the hijab I was just some ordinary white girl from New York City."[7] At the 2015 census forum, with Thompson and Ramirez lending their ears, she did not hold back.

As with other pan-ethnic categories, MENA was about political power, thwarting the assimilation process, getting the benefits that come with racial preferences, and changing America. Sarsour and the others made this clear. It was not about counting actual residents, in which they had no interest—the rationale that activists always trot out to justify categorization. Indeed, comparisons with the creation of the Hispanic collective abounded. It was the model. Lest anyone question that this was about replicating that earlier success, another expert present at the meeting was Cristina Mora.

It's Not About Counting

"Like, I don't really care about just counting how many people there are who are quote MENA," Sarsour comments at one point, "it's how we utilize this information that can be beneficial to our community." Responding to a question from another participant on whether American residents of Middle Eastern origin, when answering the census, should be able to respond that they were both Arab and white, Sarsour reminded her audience what things were really about. "For me it's *no*, because we have to understand that the way that people respond is based on the political context that we live in. So, in 2010 we actually started a national campaign that [told respondents] 'check it right, you ain't white.' And we actually asked people to go into the other category and identify themselves as whatever, Yemen, Arab-American, whatever they wanted to say, even though we knew eventually those others go back in the white category." Then Sarsour got specific about what the matter was about: "As folks are thinking about the feedback, what benefit do we get as a community from being white in the current political context as Arab-Americans in the United States of America, does it serve us right to call ourselves white and put ourselves back in the white box?" Just to make sure she wasn't being too subtle, she reinforced her point: "When we look at accessing federal, you know, any types of federal support, for example, we lose out *dramatically* because we don't have the separate category.... We're not seen as a priority area for city or state or federal funding."

And what about those rank-and-file Arab Americans and others from the Middle East who have joined the mainstream, and have zero interest in being considered marginalized—like the Mexican Americans canvassed by the UCLA researchers in the 1960s? Another participant in the forum, Morad Ghorban, of the Public Affairs Alliance of Iranian Americans, warned, "I think for the Iranian American community, the most important thing for them, is to be counted as Americans of Iranian or Persian ancestry." Did they consider themselves white? The reason this question is important is that it is often a proxy for the degree of marginalization a person actually feels. "I think you'll see a split in the community, whether they want to be identified as white or not," said Ghorban. Sarsour came back to this idea later on in the conversation, complaining about the lack of consciousness of such people: "I mean, these people really have to understand the deep impact this has by considering being able to say I'm Palestinian but then still having to go and say I'm white. Like, I'm personally not cool with that."

Sarsour was not alone in her opinion. Khaled Beydoun, a law professor from Detroit, said he wanted to "echo Linda's sentiment" and disagreed with giving the people in question the opportunity to categorize themselves as white. "To your surprise ... there are significant elements within the broader, specifically Arab American community, who want to maintain whiteness," he said. But "even though there's strong sense on the ground to maintain, you know, your ceremonial whiteness," changes could be expected after racial preference benefits were dangled. Beydoun explained: "Maybe there might not be considerable buy-in immediately after the classification is framed and adopted. But there's a cascading effect, *right?* These classifications are going to be adopted on college applications, on employment forms.... And when that happens, and people tie in ticking that classification with a specific interest, then there's going to be buy-in. So, in the long term, the buy-in is going to come, especially when the classification is echoed, endorsed, and adopted by alternative mediums in the educational context, the employment context, and so on.... And again, really important to be forward-thinking."

Yes, Sarsour, Beydoun, and the others were actually being this transparent. They were spelling it all out, in a government building, no less. No, the category was not being created *because of* grassroots demand, but *in spite of* grassroots ambivalence, if not rejection. Yes, their plan was to prevent assimilation. Yes, they understood that, in order to make the category permanent, they had to seduce people with benefits. It was all there, expressed in American colloquialisms.

The Census Bureau, in the person of Roberto Ramirez, couldn't agree more. Ramirez jumped in at this point and exclaimed, replying to Beydoun, "You know, I'm actually happy that you said that, because I just wrote it down—you know, the buy-in. So, I think this is something that's really important to understand." The buy-in that took place with Hispanics was his handy point of comparison, as Ramirez pointed out at another point in the session. "You know, I want to disclose this...one of the reasons why I invited Dr. Mora to come talk to us is because a lot of her research and books that she's done, is look at the pan-ethnicity development of the Hispanic term. As she mentioned, in the '70s, where you had Cubans and you had Venezuelans and you had Puerto Ricans, who said, 'I'm not Hispanic. I don't know what the heck that is. So why are you trying to put me under that umbrella?'" At this point, Mora piped up gamely, "And there's no Hispania!" Ramirez forged ahead approvingly, "Yes, exactly. So, there's a lot of parallels that what's happening here with the Middle Eastern and North African category, if you will, right? Same things we're hearing with you right now. Like, 'What the heck is that? What do you mean? That doesn't even exist, you know.'" Mora agreed that "MENA doesn't exist as, sort of, an identity or what people call themselves." But, she added, "nothing exists before it's created."

That, of course, is not true. Her remark conveniently ignores that ethnic groups, clans, tribes, and nations can be the organic result of spontaneous order. Most identities are not the product of government fiat. Historically, ethnicities have come into being through bottom-up coalescing of tribes and clans (think the Kurds, Berbers, Basques), while others may share common ancestors. As we will see in chapter

6, on demography, in the United States bureaucrats created synthetic groups as a frightened response to the race riots of the 1960s, in a search for mediators. But the mediators are always self-serving individuals such as Sarsour, for whom the actual desires of the people in question are secondary at best. Pace Mora, not every group emerges in the petri dish of a neon-lit federal building. To be sure, the fabrication of Hispanics—Mora's model for what was being attempted at the 2015 forum—was the result of such a process. And she thought that could be replicated with other people. She reminded those gathered that, with some elbow grease, things could get accomplished and those pesky, reluctant people they were discussing would give in. "When the Hispanic category—Latino category—was being discussed in the 1970s, lots of people did not know what this was. This is a huge effort throughout the 70's to get people to actually recognize this. It involved the media. It involved activists. So, if we're unsure about whether it exists or not, these things will take on a life of its own."

Despite Ghorban's view that people of Iranian ancestry preferred to see themselves as Americans and that on the census at least half would identify as white, the leadership of the activist organizations—as we have seen again and again—preferred confecting another category. Not coincidentally, that would have led to unending employment opportunities for said leaders. Unsurprisingly, when the Census Bureau announced in January 2018 that MENA would not be included in the 2020 census, the National Iranian American Council (NIAC) expressed frustration: "Rather than limiting Iranian Americans to a racial category that includes 61% of the U.S. population"—that is, white—"a MENA category could lead to the same benefits for Iranian Americans as the 'Hispanic or Latino' category created for Latino Americans."[8] The statement was not just transparent but translucent.

Other advocacy groups expressed similar irritation with the 2018 decision. Samer Khalaf, president of the American-Arab Anti-Discrimination Committee, told a reporter for the *Arab Weekly*: "'Federal, state and civil government divide their funding for various communities based on the census.... There is also the big question of whether we are an ethnicity or a race. I don't consider myself from the white race even though my skin tone is light.'" Speaking to the same reporter, Rashad al-Dabbagh, the executive director of the Arab American Civil Council, went straight to the point: "the Trump 'administration does not want us to have an accurate count and have the same benefits other communities get.'"[9] And the benefits are substantial, as Maya Berry of the Arab American Institute made clear to *Middle East Eye*: "What's at stake here is a tremendous amount—it is how we allocate every single dollar of our multi-billion dollar budget, it's how we draw congressional districts in terms of representation in Congress."[10] According to an NPR story, Helen Samhan, a cofounder of the Arab American Institute, began advocating for MENA in the 1990s.[11]

The thrust of the debate that day at the Census Bureau headquarters made clear that creating MENA was more than just a mere hustle for dollars. The list of participants included not just leaders of militant advocacy groups for whom the creation of yet one more group was the equivalent of the full employment act, but also replete with professors of critical theory and other identity "studies" courses, for whom transforming America is job one. Thus, the very idea of the melting pot, with immigrants and their children progressively becoming and feeling American, was seen as anathema. "One way that you might determine whether these categories will have some longevity into future generations is whether you're seeing communities completely defined around it," said Sahar Aziz of Texas A&M School of Law. "So if you're seeing churches that are defined around a certain ethnic identity more than likely that's going to stick. That's going to stay for multiple generations because people are going to be going to this church or to this, you know, whatever it is that mobilizes them that will preserve that identity over generations as opposed to becoming kind of, I hate to use melting pot, but that will melt away over time."

Merarys Rios, then the newly appointed chief of the Ethnicity and Assets branch at the bureau, agreed, and decried that Americanization was happening among immigrants from Central America. When the bureau did further inquiries, she said, some people responded with answers such as "'well, you know, I'm Salvadoran, but my child was born here so he's American.' So we already lose that!"

John Tehranian, of Southwestern Law School, went further when he remarked that, once MENA was created—as all thought it would be at that point—the bureau should not stop there but go ahead and recategorize whites as Europeans. "I would want to encourage maybe a bit of a radical proposal," he said. "If we're disaggregating the white category and taking Middle Eastern and North African out of it, why keep that term white on the census? Why not just simply put European and go to the origins directly. The term white is deeply problematic. It's deeply political.... So let's go with European and disaggregate the category. I think that would be a tremendous service to diversity in our country and to the future of our country."

For Tehranian, the possibility that creating a "European" category would enhance "diversity" was all to the good. But Samuel Huntington, the noted political scientist, feared that creating a "Euro-American" identity would lead to long-lasting social division. Huntington foresaw that, once whites merrily jumped on the identity-group bandwagon, they would cement identity politics. Once they begin to define themselves as Euro-American, Huntington wrote in his 2004 book *Who Are We?*, "the cultural divide in America will be formalized."[12]

For all these reasons, I made it my business to stymie the MENA project. Even before Hillary Clinton went down to defeat, I started writing about the folly of designating yet one more synthetic group, and I wrote about it often. "One day in the not-too-distant future," I said in *National Review*, "you may be asked to stand at attention at your local ballpark—Busch Stadium, perhaps—to celebrate Mena Heritage Day. The organist will do his level best to play traditional Mena music, vendors will sell Mena delicacies, and a chorus of Mena-American children will sing the national anthem." That the category is fictitious "wouldn't stop pride in Menaism from being progressively drilled into the young and unsuspecting by our schools or from being embraced by corporations and sports leagues that want to buy a little peace. And, of course, let's not forget how government would bribe people to tick the Mena box with the full array of benefits that come from the affirmative action cornucopia."[13] In a piece written for the *Washington Post* before the 2016 election but not published until December 12, I urged the Obama administration to do the right thing and withdraw the proposal before leaving office, warning that balkanization would get worse if we kept adding groups and sought to make them permanent: "These phenomena have caused much of the social churning of the past 18 months. And yet, the same elites who helped brew that dangerous potion want to create new spirits to toss into the mix."[14]

Rules proposals made by government must be accompanied by a public comment period, and I rallied conservatives to voice their opinions about adding MENA to the census before the commenting period was to end. In a post at the Heritage Foundation site the *Daily Signal*, I wrote, "For conservatives who care about promoting a united country with a national purpose, and who want to put a stop to the reinterpretation of America as a nation of adversarial groups, the answer should be no." The second proposal by Obama's OMB, on Hispanics,

> would effectively mean that people of Latin American or Iberian origins would no longer be able to declare whether they are also black, white, or 'some other race.' This change would practically make 'Hispanic' their only racial identifier. It would do so by collapsing what are now two separate questions—Are you Hispanic or not? What race are you?—into one: What is this person's race or origin?... Proponents say responders can always check more than one box. The reality is that given the way the questions are framed that is unlikely to happen.

I pointed to a long study that the government had released that February, which made clear that "the growing number of Americans of Spanish or Portuguese ancestry who are checking the 'white' box— more than 29 million out of 56 million in the 2010 Census—would be nudged away from doing so." Finally, I quoted my own comment in response to the proposed rule change: "Dangling purported advantages such as congressional redistricting would further help perpetuate divisions within the country by giving people an incentive to identify themselves as a member of a subnational group and a disincentive to build inter-ethnic coalitions."[15]

Conservatives responded with a wave of comments on the government site, opposing the MENA project and the Hispanic corollary. The effort to convince the new administration to do the right thing and back away from refueling identity politics got a boost when John Fonte discovered the video of the Census Bureau forum. He and I went on the offensive, meeting with members of the administration and writing jointly for Heritage and the Hudson Institute that they had best pay attention to their predecessors' dual proposals. "If this is to be a truly transformational administration," we wrote, "it should use the 2020 census to get rid of all the synthetic groupings." The administration did hold back from endorsing the changes in time. In January 2018, the Census Bureau announced that it would not move ahead with the proposed changes.

Earlier Middle Eastern Immigrants

What we did would have pleased generations of Arab Americans descended from immigrants who have been landing on American shores since the 1800s and who believed in personal striving and joining the mainstream. But the law professor Sahar Aziz made clear at the Census Bureau forum that he disapproved of the assimilation of these earlier immigrants, mostly from Lebanon and Syria, and their descendants: "I just wanted to give a little clarification about the quote unquote Arab identity. The implicit assumption in our conversation is that the people answering these questions are first- and second-generation immigrants who still have very strong conscious identifications with either a national origin or an ethnic origin." That was incorrect, apparently. Many more Arab Americans had been here for several generations, "and so the national identity, the national origin identity or the ethnic origin identity, starts to become diluted in terms of how they self-identify. Some of them completely pass into being white in terms of their social experience depending on their morphology and phenotype and skin color and hair texture." The reality that Aziz was bemoaning was, of course, that for many Americans of Arab descent, race isn't an issue—they simply take pride in being American. One such descendant of Ellis

Island–era Arab immigrants, the late White House correspondent Helen Thomas, once remarked, "I think everybody who was born here or becomes a naturalized citizen is an American, period. You shouldn't have to have a hyphen between your nationality and your ethnic background."[16] Thomas, for whom I interned in the White House in 1986, was a very liberal journalist. But she was hardly alone in resisting being pigeonholed. At the time the MENA category was being considered, a reporter noted that there was not "universal support for the proposed Census change among those who could identify as Middle Eastern or North African.... 'I'm not for it,'" one such person, whose father was a Syrian immigrant, said when interviewed. "'I feel I'm a Mayflower American. We're broken down into villages and countries [where we come from]—I don't like that.'"[17]

The first wave of Arab immigration, from the lands of the Ottoman Empire, preceded the opening of the Ellis Island port of entry in 1892 by about two decades; it ended with the Immigration Act of 1924 (the Johnson-Reed Act), which established quotas based on national origin, closing the doors to Italians, Jews, Greeks, and pretty much everyone except the Irish, Germans, Scandinavians, and other northwestern Europeans. Most of the Arab immigrants came from Greater Syria (and thought of themselves as Syrians), and most were young, single, Christian men. Like other immigrants, they hoped to find prosperity in America as well as freedom from religious persecution. They prospered and fanned out across the country. By 1925, there were about a quarter of a million Arab immigrants living in America.[18]

While this first wave was mostly made up of working-class immigrants, a second wave, which included more Muslims, began in the 1950s. It attracted more intellectuals and professionals (who were therefore more likely to gain entry). They came because of the instability brought by nationalist uprisings and decolonization—the era of Nasser in Egypt and, later, the Ba'ath Party in Syria and Iraq. The military leaders who rose to power had a Marxist bent, which explains the elite and educated profile of those who fled. A third wave, following the 1965 immigration law—and the 1967 Six-Day War between Israel and Egypt, Jordan, and Syria, as well as conflicts and tensions among Arab states—brought many Palestinian Arabs. This brought the population of Americans and other residents with Middle Eastern backgrounds to nearly a million by the last quarter of the twentieth century.

Almost from the start, immigrants who identified as Syrian, Lebanese, or other Arab ethnicities were considered white, as opposed to of the "yellow race," at a time when Chinese and certain other Asians were barred from citizenship. As whites, Arabs could become naturalized. A few legal challenges in the early twentieth century helped to settle the racial question. In one such case, in 1909, a man was arrested for a minor infraction in Venice, California, by a police officer originally from what today is Lebanon. At trial, the defendant claimed that, since the police officer was from Asia, he was "Mongolian" and not white, and thus had no legal standing to make arrests. Arab American community leaders helped the police officer with his defense, presenting evidence that his ethnicity fit under the classification of white. The judge ruled that the arrest could stand as the officer was indeed white.[19]

In 1977, the Office of Management and Budget adopted Directive no. 15, stating that for the purposes of statistics and administrative reporting on race and ethnicity, persons with "origins in any of the original peoples of Europe, North Africa, or the Middle East" are white.[20] The matter was thus basically settled.

It was this racial regime that Linda Sarsour, Khaled Beydoun, and the other participants at the census conference were trying to undo. They wanted to *unwhite* the two million Americans with ancestry in Lebanon, Iran, Egypt, and so on in the name of an ideology that encourages group dependency on government benefits. In the first half of the twentieth century, immigrants from Middle Eastern and North African regions aspired to become part of the American mainstream; like the activists discussed in chapters 1 and 2, Sarsour and her colleagues in 2015 sought to carve out a group identity as a rejection of that mainstream.

A strange logic is at work here. Sarsour and others decry "white privilege" and the people who supposedly benefit from it. At the same time, they oppose viewing MENA people as white, which, according to their thinking, would confer privilege. Recall Sarsour's comment that, without a hijab, she would be seen as "just some ordinary white girl." Does she believe that it is being a member of a *minority* group—signaled by the wearing of the hijab—that confers privilege?

Sarsour and the other forum participants were fighting against the value of personal aspiration, as enacted by individuals and families, that has so rankled those who seek to use collective activism to transform society, from Gramsci and Marcuse to Samora and Ichioka. This time, they had at their disposal a trait that, though not exactly immutable, is not entirely and always a matter of choice, either: religion.

While Christians, mostly Maronites and Copts, had dominated the earliest waves of immigrants, for the past fifty years, Middle Eastern immigrants have included greater numbers of Muslims. What the Obama-era task force, and the census forum participants, wanted to do was to racialize the religion of Islam. We see examples of this every day, when criticism of Islamic practices or of any Muslim is met with cries of "racism," as if Islam were not practiced by people of all races and in many geographical locations. It is the religious version of the racialization that took place with Mexicans and then the larger group, Hispanics. Arabs and Islam played a strong role in creating the identity and culture of today's Spain, so there is some irony in the would-be architects of MENA using the creation of the Hispanic category as their blueprint. If you can racialize different people who only share a history of colonization by the Spanish Empire, you can racialize how people pray to God.

But we shouldn't duck an important issue. Whether the earlier waves of Middle Eastern immigrants found it easier to assimilate in America because of their Christian faith, and the latter wave will find it harder because they are Muslim, is a valid question.

An American Islam?

That America was first settled by Protestants, specifically the Puritans—protesting Protestants—is one of the most important aspects of the American character. To Edmund Burke, this Protestantism was one of the main factors that gave Americans from the start their "fierce spirit of liberty."[21] The influence of religion was felt not just in the churches but in all aspects of everyday life. Alexis de Tocqueville, an early analyst of the nation, noted in the 1830s that "in the United States religion is…intermingled with all national habits and all the sentiments to which a native country gives birth; that gives it a particular strength."[22] As Burke observed of the immigrants who set out for America from Germany, Switzerland, France, and other countries, the "stream of foreigners which has been constantly flowing into these colonies has for the most part been composed of dissenters from the establishment of their several countries, and has brought with them a temper and character far from alien to that of the people with whom they mixed."[23]

The expectation that people with a particular religion would have a particular political culture had an unfortunate by-product: religious bigotry. It was directed early on against Catholics, whose hierarchical proclivities, many thought, would not mix well with the demands of a constitutional republic. Already in colonial times there had been anti-Catholic animus, which had roots in doctrinal differences as well as in concerns about national security—the fear of invasion from the Spanish colonies to the south. After independence, the identification of Protestantism with freedom made this antipathy worse. "The Catholic Church," wrote Huntington, "was seen as an autocratic, anti-democratic organization and Catholics as people accustomed to hierarchy and obedience who lacked the moral character required for citizens of a republic. Catholicism was a threat to American democracy as well as to American Protestantism."[24] We saw in the first chapter how the Catholicism of the Louisianans was held against them. The arrival of largely Catholic immigrants from Ireland and Germany in the mid-nineteenth century led to the rise of bigoted groups such as the Know-Nothings, which by the 1850s had elected six governors, controlled nine state legislatures, had forty-three members of the House of Representatives, and ran a former president, Millard Fillmore, for president in the 1856 election. A part of their platform was to make immigrants wait twenty-one years before they could naturalize and be able to vote. The history of anti-Semitism in this country is well known and need not be chronicled at length here. As recently as just a few decades ago there were neighborhoods in America where Jews could not buy a house, and there are still private clubs that do not accept Jewish members. As we have noted, quotas were put in place to keep Jews out of elite colleges, and many Jews felt they needed to change their names in order to get ahead in this country. The years 2018 and 2019 were grotesquely marked by violent attacks on American Jews. (Of course, it bears remembering that the American version of anti-Semitism has always been far more benign than that in the other two regions where Jews were found in large numbers—Europe and the Middle East.)

Over time, however, whether because of bigotry or in spite of it, all religions in America have assumed a somewhat Protestant form. American Catholics believe they have "a personal relationship with God," are more likely to have read scripture than Catholics in other lands, and find alien the street processions that are part of the traditions of Catholics in southern Europe and Latin America. As Huntington reminds us, "because they are central to American culture, Protestant values deeply influenced Catholicism and other religions in America."[25] Protestantism even affected Judaism. Writing of the East European Jews who had immigrated to America during the Ellis Island period, as opposed to the German Jews who had come earlier, the historian Thomas J. Archdeacon notes that they "developed an amorphous, pragmatic Conservative Judaism, which reflected the needs of lay men and women desirous of balancing public involvement in a gentile society with their private identities as Jews." In America, Conservative synagogues and Reform temples "transformed rabbis...into liturgical leaders like Protestant ministers and Catholic priests."[26] By the mid-twentieth century, Huntington says, Catholic leaders "had become fervent American nationalists, and the Irish-American Catholic became the prototype of the patriotic American."[27]

The reason to go into this history should be obvious. Over time an American Catholicism developed that was very different from the church in Sicily, Andalusia, or Mexico, as well as an American Judaism that differed from the one practiced in the East European shtetl. Whether we can have an American Islam is, of course, a point to be debated. It would not be easy, and one can see Islamic leaders resisting it—just as Irish Catholic priests and Greek Orthodox ones fought against the assimilation of their parishioners, and as Orthodox rabbis have of members of their congregations. Yet it is important to remember that this assimilation of the parishioners and of their respective churches was to their benefit. The fierce spirit of liberty that Burke extolled, and the mingling of religion with patriotism that Tocqueville observed, made America exceptional, uniquely attached to freedom, a place where man is able to carry on the pursuit of happiness according to his interests.

It is important, too, to bear in mind that what has worked in the past is the opposite of the special benefits that the proponents of a MENA category were trying to arrange for themselves. The fact that the Census Bureau even seeks the self-serving input of the leaders of advocacy groups who will be the direct beneficiaries of group creation—through jobs and political power—and of far-left academics who seek the transformation of America, is just another sign that advocacy groups and other militants have captured this agency, as they have many others. (The final chapter offers a solution to this and related problems.)

In 1819, John Quincy Adams, while serving as secretary of state, made clear that America was based not on privilege but on equal rights. In a letter to a German considering immigrating, he wrote:

> There is one principle which pervades all the institutions of this country, and which must always operate as an obstacle to the granting of favors to new comers. This is a land, not of *privileges*, but of *equal rights*. ... Emigrants from Germany, therefore, or from elsewhere, coming here, are not to expect favors from the governments. They are to expect, if they choose to become citizens, equal rights with those of the natives of the country.[28]

The other side of the coin was that immigrants would be granted the same protection as natives, which was at the time of the founding an unheard-of privilege and remains rare to this day. George Washington, in his August 21, 1790, letter to the Hebrew Congregation of Newport, Rhode Island, assures them that the United States is a nation that protects freedom of conscience for all its citizens:

All possess alike liberty of conscience and immunities of citizenship. It is now no more that toleration is spoken of, as if it was by the indulgence of one class of people, that another enjoyed the exercise of their inherent natural rights. For happily the Government of the United States, which gives to bigotry no sanction, to persecution no assistance requires only that they who live under its protection should demean themselves as good citizens, in giving it on all occasions their effectual support.... May the Children of the Stock of Abraham, who dwell in this land, continue to merit and enjoy the good will of the other Inhabitants; while every one shall sit in safety under his own vine and figtree, and there shall be none to make him afraid.[29]

Muslim Americans should be able to expect the same exercise of their natural rights. The proposed MENA category, which was tabled— at least for the time being—would have brought them no closer to that standard. The fierce spirit of liberty may influence American Islam, as with all religions practiced by Americans. Of course, like all religiously observant Americans, they are likely to face the kind of attack on family, tradition, and religiosity that we will see in the next chapter.

CHAPTER 4

★ ★ ★

Sex

The scene was a New York apartment in 1969. Mallory Millett, recently returning from several years of living in Southeast Asia, was invited by her sister Kate Millett, who would become one of the legendary figures of feminism, to join a gathering. Decades later, Mallory Millett recounted the event:

> They called the assemblage a "consciousness-raising-group," a typical communist exercise, something practiced in Maoist China. We gathered at a large table as the chairperson opened the meeting with a back-and-forth recitation, like a Litany, a type of prayer done in Catholic Church. But now it was Marxism, the Church of the Left, mimicking religious practice:
> "Why are we here today?" she asked.
> "To make revolution," they answered.
> "What kind of revolution?" she replied.
> "The Cultural Revolution," they chanted.

The back-and-forth went on, including vows to "destroy the family," "destroy the American Patriarch," and "destroy monogamy." These twelve women were "privileged graduates of esteemed institutions" who appeared "cogent, bright, reasonable and good." That they planned to accomplish their goals "by promoting promiscuity, eroticism, prostitution," as they chanted, left Mallory Millett "dumbstruck."[1]

Is Mallory Millett an objective observer? She has admitted to having issues with her sister. But we have in the past taken note of the witness of family members of historic figures, such as Stalin's daughter Svetlana and Juanita Castro—to whom Mallory Millett compares herself—who also broke with their relatives. It is certainly the case that the women's liberation movement was explicit in its antipathy to the family as the central unit of society, which it portrayed as a patriarchal institution that oppresses women. It is also true that, in her writings and activism as part of the National Organization for Women, Kate Millett borrowed heavily from Friedrich Engels, whose work called for overturning the free-market system that underpins the Western world. Like the elite women at that 1969 gathering, many adherents of Marxism, starting with Engels, who bankrolled Marx and coauthored the *Communist Manifesto*, have been wealthy elites—one of the enduring ironies of the Left's obsession with "oppression."

Just as the categories of Hispanics, Asians, and other groups were created by people with Marxist, neo-Marxist, and postmodernist ideologies and the goal of transforming America, so it became a project to cast women as an oppressed class. That project was later extended to homosexuals, people who say they are members of the opposite sex, and those who've tried to achieve a "transition" to the opposite sex through various methods, including surgical mutilation. Municipalities, corporations, and other entities from coast to coast officially designate dozens of "genders" and demand that others follow suit (with penalties for noncompliance); the binary classification of male or female is condemned by woke academics and others as a form of "structural violence." Although identity politics is mainly based on racial and ethnic issues, many of our worst cultural fights today have to do with sex, sexual orientation, same-sex marriage, gender identity, transgender "reassignments," and the rest. They all have at root the urge not just to change our politics, governmental institutions, and policies but to reorder fundamentally our society and culture. In the case of the women's movement, radical feminists went beyond the (laudable) goal of achieving equality to that of smashing the family. Women who just wanted equality of opportunity had to be convinced that marriage and motherhood were in themselves oppressive and ignoble. As we will see in this chapter, this approach had deep ideological roots.

Kate Millett's first book, *Sexual Politics*, published in 1970, was one of the key events in the founding of the so-called women's liberation movement, which was a product of second-wave feminism. The first wave, at the turn of the twentieth century, had sought to obtain rights that women had been denied, such as voting, divorce, and owning property. The second wave, in the 1950s and especially the 1960s, was a reaction to the first. To the members of the second wave, women hadn't made the right choices after being given the right to divorce and vote—the overwhelming majority still married and stayed home to raise children! The reason women were making these bad choices, they held, was that they were psychologically trapped in the patriarchal culture—whether they realized it or not—and had to be "liberated"— whether they wanted it or not.

In a 2017 paper, political science professor Scott Yenor traces the intellectual history of feminism's role in the attempt to remake culture. Second-wave feminists set out to create the economic and cultural environment that would free women to lead atomistic (free, in their view) lives. They supported state-funded daycare, the curtailing of parental rights over children— Yenor quotes a remark by "the mother of second-wave feminism," Simone de Beauvoir, that "'women will not be liberated until they have been liberated from their children'"—and the idea that infidelity and promiscuity are good for girls and women. One of the tools of men's subjugation of women is "the tradition of romantic love," which men fiendishly used to ensnare women in a subordinate position; therefore feminism had to dispense with it. As Yenor describes the feminist view, "sexual revolutionaries must shun sexual modesty and domesticity, adopt independent careers, and develop the qualities of character needed to pursue them." To second-wave feminists, simply restructuring the economy was not sufficient; the culture and its institutions needed to be overhauled completely. "Legal freedom was not enough to provide substantive equality for women," Yenor writes. "Getting women to choose differently would require a more fundamental cultural reformation centered on encouraging women to shed their maternal, wifely personalities."[2] Society would have to be remade.

Beauvoir, the author of the influential 1949 bestseller *The Second Sex*, in 1984 looked back at that book's themes in interviews published as *After the Second Sex*. In the later book, quoted by Yenor, she states: "I think that the family must be abolished."[3] Perhaps in illustration of her views, her lifelong relationship with the philosopher Jean-Paul Sartre, a sometime Marxist, was open and resulted in no children. In the 1984 interview, she identified Millett as one of her worthy successors in America (another being Betty Friedan, the founder of the National Organization for Women). The family, for Millett, was simply a structure that allowed men to subjugate women and keep them in bondage, a microcosm of the state and its institutions. One of Millett's insights, as Yenor explains, was her understanding that, to implement Beauvoir's notion of gender as separate from sex, and to end the oppression of gender roles in the family, feminists needed to ascend to power within the universities.

Millett's book had a profound impact. In *Faces of Feminism*, Sheila Tobias writes that

> Millett's analysis was unsettling both because it shed new light on so many previously accepted traditions and because it made women angry. Like the Copernican revolution that took the earth from the center of the solar system, where the ancients had thought it was, and put it in an orbit around the sun, Millett turned conventional assumptions about women's temperament, roles, and status upside down. Reading Millett or hearing her theories secondhand, women in the early 1970s began to look at the arrangements they had made in their lives, particularly in their relationships with men, and had what they called the "click!" experience, a sudden awareness of how political those relationships were.[4]

Sexual Politics became an instant success, selling ten thousand copies in its first two weeks. Upon reading it, some women felt that things had "clicked" into place and decided to leave their families. Mallory Millett recalled hearing women lament that her sister's book had ruined lives—marriages ended, children left behind.

Marxist Origin

The breaking up of relationships and families was to serve an ideological purpose. The entire capitalist system, Millett believed, was based on the patriarchal family. It was created, according to this distorted view, because fathers wanted to pass on their individual private ownership to their heirs. Profiting from the sweat of one's brow and possession of property thus were not, as Enlightenment thinkers had believed, natural rights. For Millett, they represented a mere historical stage.

Millett had not come up with these ideas on her own. The concept that the family was an evil institution that kept women in bondage was developed by Engels, the cofounder of communism. In *Origin of the Family, Private Property, and the State*, written in London in 1884, Engels theorized that individual private property had been a late development. Property had been at first held communally, he wrote, then by the village, then the tribe or clan, and then the *gens*, or expanded family. When property finally began to be conceived as personal, then there was a need for the monogamous, patriarchal family, according to Engels: "It is based on the supremacy of the man, the express purpose being to produce children of undisputed paternity; such paternity is demanded because these children are later to come into their father's property as his natural heirs." (Engel's wild and false ideas are dealt with in more detail in the next chapter.) With individual property came those greatest bugaboos of all communists: "the rise of the inequality of property," "wage-labor"—which in the communist mind is always equated with or placed near slavery—and class differences. The link between class struggle and female oppression by husbands was clear and described by Engels in stark terms: "In the family he is the bourgeois; the wife represents the proletariat." By collectivizing child rearing through social services, and ensuring that "society takes care of all children equally, irrespective of whether they are born in wedlock or not," monogamy and morality would be eroded over time. The result would be "unconstrained sexual intercourse and with it a more tolerant public opinion in regard to a maiden's honor."[5]

Millett drank deeply from these wells. Engels is quoted widely throughout *Sexual Politics*, as are Marx and Stalin. Not for nothing did *Time* magazine once dub her "The Mao Tse-tung of Women's

Liberation."[6] Millett is not without some criticisms of Engels. She believes that he does not do an adequate job of demonstrating the "patriarchal takeover" that happened in human development. But his analysis was clearly a lodestar to her and other feminists.

"It could be demonstrated," she wrote, "that patriarchy was accompanied by all the ills Engels deplored, the ownership of persons, beginning with women and progressing to other forms of slavery, the institutions of class, caste, rank, ruling and propertied classes, the steady development of an unequally distributed wealth—and finally the state." The great value "of Engel's contribution to the sexual revolution lay in his analysis of patriarchal marriage and family." In treating patriarchal relationships "as historical institutions, subject to the same processes of evolution as other social phenomena, Engels had laid the sacred open to serious criticism, analysis, even to possible drastic reorganization."[7] The emphasis was on drastic. John Stuart Mill is also quoted throughout the book, but only to be dismissed as pusillanimous. Mill's hypothesis, posited in his 1869 essay, *The Subjection of Women*, that the condition of women could be alleviated by advancing laws is brushed aside in favor of Engels's preferred outcome—burning it all down, the scorched lives of men, women, and children notwithstanding.

For Millett and other radical American feminists, women did not just constitute an oppressed class, they were the original class in the story of class warfare. She quotes Engels: "The first class antagonism appearing in history coincides with the development of the antagonism of man and wife in monogamy, and the first class oppression with that of the female by the male sex. Monogamy...develops the welfare and advancement of one by the woe and submission of the other." Given that she saw "the subjection of women" as "a total social and psychological phenomenon, a way of life," it's no wonder that she was calling for a sexual revolution.[8]

NOW Is Born

In 1966, Millett and other radical feminists began to gain real political and administrative power; they were able to translate their ideology into law and the all-important regulations that bureaucrats use to implement laws according to their own interpretations. That was the year that Betty Friedan and about two dozen other women attending the Third National Conference of State Commissions on the Status of Women formed the National Organization for Women (NOW), with Friedan famously scribbling the acronym on a napkin. The new organization was needed, they had concluded, to end sex discrimination in hiring and in society in general. Millett was named the first chair of NOW's education committee, an area she would use to influence her own and future generations of women.

From its inception, NOW burrowed into the administrative state and began to play a leading part—perhaps the leading part—in intimidating first the Johnson and then the Nixon administrations into drawing an analogy between women and blacks, and then between women and the "official" minority categories such as Hispanics and Asians. As explained by John Skrentny in his authoritative administrative history of the period, NOW had a powerful ally in Democratic congresswoman Martha Griffiths, who challenged the head of the Equal Employment Opportunity Commission (EEOC) over the agency's failure to uphold the equal treatment of women, using the black civil rights struggle as a model. Griffiths wrote a letter to the commissioner in which she cited a law review article—pointedly titled "Jane Crow and the Law"—on "the obvious fact that the rights of women and the rights of Negroes are only different phases of the fundamental and indivisible issue of human rights." Quoting NOW's official statement of purpose, Skrentny writes: "NOW would be a 'civil rights movement for women' that would create a 'fully equal partnership of the sexes, as part of the world-wide revolution for human rights now taking place within and beyond our borders.' NOW rapidly became *the* voice of women's rights, patterned after the African American civil rights movement."[9] One of the goals of making half of America into an official oppressed category that required protection and affirmative action was to beckon (or shame, if necessary) every woman out of the house and into the labor force.

Women had first become a "protected class" with the 1964 Civil Rights Act. The act's Title VII protects individuals from discrimination based on race, religion, national origin, or sex, thus making it illegal for employers to discriminate against women in hiring, firing, promotions, raises, and other actions. Both Title VII and the Equal Pay Act forbid employers from discriminating on the basis of sex in the payment of wages or benefits. From the beginning, there was much official and public opposition to the analogy between blacks and women; this manifested in bureaucratic pushback against extending to women the same protections that were offered to blacks.

In addition to demanding that the EEOC enforce Title VII, in 1966 NOW asked President Johnson to amend his 1965 Executive Order 11246, "requiring nondiscrimination and an undefined 'affirmative action' by all government contractors on the basis of race, color, religion, and national origin," but did not include the basis of sex. As noted by Skrentny, it helped that, "though the organization was new and had almost no membership," many of NOW's leaders came "from within the government [and] clearly understood the dynamics of administrative politics." Thus, by means of personal and bureaucratic cajoling, filing complaints against government contractors, participating in hearings, sending telegrams to senior officials, staging protests, and so on, NOW won fight after fight. The EEOC determined that discrimination on the basis of sex was in fact in conflict with Title VII, and in 1967 Johnson signed Executive Order 11375, which amended 11246 to include sex. That year NOW wrote up a "Bill of Rights for Women," demanding, among other provisions, state-funded childcare centers, a general recognition of "societal responsibility for child care," and abortion on demand.[10] These were key requirements to every second-wave feminist beginning with Beauvoir, who had championed an escape from motherhood and family life.

In 1971, during the Nixon administration, NOW won a decisive battle when it convinced the Labor Department's Office of Federal Contract Compliance (OFCC) to revise its Order No. 4 to add women to its list of racial minorities for whom it required action. The order required government contractors with more than fifty employees, and whose contracts were worth at least $50,000, to supply hiring goals and timetables for racial and ethnic minorities. Contractors had to show that they employed members of minority groups, or had a viable plan to do so, based on "the percentage of the minority work force as compared with the total work force in the immediate labor area." Women were at least 50 percent of the labor force in any area, and many women either chose to stay home or would decline to do certain jobs—say, roof repair; to officials in Nixon's Labor Department, the inclusion of women in an order that intrusively required companies to demonstrate their efforts to hire members of protected minority groups made no sense. In 1970, Secretary of Labor James Hodgson wrote, "The work force pattern of women and racial minorities differs in significant respects. Many women do not seek employment. Practically all adult males do." This sensible acknowledgment of reality enraged NOW. They won the argument, and in December 1971, the "'Revised Order No. 4,' equalizing women and racial minorities with respect to goals and timetables, became binding."[11]

As a result, government contractors were required to recruit women so that their proportional representation in the workforce would mirror that in the total population, though, as Skrentny notes, "these would be based on studies of the pool of women workers and rarely be 50 percent." It turned companies into instruments to implement the plan to recruit women into the labor force. Skrentny quotes a 1968 interview with Mary Keyserling, director of the Labor Department's Women's Bureau, which reveals how decisive a victory it had been for NOW. "Though formerly a relatively conservative women's advocate, by 1968 her views fit with the incipient ideology of NOW," he writes. The government now not only had to make sure that doors were open, but "find out *why* women aren't going through those doors...." As Skrentny says, "For Keyserling, as for many civil-rights advocates, the only way to know if an opportunity existed was if someone successfully pursued it. In this view, women could not, therefore, simply miss an opportunity or prefer not to seize it."[12] The new Order No. 4, then, sought to fix the shortcomings that second-wave feminists saw in society by insisting that it conform to their ideology.

NOW made its gains with few members. In this, it resembles other insider networks, organizations such as La Raza and Asian

Americans Advancing Justice: they have little connection to the grassroots but are all-stars in playing the inside-the-Beltway game because they have on their staff many former bureaucrats (and many sympathizers inside the permanent bureaucracy). From the beginning, and to this day, NOW has also been funded by leftist foundations and Fortune 500 corporations. As of this writing, NOW continues to assert that it is the largest feminist group in the country, yet an analysis of the dues it says it receives from members would put the number much lower.[13]

The impact of NOW on the American family was direct. While policy thinkers from Oren Cass to Elizabeth Warren have blamed the steady demise of family formation in America on the fact that a typical man with a high school degree can no longer keep a family of four above the poverty line, not enough attention has been paid to the ideological attack that has been perpetrated on the family since the 1960s.[14] Men's employment problems are attributed to various factors, among them robotization, the importation of Mexican labor, and outsourcing. But the introduction of female competition in labor markets and women's educational advances (coupled with the curious fact that women refuse to marry down educationally) are often overlooked. A glance at any graph on the decline of marriage will reveal that the delta sharpens in 1970, when the rate of married adults above age eighteen was around 70 percent, five percentage points higher than in 1960 but ten percentage points lower than in 1980.[15] It is true that the decline has been steeper among those with only a high school degree than those who have completed college (which would vindicate Cass and some others). But let's not pretend that Millett and other ideologues with a political agenda did not have the huge impact on society that they openly sought. The leftist elites have always understood the economic impact of marriage, the stability it offers to the spouses and their children. While they may agree with Engels, Beauvoir, Millett, and others that this stability must be smashed, they still want their children to go to Cornell, get married, succeed, and produce grandchildren. But these elites have been adept at using the popular culture to spread a different message among the less-well-off.

More Than a Catchy Tune

Remember *9 to 5*? It was the second-highest-grossing movie of 1980 (after *The Empire Strikes Back*). Its catchy theme song made it to No. 1 on three Billboard charts and ever since has been something of an anthem for working women. It was the song that candidate Elizabeth Warren used when she walked out to announce her candidacy for president in 2019. The movie plot was simple (on purpose). Three office workers, played by Dolly Parton, Lily Tomlin, and Jane Fonda, are terrorized by their ogre of a boss, played by Dabney Coleman. The three women join forces and end up getting the upper hand, humiliating the Man. The idea of women wronged by awful bosses who took credit for their work, harassed them sexually, and ignored them in between, struck a nerve with some women, and that was no accident. Workplace discrimination was real for many women who, lest we forget, had entered the labor force en masse only in the previous few decades. There was real discontent felt by many, which ideologues seized upon. In truth, the movie is not just a simple comedy, but one freighted with ideological content. It was a project conceived by Fonda, a committed leftist who wanted to use entertainment to bring a taste of revolution to the masses.

Before the movie came the organization 9to5, started by Karen Nussbaum, a Chicago radical who knew Jane Fonda from the anti–Vietnam War movement. In 1970 Nussbaum traveled to Cuba in a program begun by Fidel Castro to bring Americans to the island to imbibe the revolution while cutting sugarcane. In a 2003 interview, Nussbaum hailed Cuba as "a society that was combating racism, that had provided free health and educational care to every person in society, that had reduced income inequality more dramatically than any place else on earth." Back in the States, she met Fonda and Fonda's husband Tom Hayden when her Boston-based antiwar group allied itself with the Indochina Peace Campaign organization led by the leftist power couple. The IPC's mission was to cut US aid to the governments of South Vietnam and Cambodia. Leftist radicals like Nussbaum and Fonda aligned themselves with the communists and guerrillas, imagining themselves as revolutionaries. They trained their gaze toward the United States and attempted to create revolution here, too. In the 2003 interview, Nussbaum said, "When the war really did end in 1975, Jane was looking more toward working on issues in our country, you know, some domestic issues. 9to5 had already been active for a couple of years by then and Jane was intrigued by it and so she came to me and she said she wanted to make a contribution to our work in the best way she knew how, and that was to make a major motion picture. So, that sounded great to us!"[16]

But it was just a movie and a song, right? Isn't it crazy to think there was an ideological component to it? In 2019 Nussbaum told National Public Radio that the song "is brilliant. It starts with pride: 'Pour myself a cup of ambition.' It goes to grievances: 'Barely getting by.' It then goes to class conflict: 'You're just a step on the boss man's ladder.' And then it ends with collective power: 'In the same boat with a lot of your friends.' So in the space of this wildly popular song with a great beat, Dolly Parton just puts it all together by herself." NPR, which helpfully gave its online article the subtitle "9 to 5 Unites Workers Across Decades," quotes Rebecca Traister, a writer on "feminism and politics [and] the power of women's anger," as saying, "It's a song that contains complaints about so many frustrations and inequities and injustices within a workplace—some of them gendered, some of them capitalist, some of them about how power is so unequally distributed."[17]

That's because Nussbaum kept her hands on the project from the start, from the planning to the writing of the script. She invited Fonda to come to Cleveland, where she was then living, and through her 9to5 chapter "set up a meeting with about forty...women office workers." These women told Fonda and Nussbaum about "problems that they faced on the job" and their dreams of "getting even with the boss.... Every detail in the movie, with the exception of hanging the boss up by a garage opener system, actually came from these women." Nussbaum added that after 9 to 5 came out "I sat in the movie theaters many times watching the movie and in every instance, you'd get the same feeling. The place was electrified. The women would be shouting and clapping...." Nussbaum felt that "the most important effect of the movie was to change public consciousness" of workplace discrimination. "The debate then became what we should do about it. And that is exactly what I think the role of popular culture can be in a social context, and I think it's really the best example that I know of, of making that happen."[18]

In other words, the movie's long-term impact—the focus on women's grievances against men, the class conflict, the feelings of injustice regarding the distribution of power—was not happenstance, the result of an innocent outburst of Hollywood creativity. It was well calibrated by people who had cut their political teeth in Hanoi and Havana. The decision to make the character of the insufferable boss "the object of ridicule," in Nussbaum's words, was a way to slay the patriarch, to unite the worker and herd women into an oppressed class, whether they felt that way or not. This effort was very successful. Nussbaum's organization soon expanded to twenty-five chapters. In 1993, the first year of the Clinton administration, she became the director of the powerful Women's Bureau in the US Department of Labor, the same position that, when occupied by Mary Keyserling, NOW had used to push its ideological agenda. Three years later, in 1996, Nussbaum took a senior position at the AFL-CIO and now serves as the head of its political organizing arm, spreading the false message that women in America get paid less than men for doing comparable work. The campaign to recruit more women into the labor force, and convince those who would otherwise not want to forgo wifely and motherly roles to get on the corporate ladder, continues.

The Third Wave Revolution

During the Clinton years, feminism's third wave took shape. Turbocharging the ideas of second-wave feminism, the third-wave feminists questioned not just gender roles but the fact that biological sex exists at all. In the process, third-wave feminism has produced policies and ways of thinking that challenge the rights won by the first-wave feminists of a century ago and those of the second wave half a century ago. When gender is thought of as just a "social construct," the idea that women are equal to men suddenly becomes shaky. The hard-won victories of the second wave, such as Title IX protections of women's equal access to sports at schools and universities, increasingly have been turned on their head, as men saying they are women are claiming those protections. Women are now forced to compete against biological males, obviously putting them at a disadvantage. "After all," Yenor writes, "women's sports are based on the seemingly benighted assumption that there are women."[19] The idea that women have an identity as a class took a knock as well: in the twisted logic of identity politics, the notion that sex and gender are constructs undermines women's very claim to an identity. In the 1970s the rallying cry was "I am woman, hear me roar!" Now, we have Facebook's seventy-one gender categories (New York's leftist mayor Bill de Blasio has been more modest, officially designating only thirty-one) and the ever-expanding alphabet of LGBT (QIA…).

One of the hallmarks of the new sexual revolution is the creation of nearly countless gender identities, with lesbians (butch and femme), gays, bisexuals, transgenders, queers, and many more having gained victim categories of their own. States and localities try to outdo each other in establishing set-aside programs in contracting and hiring for people who identify as one of the categories in LGBT. Never mind that, on average, gay men earn more than straight men, and lesbians earn more than straight women, according to one study.[20] "Disparity studies" are used to reveal instances of oppression for members of a certain category; if the owner of a company is able to claim he has been discriminated against in the past because of his sexual orientation, then his firm can be granted a set-aside. Government contracts and employment opportunities being finite, this clearly sets up a competition in which groups previously considered as needing set-asides— racial or ethnic minorities and women—will lose out. In 2018, Chicago, for example, awarded some $450 million in contracts to women- and minority-owned businesses, and the addition of LGBT-owned businesses to "supplier diversity programs" in 2019 will necessarily elbow out others.[21] Chicago and Cook County were joining Baltimore, Nashville, Long Beach, Jersey City, and others as municipalities that have changed their supplier set-aside programs within 2018 alone to include LGBT vendors.[22]

Though third-wave feminism, with its emphasis on transgender-ism, betrayed the first two waves, it cannot be thought of as a departure but rather as a product of the second wave and its sexual revolution. Its Marxist roots are just as impeccable as those of the preceding wave. Just as Millett, channeling Engels, and others had perceived monogamous, heterosexual marriage as intricately linked with indi-vidual private property and thus wage-labor, inequality, and oppres-sion, other Marxist and postmodernist thinkers had come to view gender—or how society views the roles of the biological sexes—as a construct to oppress women. As Beauvoir wrote: "One is not born, but rather becomes a woman. No biological, psychological, or economic fate determines the figure that the human female presents in society; it is civilization as a whole that produces this creature, intermediate between male and eunuch, which is described as feminine."[23] Once free of gender expectations, women would be liberated—that was the new expectation.

As we have seen, Nixon's Department of Labor was reluctant to extend to women the same affirmative-action model that had been extended to blacks and the concocted ethnoracial minorities. One rea-son for their reluctance was that gender roles made the use of statistical data to enforce compliance tricky. While one type of job (again, say roof repair) would be of interest to men, of any race or ethnicity, that same job would attract few, if any, women applicants. Thus statistical underrepresentation of women in a particular job or career could not be a bona fide proof of hiring discrimination.

The way to get around the problem of the social expectations of gender roles, as advanced by Beauvoir, Millet, Friedan, and others, was to eliminate them. The second wave, in doing so, thus planted the seeds of the third-wave emphasis on homosexuality and transgender-ism. Millett herself had written that sexual liberation required "an end to traditional sexual inhibitions and taboos, particularly those that most threaten patriarchal monogamous marriage: homosexual-ity, 'illegitimacy,' adolescent and pre- and extra-marital sexuality."[24] But once second-wave feminists separated gender from biological sex, they split some sort of cultural atom and could not control what would happen next.

All these second-wave notions "prepared the ground for a more radical vision in the 1990s by scholars like Judith Butler, who extended the idea to include advocacy for transgender rights," as noted by Yenor.[25] Butler, one of the progenitors of third-wave feminism, and her cohorts merely took second-wave ideas to their logical conclusion. Basing their ideas on the writings of European poststructuralists such as Michel Foucault—who we will discuss further in the following chapter—they rejected all universal truths, particularly fixed notions of gender or sex, because, in their view, it entrenched the oppressor group's grip on power. Thus they embraced queer theory, which holds that everything to do with sex or gender is socially constructed. But, as Ryan Anderson writes in his book *When Harry Became Sally*, "for some radical feminists, to say that gender is socially constructed and not naturally linked to the body doesn't go far enough. Thus, Judith Butler maintains that even the body is a 'social construct.' In her view, a conception of the body as something fixed and indisputable is pernicious because it 'successfully buries and masks the genealogy of power relations by which it is constituted.' In short, 'the body' conceived as something in particular is all about power."[26]

The mental contortions of the third-wave feminists have put them in some uncomfortable positions, to say the least. They can even be, for example, at odds with "sex reassignment" surgery. Explaining why requires a trip back to the 1960s.

The idea that gender is fluid, and that individuals can transition from one sex to another, received its impetus in 1965, when John Money cofounded the Johns Hopkins Gender Identity Clinic and Robert Stoller founded the Gender Identity Center at UCLA. As recounted by Yenor, "Money was involved in winning approval for sexual reassignment surgery in 1966 and in creating the transsexual category." He became famous for the case of a boy who was brought to the Johns Hopkins clinic because a botched circumcision had severely damaged his penis; according to the clinic's advice, the boy was castrated, with no vagina added, and raised as a girl. Critically, "Money thought this case proved that 'the gender identity gate is open at birth for a normal child no less than one born with unfinished sex organs...and that it stays open at least for something over a year after birth."[27] For second-wave feminists, Money opened "the door...to a greater role for human choice concerning the creation of identity.... [His] ideas about femininity and masculinity seemed malleable." Politically, such fluidity destabilized "male supremacy" and "the biological basis of identity."[28]

But to Butler and other third-wave feminists, sex-reassignment therapy or even correcting natural sexual abnormalities is wrong because "these treatments presuppose a particular bodily form that is correct or optimal."[29] Sex reassignment, in fact, has led to an outbreak of legal clashes and intellectual skirmishes, and to a new epithet, TERF, for "trans-exclusionary radical feminist." Such feminists are considered trans-exclusionary or anti-trans because they take umbrage at the idea that men who think of themselves as women must be recognized as such; feminists who dissent from this idea are subjected to social-media attacks and in some cases face being fired or legally prosecuted for expressing their beliefs.

The *College Fix* reported on one such case of a doctoral student in the department of feminist studies at the University of California at Santa Barbara. Laura Tanner, a self-styled radical feminist and expert on "intersectionality," found herself in the crosshairs of transgender students and "allies." What were her sins? Her Twitter header image says it all: "A woman is someone with a female body and any personality...not a 'female personality' and any body. Any other definition is sexism." Social media exploded as student after student denounced Tanner for her "transphobia"; on Twitter, there were demands that she be "removed from teaching or worse, with some lobbing personal insults at Tanner such as 'absolute trash' and 'dumb bitch'.... One declared 'that bitch needs to die,' and others have targeted her for being white."[30] Some students threatened to file complaints with the university's Title IX office. The university launched an investigation into the matter, with its conclusion not yet known at the time of writing. Notably, her Twitter bio concludes with the words, "I will not be silenced."[31]

Same-sex marriage can be another battleground between second- and third-wave feminists. Some feminists embrace same-sex marriage because it "problematizes" traditional roles and institutions. As

Anderson points out, many same-sex marriage advocates view it as a way to change marriage beyond recognition—in fact, to bring about its end. They "would leave marriage with no essential features, no fixed core as a social reality."[32] According to Yenor, Judith Butler "embraces same-sex marriage because it creates gender trouble for marriage."[33] But to many new third-wave radicals, when gays and lesbians marry what they are doing is simply copying, and therefore affirming, the "heteronormativity" of the dominant male group. As Canadian feminist legal scholar Susan B. Boyd notes, "[R]adical feminists...have suggested that the emphasis on marriage and coupledom stigmatizes alternative models of intimacy, including communal living, chosen families that fall outside of the nuclear dyadic model, and non-monogamous and polyamorous relationships."[34]

Friedan, NOW's founder and first leader, had foreseen how the nascent gay rights insurgency would fragment the feminist movement she was trying so hard to build. Her fear of it contributed to a rupture between her and Millett. In a celebrated incident in late 1970, after *Time* had outed Millett as a lesbian, a rally was held in her support. One of the demonstrators urged Friedan to don a lavender armband, which had become a symbol of support for lesbians. Friedan grabbed the armband, threw it on the ground, and stomped on it. In her last interview, Millett said that Friedan "hated the gay kids. They were messing up her program....I felt sorry for her."[35]

These clashes between competing visions of what constitutes sexual categories bring to mind PayPal founder Peter Thiel's dictum that, under the rules of identity politics, the conflicts that inevitably arise among the groups will be adjudicated in the way that most benefits the Left. That does not bode well for gay couples seeking domesticity or for aging second-wave feminists who want their granddaughters to be able to play soccer competitively (that is, in a league that would have to exclude boys, even those who insist they are girls). But we would all do well to remember that the ultimate object of identity politics is not to protect gay families or little girls who want to grow up to powerful, but to turn society upside down. As postmodernism has percolated out of the universities and into everyday life, this has finally become clear, and it irritates those who actually did believe that the goal of transforming American society through collectivist effort was to protect victims of oppression.

"For the oppressed, class awareness is essential for resistance," said the feminist Ti-Grace Atkinson at a presentation at Harvard in March 2014. "It's the commonalities between formerly differentiated individuals which form the basis for solidarity and political change. Oppressed individuals by themselves are relatively powerless; together, it's a different story.... It is only as this class mobilizes around these grievances and forms political groups that meaningful social change can be achieved." But postmodernists were spoiling everything, Atkinson added. "Differences are not what we organize around. The fact that Postmodernism emphasizes 'difference' gives their political game away." Beauvoir had warned her in Paris in 1975, Atkinson said, to "watch out for the anti-feminist differentialists." Atkinson then added, "I finally understood, in the late 1980s, what Beauvoir was talking about."[36]

Engels had already commented on the value of polyamorous relationships to destroy the patriarchy—and with it the entire state—back in 1886, so we can fully expect it to be the next challenge on the horizon. In fact, in 2019 the American Psychological Association launched its Taskforce on Consensual Non-Monogamy to promote "awareness and inclusivity about consensual non-monogamy and diverse expressions of intimate relationships. These include but are not limited to: people who practice polyamory, open relationships, swinging, relationship anarchy and other types of ethical, non-monogamous relationships."[37]

As it should be clear by now, the identity battles that have torn up society—from the early ones that NOW waged to the recent ones over unisex bathrooms, women's sports, and pronouns, have not been about protecting women, gays, or anyone else, but about tearing society apart in order to install another system. The creation of identity groups has not been a project to upend the hegemonic hold on power of Protestant, white, male America to give subordinate groups a share of the pie. It was a far more ambitious and encompassing enterprise; it was about destabilizing, or "problematizing" in the language of its entrepreneurs, all social norms. It wasn't just a patriotic, national identity that was under the gun. Private property, the free market, the family, religion, assumptions not just about sexual roles but about fixed biological sexes—all these verities needed to be destroyed, and individuals, society, and legal authorities had to recognize and affirm the new realities. The imperative to make revolution continues.

PART II
LIBERTY AT RISK

★ ★ ★

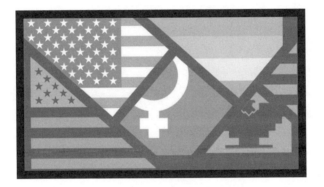

CHAPTER 5

★ ★ ★

Marxism by Any Other Name

Wasting away in a fascist prison in the 1930s, the Italian communist leader Antonio Gramsci had time to write down thoughts he'd been having for over a decade. It had long since dawned on him that, though Marx had promised almost a century earlier that the working class would rise up, overthrow the capitalists, and establish the dictatorship of the proletariat, until that time revolutions had been few. In Europe, the revolutions of 1848 had failed. The Bolsheviks had succeeded in Russia in 1917, but the rest of Europe was run by capitalists. America was even more hopeless. There, as Friedrich Engels had written in 1892, "society at the very beginning started from a bourgeois basis," though he added, wrongly as it turned out, that things were about to turn.[1] Where had Marx and Engels gone wrong? Gramsci came up with a useful meta-explanation. The bourgeoisie had acculturated the working-man to do its bidding, giving him "false consciousness." In this manner, the bourgeois did not even have to coerce the worker into submission. The cure, Gramsci thought, was to carry out a "consciousness raising" indoctrination campaign that would convince the proletariat of his having been duped by tradition, religion, the family, the educational system, and all the cultural trappings of society. Consciousness raising would let the worker understand his true interest and induce him to renounce any idea of succeeding individually; he would thus join with those in his class in a collective effort to transform the system.

Gramsci envisioned this revolution as bloodless; it would not be Russia in 1917. This campaign would require a determined effort to take over the culture-making industries, what the 1960s radical Rudi Dutschke later termed the "long march through the institutions."[2] To Gramsci, this reeducation would overcome the resistance of those workingmen "who think only of solving their own immediate economic and political problems for themselves, who have no ties of solidarity with others in the same condition."[3] Struggle sessions would transform "the facts of vassalage into the signals of rebellion and social construction."[4] Once cultural institutions had been taken over, they would stop promoting traditional culture—known to Gramsci as the "hegemonic narrative." Dissent would be crushed through what Herbert Marcuse later called "repressive tolerance."[5] This is how we get the Rev. Jesse Jackson joining students at Stanford in 1987 in the chant, "Hey, hey, ho, ho, Western Civ has got to go!"[6]

Gramsci, Marcuse, and Dutschke represent three generations of so-called Western Marxists associated with critical theory and the attempt to remake society institution by institution. Marcuse, as we have seen, was a member of the Frankfurt School, which had an enormous impact on the founders of today's identity politics. Marcuse personally tutored the Black Panther leader Angela Davis and took part in student demonstrations. Today, many of the academics who teach young minds at our universities are critical theory professors, as are many of the members of the Census Bureau's National Advisory Committee on Race and Ethnicity. The Frankfurt School thinkers were not the only major influence on today's purveyors of identity politics. The postmodernists are the other camp of European philosophers and academics, many of whom were based in Paris, to which identity politics traces its origins. Both Marxist camps repackaged Marx for mass culture, taking his analysis out of economics and putting him in Disney. They employed similar methods and approaches: a systematic attack on Western democratic societies and their cultural norms; the belief that morality, and reality, are culturally relative, with the related rejection of universal truth and objectivity and the belief that individuals and groups have separate and equal "truths" which must do battle with the hegemonic narrative, or "episteme"; the Marxist emphasis on conflict between oppressors and subordinates; and the expansion beyond economics to culture, which is why practitioners of both schools are called cultural Marxists.

To these two schools we owe the view, so ubiquitous in our society today, that certain groups—workers, minorities, women, and others—are "marginalized," and that these groups participate in their own oppression when they perpetuate the hegemonic metanarrative of the privileged. This is why students in American universities, and increasingly in secondary and even primary education as well, are taught that the assimilation of immigrants is a capitulation to the oppressors. Both the Frankfurt School thinkers and the postmodernists believed that members of subordinate groups lack unity and foolishly put their faith in success through individual effort; instead, they need to be organized into a collective. Thus, Mexican Americans in Los Angeles in the late 1940s needed Saul Alinsky and Fred Ross to come along to teach them how to organize, and women needed to be awakened from their submissive torpor by Kate Millett's "click." The children of Chinese and Indian immigrants succeeding individually through hard work and virtuous living are, on the other hand, an inconvenient threat.

The American founders were inspired by the ideas of the Anglo-Scottish Enlightenment, an intellectual tradition that underlies America's attachment to freedom. But the influence of certain Continental philosophers on Western, and specifically American, society are reshaping America in pernicious ways. Critical theory and postmodernism derive from Continental philosophy and its successors. These thinkers are the intellectual heirs of the French terror and communist totalitarianism, and despite this sorry record, their ideas have been a beguiling temptation to academics and activists for decades on this side of the Atlantic. To understand what has happened to America, its universities and its politics, we have to understand these philosophical antecedents.

Marxism's First Experiments

Before Gramsci, Marcuse, Millett, Samora, and the rest, there were Marx and Engels. In terms of our identity politics today, the influence of Marx and Engels was mostly distilled through the cultural iterations discussed so far (with more to come). The exception is feminism, where the hit was direct. Millett and other feminists were especially influenced by Engels, who had the most to say about the family (very little of it good). To the coauthors of the *Communist Manifesto*, economics was everything and individual private property was the original sin. They believed that the emergence of private property among the ancient Athenians had made it necessary for men to know who their heirs would be, and only the monogamous family could supply that (though Engels contradictorily also insists that Athenian women cheated on their husbands as much as their husbands cheated on them, which was quite a lot, and that made men fall "into the abominable practice of sodomy"):

> This is the origin of monogamy as far as we can trace it back among the most civilized and highly developed people of antiquity. It was not in any way the fruit of individual sex-love, with which it had nothing whatever to do; marriages remained as before marriages of convenience. It was the first form of the family to be based, not on natural, but on economic conditions—on the victory of private property over primitive, natural communal property.[7]

Only communal property could be natural to Engels, whereas individual property led directly to "the rise of the inequality of property," to "wage-labor"—which in the communist mind is always equated with or placed near slavery—and to class differences. The sequence to Engels appeared like this: "the productivity of labor increasingly develops, and with it private property and exchange, differences of wealth, the possibility of utilizing the labor power of others, and hence the basis of class antagonisms." What follows "as its necessary correlate" is "the professional prostitution of free women" and the creation of the monogamous family unit. Engels quotes Marx as adding that "'the modern family contains in germ not only slavery (servitus), but also serfdom, since from the beginning it is related to agricultural services. It contains in miniature all the contradictions which later extend throughout society and its state.'"[8]

What is astonishing is that Marx and Engels borrowed their ideas on the family from the nineteenth-century American anthropologist Lewis Henry Morgan, whose theory of cultural evolution as moving from promiscuity to monogamy has been discredited. Yet the consequences of these ideas, both in Russia early on and in America because of their adoption by the feminists of the later twentieth century, have been grave. The economically rooted aversion to the "patriarchal" family, the notion that it was merely a transitory stage instituted to sustain capitalism, inspired Lenin and the other Bolshevik leaders: as Lauren Kaminsky observes, "Lenin imagined a future when unpaid housework and child care would be replaced by communal dining rooms, nurseries, kindergartens, and other industries."[9] Immediately after the revolution, the Bolsheviks passed a series of laws to begin their project of remaking society. An anonymous "Woman Resident in Russia" wrote in the *Atlantic* in 1927 that, in one of the Soviet government's first decrees, it "abolished the term 'illegitimate children.' This was done simply by equalizing the legal status of all children, whether born in wedlock or out of it," so that the Soviet Union could "[boast] that Russia is the only country where there are no illegitimate children"; divorce was made to be "a matter of a few minutes, to be obtained at the request of either partner in a marriage." The result was "chaos," added the anonymous writer.[10] She recounts men with multiple wives, uncared-for children forced onto the streets, rampant promiscuity, and other ills, to the point that the Soviets were induced to undo their changes and return to the status quo ante. Even Soviet commissars had a modicum of wisdom lacking today among American academics, activists, and political operatives.

Seeing everything through the lens of economics and property produced blind spots for Marx and Engels and their followers, notably the role that race and ethnicity could play (and would go on to play) in the revolution to overthrow the ruling class. One exception to this blind spot was Marx's observation that, in English manufacturing cities, mutual hostility kept working-class English and Irish apart despite their supposed common interests. Marx never used the phrase "false consciousness," but in the following passage from a letter he wrote in 1870 we can see that he deduces that something like it has made the English worker a willing accomplice in his own subjugation:

> Every industrial and commercial center in England now possesses a working class divided into two *hostile* camps, English proletarians and Irish proletarians. The ordinary English worker hates the Irish worker as a competitor who lowers his standard of life. In relation to the Irish worker he regards himself as a member of the *ruling* nation and consequently he becomes a tool of the English aristocrats and capitalists against Ireland, thus strengthening their domination over himself. He cherishes religious, social, and national prejudices against the Irish worker.... *This antagonism* is the secret of the *impotence of the English working class*, despite its organisation. It is the secret by which the capitalist class maintains its power. And the latter is quite aware of this.[11]

Marx's mistake was in thinking that revolutionary consciousness would emerge from "the objective (and oppressive) material conditions of working class life," writes John Fonte.[12] A refinement of this way of thinking would have to wait for the next wave of Marxist thinkers ushered in by Gramsci.

We Are All Gramscians Now

Gramsci was born in 1891 to a literate Sardinian family—at a time when nine out of ten people in that Italian region could not read or write. He went on to become the preeminent European communist intellectual of the twentieth century, and certainly the one with the biggest impact in the United States of the present century. Whether they realize it or not (and the overwhelming majority most certainly do not), Americans today make decisions or attach themselves to identities because of what Gramsci wrote. The identity politics in which we all bathe daily is partly a Gramscian invention. Venezuela and other parts of Latin America are the messes they are today not just because of Marxian socialism, but because Gramsci refined Marxism and created ideological vectors through which entire societies could be clandestinely infected with Marxist pathologies. As the famed British Marxist scholar Eric Hobsbawm rightly put it, Gramsci has become known as the "communist thinker who provided a Marxist strategy for countries in which the October Revolution might have been an inspiration, but could not be a model, that is to say for socialist movements in non-revolutionary environments and situations."[13]

Despite a spinal deformity (which gave him a hunchback later in life), Gramsci had to work early because his father, a local bureaucrat, was accused of corruption and thrown in prison. At the age of fourteen he began receiving issues of *Avanti!*, the Italian Socialist Party (PSI) organ, from his older brother, who was in military service in the industrial hub of Turin. In 1913, he became an activist for the PSI, and a few years later he began to write articles for *Avanti!* supporting the Russian Revolution, winning the praise of Lenin. Breaking from the PSI the following year, Gramsci and the radical wing of the party founded the Communist Party of Italy, and he rose to a leadership position, spending two years in Moscow. In 1924, he was elected to Italy's parliamentary government. His party having been outlawed by Mussolini, in 1926 he was arrested, and in 1928, following the prosecutor's urging that "we must stop his brain from working for twenty years," he was sentenced to twenty years in prison.[14] Gramsci was not released until April 1937, a few days before his death.

But his brain did not stop working. It was while under arrest that Gramsci, rather like Paul, wrote his famous *Prison Notebooks*, which were whisked out of his cell by his sister-in-law and published posthumously. In prison he developed his "philosophy of praxis" (a term that some historians believe he used to confound fascist censors, but which means putting abstract philosophical ideas into concrete political action). Marx had already argued, "the philosophers have only interpreted the world in various ways. The point…is to change it"; Gramsci kicked that notion into high gear. Praxis is implemented from the top down, the antithesis of conservatism's tenet that things are real only when they arise from the bottom up. Praxis was needed, said Gramsci, "in order to destroy one hegemony and create another, as a necessary moment in the revolutionizing of praxis."[15]

To realize this goal, Gramsci over the course of his long incarceration fine-tuned his already existing ideas on cultural hegemony, by which he meant that the oppressed were complicit in their oppression when they accepted traditions, norms or—in the language of the self-regarding pedant of today—"scripts." This oppression was enforced through "a multitude of other so-called private initiatives and activities…which form the apparatus of the political and cultural hegemony of the ruling classes."[16] The hegemonic narrative of the rulers had to be destroyed, and replaced with a counterhegemony.

Replacing one narrative with another meant fundamental, root-and-branch transformation, Gramsci made clear. In one of many examples, he berates labor leaders for being too moderate and not seeking the complete overhaul of society:

> What is at stake is a rotation in governmental office of the ruling-class parties, not the foundation and organization of a new political society, and even less of a new type of civil society. In the case of the theoretical syndicalist movement, the problem is more complex. It is undeniable that in it, the independence and autonomy of the sub-altern group which it claims to represent are in fact sacrificed to the intellectual hegemony of the ruling class, since precisely theoretical syndicalism is merely an aspect of laissez-faire liberalism—justified with a few mutilated (and therefore banalized) theses from the philosophy of praxis.[17]

Gramsci was not interested in changing policy but in transforming Italy.

It was essential for the worker to understand how he had become part of the problem by signing up for the moral code of the ruling class (or, as today's identity politics promoters of groupism would put it, "acting white"). He would have to have his class consciousness raised through struggle sessions:

Critical understanding of self takes place therefore through a struggle of political "hegemonies," from opposing directions, first in the
ethical field and then in that of politics, in order to arrive at the
working out at a higher level of one's own conception of reality.
Consciousness of being part of a particular hegemonic force (that
is to say, political consciousness) is the first stage towards a further
progressive self-consciousness in which theory and practice will
finally be one.[18]

Only then could the marginalized ascend to his new, dominant
role. But for that he would have to repudiate any idea of individual
success. "The proletariat cannot become the dominant class if it does
not overcome this contradiction through the sacrifice of its corporate
interests. It cannot maintain its hegemony and its dictatorship if, even
when it has become dominant, it does not sacrifice these immediate
interests for the general and permanent interests of the class."[19]

Gramsci was not the first communist to understand that Marx
had erred in thinking that the working class would spontaneously rise
up and overthrow capitalism. Lenin, too, had come to believe that a
revolutionary vanguard made up of intellectuals would have to instruct
the proletariat on their oppression and guide them into toppling the
bourgeoisie. Gramsci's notion of cultural hegemonic oppression was an
innovation without which the advances of the Left in America would
not have been possible. One of his main targets was Christianity, and
specifically the Roman Catholic Church, which along with the educational system stood in the way of class consciousness. Christianity
offers hope, and therefore prevents a feeling of desolation; one who has
religious faith need not transfer his faith to an ideological vanguard
indispensable for bringing about revolution.

Gramsci even gave instructions on how to make a global revolution appear particularistic. The proletariat was an international class,
Gramsci averred, but the ideological vanguard—the intellectuals,
activists, and organizers—would have to learn how to go undercover
as a national one in order to overthrow systems throughout the West.
"A class that is international in character has—in as much as it guides
social strata which are narrowly national (intellectuals), and indeed

frequently even less than national: particularistic and municipalistic (the peasants)—to 'nationalize' itself in a certain sense,"[20] he wrote. The methods required to upend society in Europe and the United States would have to be different from those that had been employed in Russia, but the goals remained the same. As David Forgacs, the editor of *The Gramsci Reader*, writes, Gramsci's argument was that revolution "in the West . . . must involve the building of hegemony between the working class and its allies. It must involve ideological struggle. It must involve the construction of a mass democratic movement. But this does not add up to an abandonment of the revolutionary goal of socialism and its replacement by a strategy of piecemeal reforms."[21]

Gramsci had already written in 1916, when he was twenty-five, that culture was not the result of spontaneous order over the course of time. Culture had to be directed, by ideological elites at first; the hegemonic narrative had to be replaced with a counterhegemony, or socialism would continue to be put off. It was through culture, he wrote, that "we can come to understand our value and place within history, our proper function in life, our rights and duties." Change was not going to happen by itself. Man "is primarily a creature of spirit—that is, a creation of history, rather than nature. Otherwise, it would be impossible to explain why it is that, when the exploiters and the exploited have always existed, socialism has never yet come into being." The vanguard was needed initially. "This consciousness," he wrote, would not be formed "under the brutal goad of physiological necessity, but as a result of intelligent reflection, at first by just a few people and later by a whole class, on why certain conditions exist and how best to convert the facts of vassalage into triggers of rebellion and social reconstruction." That is why there was a need for consciousness raising, for struggle sessions, for reeducation of the worker and peasant. "Every revolution has been preceded by an intense labour of criticism, by the diffusion of culture and the spread of ideas amongst masses of men who are at first resistant, and think only of solving their own immediate economic and political problems for themselves, who have no ties of solidarity with others in the same condition."[22]

Without critical thinking, man would fall into the groups in which the happenstance of his birth had placed him, and be trapped by a narrative of the universe that kept the privileged class in power. Gramsci asked rhetorically,

> [Is] it better to "think," without having a critical awareness, in a disjointed and episodic way, to take part in a conception of the world mechanically imposed by the external environment, i.e. by one of the many social groups in which everyone is automatically involved from the moment of entry into the conscious world (and this can be one's village or province; it can have its origins in the parish and the "intellectual activity" of the local priest or ageing patriarch whose wisdom is law, or in the little old woman who has inherited the lore of the witches or the minor intellectual soured by his own stupidity and inability to act) or is it better to work out consciously and critically one's own conception of the world and thus, in connection with the labours of one's own brain, choose one's sphere of activity, take an active part in the creation of the history of the world, be one's own guide, refusing to accept passively and supinely from outside the moulding of one's personality?[23]

As Fonte puts it, "Gramsci's main legacy arises through his departures from orthodox Marxism. Like Marx, he argued that all societies in human history have been divided into two basic groups: the privileged and the marginalized, the oppressor and the oppressed, the dominant and the subordinate. Gramsci expanded Marx's ranks of the 'oppressed' into categories that still endure."[24]

Gramsci's prose can be turgid, as writing on the Left tends to be, but he must be quoted in full so the reader can start to discern the origins of today's disorders, the constant talk about "privilege," the use of the benign-sounding term "community organizer" by radicals who wanted to upend society, the denigration of American history, and the insistence that America was rotten from the start. Gramscian theories, applied through praxis in the twentieth century here in America, led to the organizing of Mexican Americans, the creation of the categories of Hispanics and Asian Americans, and the instilling of a sense of victimhood and grievance in those groups; if people in those groups still wanted to strive for success on their own terms, they were told they suffered from false consciousness. Gramsci's influence underlies the consciousness-raising sessions introduced by major corporations like Starbucks; and it underlies, too, the reinterpretation of American history, by Howard Zinn and others on the Left, as a long and bloody tale of perfidy, an attempt by bourgeois colonial elites to keep their property by assimilating workers, native- and foreign-born alike, to their worldview. The spread of leftist governments in Latin America, by Cuba after the 1990s to Venezuela to Bolivia to Nicaragua, achieved through the region-wide assemblage of socialist parties, the Foro de São Paulo, was explicitly inspired by Gramsci's ideas about cultural hegemony. Gramsci essentially provided the field manual for taking over countries.

The Frankfurt School and Critical Theory

But the final execution of Gramsci's ideas would have to wait for another evolution, a further refinement. That was left to the Frankfurt School, a movement of Marxist philosophers and sociologists that began in the 1920s at the Institute for Social Research in Frankfurt. Many of these thinkers left Nazi Germany for America, establishing a base at Columbia University and from there becoming a major influence on American academia. Though they were disillusioned by the American worker's utter refusal of revolutionary consciousness, Marcuse found a way around the problem.

The Frankfurt School was both a Marxist response to the failure of the German Revolution of 1918–1919 to turn Germany into a soviet-style state and to the perceived need for a leftist intellectual analysis of the forces that led to the formation of the Weimar Republic. The historian Martin Jay, who is sympathetic to the school and is probably its foremost expert, writes in his history of the Frankfurt School that there were three options left to German Marxists: "First, they might support the moderate socialists and their freshly created Weimar Republic, thus eschewing revolution and scorning the Russian experiment; or second, they could accept Moscow's leadership, join the newly formed German Communist Party, and work to undermine Weimar's bourgeois compromise." The third course of action "was the searching reexamination of the very foundations of Marxist theory, with the dual hope of explaining past errors and preparing for future action."[25] This was what the Frankfurt School set out to do, and its biggest impact was not on Weimar but on the United States, as we will see.

The institute's model was the Moscow-based Marx-Engels Institute. It was originally going to be called the Institute for Marxism, but its founders thought it prudent to adopt a less provocative name, according to Jay. Jay also notes that it maintained close ties with the Soviet Union in its early years, though the school itself was kept free of party affiliations.

Interestingly, then, the two states where communists had failed to take power after World War I and later turned fascist, Italy and Germany, produced Marxist thinkers who theorized on how to achieve political conquest surreptitiously through cultural means. One of the Frankfurt School's innovations was to integrate Marxism with Freudianism, out of the belief that man did not just act out of material interest, but that psychology, too, played a role. The fusion was potent, and the School attracted to its ranks such well-known psychoanalysts as Erich Fromm and Wilhelm Reich.

In 1937, the second director of the Frankfurt School, Max Horkheimer, published the school's manifesto, *Traditional and Critical Theory*. Traditional theory, Horkheimer claimed, had fetishized knowledge and objectivity. Traditionalists saw truth as empirical and universal, and they applied a scientific method that was overly reliant on the possibility of objectivity. Critical theory, its opposite, held that man could not be objective and that there are no universal truths. This relativism was nothing less than an assault on Western civilization, its tenets and traditions. "The facts which our senses present to us," Horkheimer wrote, "are socially preformed in two ways: through the historical character of the object perceived and through the historical character of the perceiving organ."[26] For him and other early critical theorists, dialectic criticism was a way to tear down societal norms— but only those of the West. The School "maintained an almost complete official silence about events in the USSR,"[27] notes Jay, and its leaders' faith in the Soviet Union did not begin to crack until the Stalinist purge trials in the 1930s. Another major figure of the Frankfurt School,

Theodor Adorno, in 1950 published *The Authoritarian Personality*, a book that pathologized a respect for authority, tradition, religion, and honor as a psychological type especially susceptible to fascism. On the faculties of universities across America today, critical theory's ideas have become weapons to replace the narrative of America's founding principles with the counternarrative of Marx.

The critical theorists' critiques and methods owed a great deal to G. W. F. Hegel (discussed further below), perhaps the most important philosopher since Immanuel Kant and the most influential after Marx. Marx and Engels, as disciples of Hegel, appropriated his concept of the dialectic—a thesis confronted by an antithesis, reconciled in a synthesis—into their dialectical materialism, which they employed to critique economic forces.

With the rise of Nazism in the early 1930s, Germany was no longer hospitable to the members of the Frankfurt School, many of whom were Jews. Horkheimer moved the institute first to Geneva, and then to New York in 1935. From their perch at Columbia, the Frankfurt School thinkers began to directly influence the United States. In the early 1940s, intuiting early on the value of the film industry for spreading messages into the popular culture, Horkheimer moved from New York to Southern California, where he joined other Germans in exile such as the writer Thomas Mann, the playwright Bertolt Brecht, and the composer Arnold Schoenberg. Adorno, Marcuse, and others followed, and in their work endeavored to apply their critical analysis to Hollywood. Horkheimer and Adorno teamed up to write *Dialectic of Enlightenment*, an influential book in which they coined the phrase "the culture industry" in a chapter titled "The Culture Industry: Enlightenment as Mass Deception." The book, a long tirade against the Enlightenment ("philosophers ally themselves in practice with the powers they condemn in theory.... Moral philosophies are acts of violence performed in the awareness that morality is nondeducible"[28]) and capitalism. Disdaining the culture of the country that had given both men asylum from the Nazis, the book amounted to a long dissertation on the concept espoused by Gramsci that the modern worker had assimilated into the morality of the ruling class and thus, without a need for coercion, had become its willing slave.

In American society, Horkheimer and Adorno saw "a heroizing of the average" that results in a "cult of cheapness." Indeed, "for centuries, society has prepared for Victor Mature and Mickey Rooney. They come to fulfill the very individuality they destroy."[29] This brand of contempt foreshadowed the condescension that today's urban and academic elites evince for "flyover country." Average American workers had no idea of the ways in which they were being oppressed:

> Capitalist production hems them in so tightly, in body and soul, that they unresistingly succumb to whatever is proffered to them. However, just as the ruled have always taken the morality dispensed to them by the rulers more seriously than the rulers themselves, the defrauded masses today cling to the myth of success still more ardently than the successful.... They insist unwaveringly on the ideology by which they are enslaved. The pernicious love of the common people for the harm done to them outstrips even the cunning of the authorities.[30]

America's culture makers had even instrumentalized cartoons to break "the individual resistance" of the American consumer. In a sentence that cannot be parodied, they write, "Donald Duck in the cartoons and the unfortunate victim in real life receive their beatings so that the spectators can accustom themselves to theirs."[31] Mercifully for Horkheimer and Adorno, the United States defeated Germany and liberated Europe in 1945, and in 1949 the pair were able to leave the capitalist hell that was California and return to Germany to reinstate the institute. In 1953, Adorno took over from Horkheimer as its director.

Marcuse Discovers Race, Sex, and Politics

Marcuse, Horkheimer's former assistant, remained in America, teaching at Columbia and Harvard in the 1950s, at Brandeis University (1954–65), and finally at the University of California at San Diego (1965–76). He, too, was initially pessimistic about the American worker—and equally snide about him. "The people find themselves in their commodities: they find their soul in their automobile, hi-fi set, split-level home, kitchen equipment," said Marcuse in 1964, in his influential book *One-Dimensional Man* (the title itself was a putdown).[32] But Marcuse in time twigged that the revolutionary base would be formed from different building blocks. In the 1960s new groups were being created in American society—by race, ethnicity, and sex. It is here, after all the evolutions that we have explored so far, that we see the identity politics of today starting to jell, and the original dreams of Marx and Engels made real.

During World War II, Marcuse did a stint as an analyst for the Office of Strategic Services (OSS), the precursor to the Central Intelligence Agency. That a Marxist was appointed to serve in a sensitive government position may strike one as odd, but he and two other Frankfurt School members, Franz Neumann and Otto Kirchheimer, were asked to write analyses of German political culture. Though all three were Jewish, they saw anti-Semitism in an "unemotional" way, as John Bew (who lauds their work) writes, viewing it as a "cynical political tool, rather than a hatred that came from the belly of German society,"[33] for which they received criticism. The trio predictably blamed the rise of Hitler on capitalists, according to Bew, for forging an alliance with the Nazis, and not on the "landed nobility" or "Prussian militarism"—Winston Churchill's preferred view, again according to Bew. In this, Marcuse and his colleagues were harking back to Gramsci, who wrote in his prison notebooks that the German bourgeoisie were really the ones in charge, and were only pretending to let the Junkers rule through cultural hegemony; it had allowed "a part of the latter's façade to subsist, behind which it can disguise its own real domination."[34]

Although Marcuse's reliance on neo-Marxist analysis while working for the US government is notable in itself, it was the work that was yet to come that had a huge impact on our culture. During the 1950s and the social transformations of the 1960s, as Marcuse's theories were put into action, he became known as the "guru of the New Left" (and was even denounced by the pope). Two of his books, *Eros and Civilization* (1955), which Roger Kimball has called "a bible of the counterculture,"[35] and the aforementioned *One-Dimensional Man* became bestsellers and guides to the new age. Marcuse used his intellectual clout to support, and sometimes direct, the radical student movement of the 1960s.

One-Dimensional Man is essentially a second communist manifesto, written for America at a time when its religious and cultural defenses had been badly diminished by the establishment's panic over the riots—a weakening of the nation's immune system to which the book contributed. Yes, it included criticism of the Soviet Union, but it was aimed mostly at the West, and specifically America, where Marcuse saw a consumerist culture that was getting in the way of the collectivization he thought was needed. It foreshadowed today's anticonsumerism, which is to say, anticapitalism. "Today, the opposition to central planning in the name of a liberal democracy...serves as an ideological prop for repressive interests. The goal of authentic self-determination by the individuals depends on effective social control over the production and distribution of the necessities (in terms of the achieved level of culture, material and intellectual)," wrote Marcuse. "Technological rationality, stripped of its exploitative features, is the sole standard and guide in planning and developing the available resources for all. Self-determination in the production and distribution of vital goods and services would be wasteful.... In this realm, centralized control is rational...." Democracy was not working because, even if the "the laborers" were put in charge, nothing would change as they had imbibed the hegemonic narrative of the rulers. "Where these classes have become a prop of the established way of life, their ascent to control would prolong this way in a different setting."[36]

The fact that the American working class had become a prop for the ruling class, which advanced its interests without the need to coerce the workers, preserved "the illusion of popular sovereignty." Marcuse did admit that "this illusion contains some truth: 'the people,' previously the ferment of social change, have 'moved up' to become the ferment of social cohesion."[37] The reason capitalism was bad was, essentially, because it was so good: "It is a good way of life—much better than before—and as a good way of life, it militates against qualitative change."[38]

But there was a ray of hope. Here is where Marcuse hits on his new revolutionary base, the people who, if correctly organized and led by an ideological vanguard, can move the country toward central planning and technological rationality:

> underneath the conservative popular base is the substratum of the outcasts and outsiders, the exploited and persecuted of other races and other colors, the unemployed and the unemployable. They exist outside the democratic process; their life is the most immediate and the most real need for ending intolerable conditions and institutions. Thus their opposition is revolutionary even if their consciousness is not. Their opposition hits the system from without and is therefore not reflected by the system; it is an elementary force which violates the rules of the game and, in doing so, reveals it is a rigged game. When they get together and go out into the streets, without arms, without protection, in order to ask for the most primitive civil rights, they know that they face dogs, stones, and bombs, jail, concentration camps, even death. Their force is behind every political demonstration for the victims of law and order. The fact that they start refusing to play the game may be the fact which marks the beginning of the end of a period.[39]

Clearly, Marcuse saw an opportunity in the civil rights movement that he was witnessing all around him: it could be used to transform American society into a socialistic one. The fact that the civil rights movement was a beautiful and necessary step to realize America's promise of freedom for all, and that its preeminent leader, Martin Luther King Jr., had cast it in precisely those terms, meant nothing to Marcuse and his followers. The original promise was a color-blind society; the original intent was not to divide society or to raise the revolutionary consciousness of groups of people by making them believe they were victims, or to make the nation hideous in the eyes of its people. The original promise had been to bring descendants of slaves, who had been excluded from America's promise, into its fold. But central planning was a necessity, and self-determination was wasteful: American society needed to be subverted from within and revamped.

Because this subversion needed to happen at all costs, the ends justified any means. So it would be the role of the new vanguard—as exemplified by figures such as Saul Alinsky, Fred Ross, Julian Samora, Lillian Fabros, Kate Millett, and Linda Sarsour—to instill grievances into people's hearts, to spread the antigospel of victimization. "All liberation depends on the consciousness of servitude," Marcuse averred, and the emergence of this consciousness could no longer be hampered by comfort. This meant that groups would have to be created and partitioned off from the rest of society, and their consciousness would have to be raised into victimhood. Otherwise, they would join the contented boobs who had been lulled into submission by happiness, and they, too, would stubbornly refuse to coalesce into a revolutionary base. To do this, the vanguard would have to quash aspiration, personal agency, and individuality. America would have to be ripped apart, group separated from group. It was the devil's work, but so be it. Alinsky did famously dedicate his book to Lucifer. The biblical injunction that "what is lame may not be dislocated, but rather be healed" was to be ignored. As we will see in the next chapter, the 1965 immigration law would be used to swell group membership, never mind that it would plainly be absurd to bestow the so-called compensatory justice benefits used to suborn people into joining the victim groups on those newly arrived. These actions did nothing but inject more poison into what is always a poisoned matter—immigration.

Given that the enemy was national cohesion, Marcuse and his followers fomented division, disunity, and strife. "Capitalist society," Marcuse wrote, "shows an internal union and cohesion unknown at previous stages of industrial civilization"—America was one-dimensional not because it had rejected a national culture but because it had one.[40] "The liquidation of *two-dimensional* culture takes place not through the denial and rejection of the 'cultural values,' but through their wholesale incorporation into the established order.... In fact, they serve as instruments of social cohesion."[41] Marcuse was not wrong that America was united around the idea of freedom—that was precisely why denying blacks their civil rights was such a sin, as those who fought segregation and, before them, the abolitionists of the nineteenth century well understood. Less than a decade before *One-Dimensional Man*, the sociologist Louis Hartz had published *The*

Liberal Tradition in America, in which he, too, groused that a bias for freedom had been so much a consensus throughout our country's history that there existed what he called a "fixed, dogmatic liberalism of a liberal way of life."[42] Marcuse and those who became his disciples saw liberalism and cohesion not as ideals but as problems to be overcome.

One area where Marcuse did want more individual freedom was in sexual mores, because it fit his plans of "problematizing" society. He had already started the work of undermining the American family a decade earlier. It was in *Eros and Civilization* that Marcuse called for the abandonment of sexual morality and monogamy. "Progress would depend completely on the opportunity to activate repressed or arrested organic, biological needs: to make the human body an instrument of pleasure rather than labor."[43] He predicted that there would come "a resurgence of pregenital polymorphous sexuality." Changing "the value and scope of libidinal relations would lead to a disintegration of the institutions in which the private interpersonal relations have been organized, particularly the monogamic and patriarchal family."[44] Small wonder that, in 1969, Pope Paul VI, in an extremely rare personal rebuke, denounced Marcuse for promoting the "disgusting and unbridled expressions of eroticism," the "animal, barbarous and subhuman degradations" known as the sexual revolution, and "license cloaked as liberty." Marcuse, to be sure, was not the first Frankfurt Schooler who had tackled the subject of sex. Wilhelm Reich in his 1936 book *The Sexual Revolution* had insisted that society's ills stemmed from a lack of sexual satisfaction. The Hungarian philosopher Georg Lukács, influential with members of the Frankfurt School, was a pioneer in the area of sex education. As an education commissar in the post–World War I Hungarian government, he established sex education programs for young schoolchildren "to undermine parental and Church authority."[45]

While Marcuse sought to liberate us libidinously, he sought to limit our other rights, such as freedom of speech. This should surprise nobody. All communist dictatorships (which is what Marcuse argues for in his works—we can at least give him credit for not hiding it) require censorship and repression. Thus, in his 1965 essay "Repressive Tolerance," he forthrightly advocates repression of conservative views.

"Liberating tolerance, then, would mean intolerance against movements from the Right and toleration of movements from the Left," he explains. He calls for

> the practice of discriminating tolerance in an inverse direction, as a means of shifting the balance between Right and Left by restraining the liberty of the Right, thus counteracting the pervasive inequality of freedom (unequal opportunity of access to the means of democratic persuasion) and strengthening the oppressed against the oppressed. Tolerance would be restricted with respect to movements of a demonstrably aggressive or destructive character (destructive of the prospects for peace, justice, and freedom for all). Such discrimination would also be applied to movements opposing the extension of social legislation to the poor, weak, disabled.[46]

Did he anticipate opposition from those squeamish about repressing speech? Yes, but he didn't share their worry: "As against the virulent denunciations that such a policy would do away with the sacred liberalistic principle of equality for 'the other side,' I maintain that there are issues where either there is no 'other side' in any more than a formalistic sense, or where 'the other side' is demonstrably 'regressive' and impedes possible improvement of the human condition."[47] This notion is aptly summed up as "free speech for me but not for thee."

How influential has Marcuse been? *One-Dimensional Man* sold 100,000 copies in just five years in the United States alone—a lot for a book of densely written theorizing—and was translated into sixteen other languages. His books were reviewed and discussed in scholarly journals and popular magazines alike. When he visited Rome, students met him with signs saying "Marx, Mao and Marcuse."

Marcuse's thinking was discussed even in the White House. Bill Moyers, the White House press secretary under Lyndon Johnson, wrote in a 1987 essay: "In 1965, I sent to the President an essay by Herbert Marcuse, the leftist philosopher so admired by the student movement, in which Marcuse applauded LBJ's objectives, but doubted the government's ability to stay the course. 'Rebuilding the cities, restoring the countryside, redeeming the poor and reforming education,' said

Marcuse, 'could produce nondestructive full employment.'" Johnson's programs could effect these changes, Marcuse said, but it would require "'the transformation of power structures standing in the way of its fulfillment.'"[48] It is hard to believe that President Johnson actually sat down to read Marcuse, but we can see that the latter's ideas on transforming power structures were being discussed at the highest levels of government.

And, as Moyers said, Marcuse was influential among the students, who became the university teachers of today. As her teacher at UC San Diego in 1968, Marcuse directly shaped the worldview of the future Black Panther Angela Davis. She spent time in prison in the early 1970s for her role in the murder of a judge, was a member of the Communist Party USA, and was awarded the Lenin Peace Prize by the East German government, one of the most repressive regimes behind the Iron Curtain; but today she holds the title of distinguished professor emerita at the University of California, Santa Cruz. Davis wrote in 2018: "As new generations of scholars and activists ponder the role of intellectuals in shaping radical movements of this era, I believe that Marcuse's ideas can be as valuable today as they were 50 years ago."[49] Today, Davis has become the doyenne of identity politics, and a guide to thousands of students uninformed as to her criminal past and instilled with an admiration for Marxism. She has told at least one university audience, "I have always been a communist," and they responded with a standing ovation.[50]

In a speech at California State University at Los Angeles in 2016, Davis made it clear that Marxist ideas animate current academic trends. Pan-African studies, she said, is "the intellectual arm of the revolution." Any version of multiculturalism "that does not acknowledge the political character of culture will not, I'm sure, lead toward the dismantling of racist, sexist, homophobic, economically exploitative institutions."[51] In a 2018 speech, presented to a packed theater in Charlottesville and sponsored by the University of Virginia's engineering school, she called for systemic transformation: "Diversity without changing the structure, without calling for structural formation, simply brings those who were previously excluded into a process that continues to be as racist, as misogynist as it was before."[52] Translation:

members of "minorities" simply cannot be allowed to assimilate into the American mainstream. Marcuse taught her well, and his influence remains strong.

It is to Marcuse, too, that we owe the censorship of political correctness, the threats of ostracism or punishment for those who do not toe the line of identity politics, and outbursts of violence against conservatives on campus and on the streets of cities such as Portland, Oregon. All this was already envisaged in "Repressive Tolerance." If the ideological vanguard is blocked from building a "subversive majority," Marcuse wrote, the response "may require apparently undemocratic means," including the "withdrawal of toleration of speech and assembly from groups and movements which promote aggressive policies, armament, chauvinism, discrimination on the grounds of race and religion, or which oppose the extension of public services, social security, medical care, etc." This, in turn, "may necessitate new and rigid restrictions on teachings and practices in the educational institutions which, by their very methods and concepts, serve to enclose the mind within the established universe of discourse and behavior—thereby precluding a priori a rational evaluation of the alternatives."[53] The essay also adumbrated the subsequent leftist takeover of schools of education, which we will discuss in chapter 7.

Marcuse also directly influenced the German revolutionary Rudi Dutschke, who as a student advocated violence during protests as a way to provoke the West German police into overreacting. Marcuse met Dutschke when he was invited to attend the "Vietnam-Kongress" that "Red Rudi" had organized in Berlin in 1968. The two grew very close, and when Dutschke was shot in an assassination attempt in 1968, Marcuse went to his bedside and pressed for him to be allowed to come to the United States in the name of academic freedom. Dutschke, however, remained in Germany, where he died in 1979. According to the British paper *Socialist Worker*, "Under the influence of Marcuse he had written off the working class of the developed countries as being unable to be the agents of revolutionary change." Dutschke believed "the working class had been bought off by a high standard of living and by the propaganda of the ruling classes and their media," and that "the student vanguard [must] use the universities as 'safety zones and as social bases from where the struggle against the institutions, the struggle for cheap student meals and for state power' could be fought."[54]

Under Marcuse's influence, Dutschke also advocated the vanguard's takeover of all cultural institutions as a way to propagandize to all of society. He called this "the long march through the institutions," in an obvious reference to Mao's Long March through China with Communist Party fighters in the 1930s. In *Counterrevolution and Revolt*, Marcuse praised Dutschke's strategy, describing it as "working against the established institutions while working with them. But not simply by 'boring from within,' rather by 'doing the job,' learning (how to program and read computers, how to teach at all levels of education, how to use the mass media, how to organize production, how to recognize and eschew planned obsolescence, how to design, etc.), and at the same time preserving one's consciousness while working with others."[55] In a 1971 letter to Dutschke, Marcuse told him he was writing a book on how to funnel the energies of the student movement into overthrowing capitalism in its late stages (for communists, again, capitalism is always about to collapse because of its supposed internal inconsistencies). "Let me tell you this," he wrote, "that I regard your notion of 'the long march through the institutions' as the only effective way, now more than ever."[56]

Philosophical Links with Postmodernism

Dutschke's strategy pleased Marcuse, but his calls for violence were too much for the Frankfurt School philosopher Jürgen Habermas, who emerged as the preeminent German philosopher of the later twentieth century. In the late 1960s, Habermas accused Dutschke of putting people at risk (Dutschke responded that he didn't care). Habermas took seriously, though also criticized, another group of thinkers, the postmodernists, whose major figures include Jacques Derrida, Jean-François Lyotard, and Michel Foucault. Marxism was the shared philosophical ancestry of the postmodernists and the critical theorists; but the line began with a luminary of the French Enlightenment, Jean-Jacques Rousseau, and ran mostly through Germany, from Kant through Hegel, Friedrich Nietzsche, Martin Heidegger, and others. Marcuse studied philosophy under Heidegger at Freiburg University from 1928 to 1932, eventually becoming his assistant. Marcuse broke with his mentor in 1932, when it was clear to all that Heidegger was a Nazi (he joined the party but a year later). Thus we can also see the line from Heidegger to Angela Davis. (As an aside, the Left has often tried to stifle criticism of the Frankfurt School by alleging that criticism of its mostly Jewish thinkers is anti-Semitic in nature. But this charge completely misses the fact that the direction the school took was due to its very Germanness.)

The intellectual legacy of the mostly German Continental thinkers included the belief that man's rights came from the state, in sharp contrast to the American founders' inheritance of the idea of natural rights from the Anglo-Scottish Enlightenment of Hume, Locke, and Smith. According to the natural rights view, man possesses certain rights at birth—such as life, liberty, and property—and the role of the state is to safeguard those rights. Limited government is needed to safeguard rights because, as Christianity teaches, man is fallen, imperfectible—avarice will pit one man against another without the mediating influence of the state. The Germans put their faith in a strong, centralized state, with government providing for man what he could not provide for himself. In the more atheistic, and in some cases antireligious, view of the Continental Enlightenment, man is perfectible; he can be instructed or induced by the state to behave well.

The Continental ideas have triumphed among our progressive left today. But the struggle to inculcate these ideas in America and eradicate the founding principles of natural rights and limited government was by no means just a twentieth-century phenomenon. The effort began in the early nineteenth century through different means. (We will explore the demographic means in the following chapter.) Charles Merriam, one of the fathers of the academic field of political science in America (and a member of the Frankfurt School's advisory committee in the late 1930s), traced the birth of the nineteenth-century Progressive movement to German-influenced thinkers. "Much of the credit for the establishment of this new school belongs to Francis Lieber, a German scientist who came to this country in 1827, and, as an educator and author, left a deep impress on the political thought of America,"[57] wrote Merriam in 1903. "Following Lieber, came a line of political scientists, many of whom were trained in German schools, and all of whom had acquired a scientific method of discussing political phenomena." As Merriam explained, the belief of the "Fathers" (the scare quotes are his) "that men possess inherent and inalienable rights...has been generally given up"; the new belief, among intellectuals at the turn of the last century, was that "it is the state that makes liberty possible.... The state...is the creator of liberty." If that was true, then it only stands to reason that liberty "is not a right equally enjoyed by all. It is dependent upon the degree of civilization reached by the given people...."[58]

Merriam and his fellow Progressives believed that deciding "who should enjoy liberty and how much of it," as the Peoria Project explains, should be left to a centralized state informed by science. "If rights are not inherent in or derived from a shared human nature, liberty or rights need not be the same for all. If rights are the gift of the state, the issue arises as to whom and when the state should give these unequal rights."[59] To the German thinkers of the nineteenth century and the Progressives they influenced, including Merriam, the answer was those guided by science and reason—and that meant the superior "Teutonic" race. Today, under the present regime of affirmative action, the state has said it is fine for members of designated victim groups to receive benefits denied to members of other groups. It is important to note in passing that John C. Calhoun, the nineteenth-century defender of slavery, subscribed to the German ideas and was himself greatly influenced by Hegel. It is also worth noting that every totalitarian system has employed this kind of thinking.

In the twentieth century, and continuing into the present one, the German ideas enjoyed even greater success in America. Kim R. Holmes calls Rousseau and Kant "the intellectual founders of the modern radical left. That is to say, they are the intellectual forefathers not only of Karl Marx, but Michel Foucault and Jacques Derrida." Kant, too, had believed that "actualizing freedom was the primary obligation of states.... Freedom is an a priori ideal to be achieved through the state's organization of people's lives, an idea that would be later taken up and expanded [by]...Hegel."[60] The same is true of the Frankfurt Schoolers. According to Jay, "Horkheimer, who set the tone for all of the Institute's work, had been interested in Schopenhauer and Kant before becoming fascinated with Hegel and Marx." It was, he added, "tempting to characterize Critical Theory as no more than Hegelianized Marxism." The origins of critical theory go to the so-called Left Hegelians, who, like the members of the Frankfurt School, "were interested in the integration of philosophy and social analysis," maintains Jay.[61] Both Left Hegelians and critical theorists developed their ideas in order to transform the social order.

The postmodernists in the 1970s and 1980s shared many of the tenets of the Frankfurt School, only they sometimes used different language. Gramsci and the Frankfurters spoke of a hegemonic narrative, the postmodernists of a "dominant discourse" (or an "episteme" for Foucault). The Frankfurters developed critiques, the Parisians practiced "deconstruction." Whatever the terminology, both schools put a premium on dismantling Western culture and were the enemies of coherence and cohesion.

To give credit where credit is due (if credit is the proper word for it), on the matter of the hegemonic narrative, Gramsci, the Frankfurters, and the postmodernists were all in fact borrowing from an earlier master, Nietzsche. In 1887, in *The Genealogy of Morals*, Nietzsche wrote that words and concepts only had the meaning given to them by the master class he thought were entitled to rule. "The masters' right of giving names goes so far that it is permissible to look upon language itself as the expression of the power of the masters," he wrote. Nietzsche was making precisely the same point as his modern followers, to wit, that there is no good and evil, and that the good is only those things that the natural aristocracy approved of and thought to be "of the first order, in contradiction to all the low, the low-minded, the vulgar, and the plebeian."[62] There was no universal good, truth, or morality.

Whereas the postmodernists embraced relativism, the Frankfurt Schoolers insisted that they were not relativists but rather historicists. "Truth, Horkheimer and his colleagues always insisted, was not immutable," writes Jay, but the Frankfurters denied relativism because "each period of time has its own truth."[63] The postmodernists went further in saying that each individual has his or her truth. The British scholar Helen Pluckrose writes that the "nihilistic" postmodernists "attacked science and its goal of attaining objective knowledge about a reality which exists independently of human perceptions which they saw as merely another form of constructed ideology dominated by bourgeois, western assumptions."[64]

Postmodernism gets its name because it is a refutation of the Enlightenment, thus the modern age, which postmodernist thinkers see as suppressive of cultural identities and an attempt to universalize Western thinking, to create a global cultural hegemony. In the introduction to his 1979 book, *The Postmodern Condition*, Lyotard writes, "I define *postmodern* as incredulity toward metanarratives."[65] These were to be replaced with multiple narratives, none of them authoritative and all in perpetual competition. Two metanarratives he named were the Enlightenment and Marxism (the latter being something the postmodernists wanted to refine). Today's identity politics promoters have embraced this thinking, viewing the Enlightenment as a narrative embraced by those in power to impose Western values on the rest of the world and to oppress women and people in the United States who are not of European origin. Writing in *Slate*, Jamelle Bouie (now a *New York Times* columnist) claims that "'race' and 'racism' are products of the Enlightenment": "Racism as we understand it now, as a socio-political order based on the permanent hierarchy of particular groups, developed as an attempt to resolve the fundamental contradiction between professing liberty and upholding slavery."[66] This rejection of the body of thought that gave us our present understanding of individual freedom, natural rights, equality, and democracy—that produced America itself—is one of the reasons identity politics, born in Frankfurt, nurtured in Paris, and flourishing in the college towns of America, presents such a threat to freedom, and why it's so important to understand its philosophical roots.

Physicists Alan Sokal and Jean Bricmont give as good an explanation of postmodernism as any when they define it as "an intellectual current characterized by the more-or-less-explicit rejection of the rationalist tradition of the Enlightenment, by theoretical discourses disconnected from any empirical text, and by a cognitive and cultural relativism that regards science as nothing more than a 'narration,' a 'myth,' or a social construction among many others."[67] As Pluckrose observes, however, some see postmodernism as within the modern tradition, just the most recent iteration of it. She elegantly reconciles these seemingly opposing views. It depends, she writes, on

> whether we see modernity in terms of what was produced or what was destroyed. If we see the essence of modernity as the development of science and reason as well as humanism and universal liberalism, postmodernists are opposed to it. If we see modernity as the tearing down of structures of power including feudalism, the Church, patriarchy and Empire, postmodernists are attempting to continue it, but their targets are now science, reason, humanism and liberalism. Consequently, the roots of postmodernism are inherently political and revolutionary.[68]

Identity politics springs from this revolutionary root. Its promoters inherited the postmodern beliefs that every individual or group has a separate and equally valid reality; that language has no fixed meaning, making what the speaker or writer intends less important than what one hears or reads (as Pluckrose observes, this is what "underlies the current belief in the deeply damaging nature of 'microaggressions' and misuse of terminology related to gender, race or sexuality"[69]); and the view that the individual matters little and has no agency but rather is trapped in power relations beyond his control. Each society has its own "episteme" or way of interpreting the world (a dominant discourse, close relative of the hegemonic narrative).

In light of Foucault's view of the individual as nothing, we can understand how flummoxed the writers of the UCLA report on Mexican Americans were when their own survey told them that individuals in the Southwest believed they did have the power to improve their own lives. Pluckrose, again, puts it well when she writes that we see in postmodernist notions a "justification for identity politics. There is an explicit denial that differences can be other than oppositional and therefore a rejection of Enlightenment liberalism's values of overcoming differences and focusing on universal human rights and individual freedom and empowerment. We see here...the idea that identity dictates what can be understood."[70] The denial that there are universal truths denies the possibility of shared human understandings. One "group truth" or another, by virtue of political correctness, gets the upper hand. As Holmes puts it, "despite the theoretical position that 'everyone is entitled to their own truths,' the reality is that whatever local truth entitlement emerges as dominant must become the *final word for everyone*."[71] Indeed, Holmes observes:

> Practically every radical cause in America today shows the influence of the postmodernist assault. From radical feminism to racial and sexual politics, postmodern leftists blend their unique brand of cultural criticism with the political objectives of these movements. In their intellectual laboratories—the cultural studies and humanities programs at American universities—they apply theories of structuralism, poststructuralism, and deconstructionism to achieving the political objectives of the New Left... Every cause in identity politics owes its existence to this bevy of critical theories."[72]

Third-wave feminism also owes several of its central tenets to Foucault and the other major postmodernist thinkers, notably Judith Butler's introduction of the idea that gender is a social construct and Kimberlé Crenshaw's introduction of the concept of "intersectionality," which views people as collections of overlapping identities, which for some (minorities, women, and so on) are victim identities.

Crenshaw can claim the extra credit of moving postmodernism from the theoretical to the practical (praxis, again) and changing its nature in the process. As she puts it in her essay, "Mapping the Margins: Intersectionality, Identity Politics, and Violence Against Women of Color," Crenshaw writes:

> While the descriptive project of postmodernism of questioning the ways in which meaning is socially constructed is generally sound, this critique sometimes misreads the meaning of social construction and distorts its political relevance.... To say that a category

such as race or gender is socially constructed is not to say that that category has no significance in our world. On the contrary, a large and continuing project for subordinated people—and indeed, one of the projects for which postmodern theories have been very helpful—is thinking about the way power has clustered around certain categories and is exercised against others.[73]

That neatly squares the circle: victim categories are constructed (and Crenshaw is certainly right about that, when it comes to Hispanics, Asians, MENA, dozens of genders, and so forth), but we have imbued them with meaning now, we have raised the consciousness of group members, who finally see themselves as victims, which in our society now bestows value and worth—and compensatory justice. So categories do indeed have value, especially when they are recognized (after being fabricated) by the state.

Ideas culled from postmodernism are leveraged everyday by those with electoral politics in mind. This is also a useful reminder that something else was at play—Marxism's influence on our identity politics today was not merely intellectual. Members of the Communist Party USA, who were always acting on Moscow's orders, were very much involved in the spread of groupism, and the plot to change America.

Not All Communists Were Intellectuals

We have dealt in this chapter with the intellectual Marxist antecedents of critical theory, postmodernism, and identity politics. But the reason we have identity politics today is not only that Marxist intellectuals had a long march through the cultural and educational institutions. The old adage from Watergate, "follow the money," also applies here. As you will recall, the money behind much of the attempt to transform America came from the Ford Foundation. Right around the same time that Moyers was sending Marcuse's writings to the Oval Office, the foundation's vice president, Paul Ylvisaker, was forking over a lot of money to make sure that Mexican Americans could be organized into a "united front," as he himself put it.[74] Whatever Ylvisaker's intention was, the concept was formulated in 1922 by the Comintern, an international unit the Soviet Union created to unite different groups into "a common struggle to defend the immediate, basic interests of the working class against the bourgeoisie." Gramsci was present at the meeting.

Was Ford a communist front? Its influential president from 1966 to 1979, McGeorge Bundy, was a committed anticommunist who had directed the war effort in Vietnam as National Security Advisor to both Kennedy and Johnson from 1961 to 1966. But we also know from Robert Schrank, a former communist who was a program officer for the foundation during the 1970s and early 1980s, that communists had strongly influenced the foundation's thinking about programs. As Heather Mac Donald reported in 1996, Schrank referred to the foundation's "secret anti-capitalist orientation." He said that "the horror stories we Marxists had put out about the capitalist system" had influenced and guided his fellow program officers.[75] By 1977, Henry Ford II, the founder's grandson, had had enough with the institution's leftist tilt, and resigned as its trustee. His resignation letter said, in part:

> The foundation is a creature of capitalism—a statement that, I'm sure, would be shocking to many professional staff in the field of philanthropy. It is hard to discern recognition of this fact in anything the foundation does. It is even more difficult to find an understanding of this in many of the institutions, particularly the universities, that are the beneficiaries of the foundation's grant programs. I'm not playing the role of the hard-headed tycoon who thinks all philanthropoids are socialists and all university professors are communists. I'm just suggesting to the trustees and the staff that the system that makes the foundation possible very probably is worth preserving.[76]

There was direct Communist Party involvement in the creation of identity politics. As noted in chapter 1, the 1949 Los Angeles City Council election of Ed Roybal was pivotal in the process of organizing Mexican Americans as a group. The most influential of the groups formed at the time was the Community Service Organization (CSO), which was financed by Saul Alinsky and supervised by Fred Ross, and was used to politicize Mexican Americans. The CSO was set up with the help of known communists Henry Steinberg, while Roybal himself was buoyed by the support of communists Harry Hay and Bert Corona. Corona always said he never actually joined the party, but he attended its meetings and praised it for its "unwavering dedication to ameliorating the terrible conditions under which poor people such as Mexicans were forced to live" and for playing "a positive role in trying to build a democratic trade union movement."[77] These assessments were made, lest we forget, while Stalin was still in power.

A critical moment in Roybal's election was also the decision by Philip "Slim" Connelly to endorse Roybal. Connelly, not just a communist but a Stalinist, was the executive secretary of the Congress of Industrial Organization's Council. He was married to Dorothy Healey, who was the chairwoman of the Southern California branch of the Communist Party USA (which her mother had helped found). Roybal, writes Kenneth Burt, was happy to receive support from "Communist Party–influenced organizations" but was understandably "wary of the negative reaction if the party itself endorsed his campaign." He therefore asked the party not to publicly take a stand. But "ignoring Roybal's request that they remain quiet, the Communist Party openly associated themselves with the candidate and his coalition." This became a campaign issue, and the influential League of Hollywood Voters issued a strong statement: "It is the position of the League of Hollywood Voters that 'Stalinists' constitute the main menace to full democracy and complete civil rights at home and abroad, and any candidate who accepts their support is automatically an opponent of free labor and good citizens alike."[78] The chairman of the union was an actor named Ronald Reagan.

That communists were involved in the campaigns of Roybal and Wallace, and in the CSO, should not be a controversial statement. As Mario T. Garcia writes, "In both the fields and factories of the Southwest, the Communists recruited adherents and admirers because of their willingness to stand up for the rights of Mexican workers."[79] Alinsky himself never bothered to deny the involvement of communists, telling *Playboy* in 1972, shortly before his death, "Anybody who tells you he was active in progressive causes in those days and never worked with the Reds is a goddamn liar. Their platform stood for all the right things, and unlike many liberals, they were willing to put their bodies on the line."[80] According to the historian Shana Bernstein, both Ross and Roybal worried about how to "escape the red label." They sidelined the most overt communists, like Carey McWilliams, whom they refused to offer a leadership position in 1948 despite "his initial assistance and their personal respect for him."[81] They also sought the backing of the Catholic Church and other respected institutions that could provide cover.

Whether the communists who participated were acting on behalf of Moscow or out of a real desire to obtain social justice according to their lights is very much an open question, or at least it ought to be in view of Vladimir Putin's continued attempts today to exacerbate our social fissures. It at least bears remembering that the Communist Party USA in the twentieth century was not in the least an independent actor, but a wholly owned subsidiary of the Soviet Union. But while it should not be controversial to openly discuss these things, the involvement of communists, whether active party members acting on the orders of Moscow or Marxist academics from Germany and France who wanted to introduce bolshevism to the West through cultural means, should be troubling. Identity politics seeks to transform the country culturally but also politically, as we will see in the next chapter.

CHAPTER 6

★ ★ ★

The Demographic Hustle

R uy Teixeira has made quite a career out of predicting that increasing diversity in America would give the Democratic Party a ruling majority in the early twenty-first century. This would enable the party to impose its policy agenda on the country even when Republican presidents occasionally won elections. As Teixeira and his coauthor, John Judis, explain in their 2002 book on political demography, *The Emerging Democratic Majority*, American politics goes in cycles "where one party and its politicians have predominated for a decade or more—winning most of the important elections, and setting the agenda for public policy and debate. . . . During these periods of ascendancy, the dominant party hasn't necessarily gotten everything it has wanted, but it has set the terms of which compromises have occurred."[1] Teixeira and Judis met in the early 1970s when they were both members of a socialist group, the New American Movement (NAM), and have remained friends since. "Hispanic support is a crucial part of a new Democratic majority," they write, adding similar comments about Asian Americans. They admit in passing that, "like the term *Hispanic*, the term *Asian-American* imputes a spurious unity of belief to a diverse group of nationalities,"[2] but that did not prevent their rosy forecast for a new Democratic majority.

While Judis has remained a socialist, Teixeira says now that he has gravitated toward democratic-socialist beliefs. He is, at the time of this writing, a senior fellow at the Center for American Progress (CAP), the intellectual hothouse of the left wing of American liberalism. In 2017 he gave an indication of the kind of leftist program he thinks will dominate in America in this century. "I favor what economists are calling a model of equitable growth," he said in an interview with Judis for the left-wing website Talking Points Memo. "It would mean substantial government investment in creating new opportunities for the middle and aspirational classes. It could include a dramatic expansion of the educational system and a Manhattan-style investment in bringing down the price of clean energy and building the infrastructure to match." He admits that such "proposals would not get through Congress now, but it is the kind of agenda that I am optimistic that the Democrats will endorse and that the country will eventually embrace."[3] The Democratic Socialists of America (which, it is important to note, were created by the NAM in 1983) are ascendant, with political stars like Bernie Sanders and Alexandria Ocasio-Cortez, because today's challenges "are simply too big to be solved by mild, ameliorative steps,"[4] Teixeira wrote for the British news website UnHerd in 2018.

So how have Teixeira's 2002 predictions held up so far? George W. Bush won reelection in 2004; during the Obama administration, the Republicans retook the House in 2010 and kept it for eight years and retook the Senate in 2014; under Obama, the Democrats lost around a thousand seats at the national, state, and local levels; Donald Trump beat Hillary Clinton in 2016; and there is a clear populist wave in the United States and throughout the West. Nevertheless, Teixeira remains optimistic. The reason? The groups he would call the minorities (which, as we will see later in this chapter, is a term of the Left that conservatives have been ill advised to adopt). Teixeira estimates that, by 2036, white voters will make up just 64 percent of the electorate, compared to 87 percent in 1980, 74 percent in 2016 and an expected 72 percent in 2020.

In June 2019, Teixeira, along with Rob Griffin and William Frey, produced a report for CAP, the Brookings Institution, a center-left think tank, and the Democracy Fund, a nominally bipartisan public policy foundation headed and funded by eBay Founder Pierre

Omidyar that makes contributions to leftist organizations and causes. The gist of the report, *States of Change: How Demographic Change Is Transforming the Republican and Democratic Parties*, was to restate the premise of the 2002 book. Again, things look very rosy for the Left because of "the growth of the nonwhite population in the United States." In the 2000 election, Hispanics made up, respectively, 6 and 5 percent of Democratic and Republican coalitions. By 2016, the report states, the gap had widened considerably, with Hispanics making up 12 percent of Democratic voters and just 6 percent of Republican voters. Asian American support for the two parties followed a similar trend. In 1980, they made up less than 1 percent of all voters; by 2016 they made up 4 percent of Republican voters and 7 percent of Democratic voters. Though Teixeira, Griffin, and Frey ran some simulations, these did not much alter the rates at which group members voted. They conclude, in fact, that those who would like to see conservative policy enacted this century had best give up hope. "Our data indicate that, while shifting turnout and support rates can be pivotal for winning elections, these changes are likely to have a relatively small impact on the overall makeup of the electorate and party coalitions in the future."[5]

An innovation this time was to develop two compositional gaps between the two parties. One was related to the ethnoracial pentagon that has been imposed on the nation since the late 1970s. The other related to college education. White voters as a whole make up the majority of both parties' coalitions, which is hardly surprising, as the United States is majority white. Thus in 2016, 60 percent of Democratic voters and 88 percent of Republican voters were white. Where it gets interesting is the difference in the behavior of white voters with four-year college degrees and those with no college. That gap is huge. In 2016 white noncollege voters made up 60 percent of Republican voters, but just 29 percent of Democratic voters. If one considers the racial gaps and the educational gaps between the parties, "2016 was the most demographically divisive presidential election in modern American history. The parties' coalitions were more dissimilar in terms of their racial, educational, and age composition in 2016 than at any point in the previous 36 years," the report states. The gap was 63 percentage points, whereas it was as low as 42 points in the 1980 election.[6]

That is the double whammy. Not only is the number of white voters declining overall as a result of the rise of the "minorities," but the number of noncollege whites is also shrinking because of "rising educational attainment." White voters with a four-year degree have risen by 12 percentage points between 1980 and 2016, and they lean Democratic, making up 32 percent of the Democratic coalition as opposed to 28 percent of Republicans in 2016. That year was the first time that noncollege white voters did not make up the biggest group in the Democratic coalition, and that was also "the first election where white college voters made up a plurality of Democratic voters. These are both significant milestones in the long-term trajectory of white voters."[7] And those with postgraduate education, another cohort that also keeps growing, vote even more overwhelmingly Democratic. In 2012, they went for Obama 55 to 44 percent, Teixeira has observed elsewhere.[8] So in an age when every barista must have a college degree, conservatism is hit with two shrinking parts of its coalition, whites and the noncollege educated.

What we are seeing, then, looks an awful lot like Teixeira's version of the vanguard leading a new revolutionary base, as Marcuse foresaw in 1964. To get a better sense of who the vanguard is, we can look to the findings of the massive Hidden Tribes Project report of 2018, which surveyed eight thousand people on demographics, partisanship, ideology, and other subjects and used this large sampling data to sort Americans into seven political tribes. Of the seven, the farthest to the Left is the one the authors label "progressive activists." They are "skeptical of traditional authority and norms. They see those values as being established by socially dominant groups such as straight white men, for their own benefit. Progressive activists seek to correct the historic marginalization of groups based on their race, gender, sexuality, wealth and other forms of privilege."[9] In other words, progressive activists are the twenty-first-century children of Marcuse and Gramsci. Virtually none of the members of this group believe in individual agency (only 2 percent disagreed with the statement that "people's outcomes are outside their control"), and more than 90 percent believe that both men and white people start out with an advantage. Just 5 percent say they are proud of America's history. They are mostly white (80 percent) and "have strong ideological views, high levels of engagement with political issues, and the highest levels of education and socioeconomic status" of all the seven groups. Although this Gramscian and Marcusian vanguard makes up only about 8 percent of the country, "they have an outsized role in political discourse…[and] they are highly sensitive to issues of fairness and equity in society, particularly with regard to race, gender and other minority group identities."[10]

This group, steeped in critical theory, ethnic studies, women's studies, and a variety of grievances as college students, have carried that academic perspective forward into their adult lives. They have formed a coalition with members of groups regarded as "marginalized" and thus boxed in by racial and ethnic categories. Loyalty to these groups is required, and adjusting to or accommodating societal norms is to be avoided. That last part is key to the enactment of progressive activists' plans: the "minorities"—racial, ethnic, sexual, gendered—must be prevented from joining the ranks of the complacent bourgeoisie that so dismayed Horkheimer, Adorno, and Marcuse in the twentieth century. For Teixeira and like-minded policy activists seeking a permanent Democratic majority, people need to be penned inside minority categories so they will continue to feel marginalized and thus look to the Democrats as their allies and benefactors. Otherwise, Teixeira's math won't work. That is why so much effort is put into making people feel like victims.

Conservatives often make this an argument against immigration (the idea being that more immigrants will become Democratic voters than Republican voters). But it should be clear that even if restrictionist goals were fully realized tomorrow, and the immigration doors were shut completely, the problem would not only not be fixed but would continue to grow. Conservatives should understand that, in the absence of a sustained effort to keep certain segments of the population perpetually aggrieved, as Teixeira and others want, the Democrats' push to swell their numbers can't work. This is because people naturally gravitate toward the mainstream as a result of what demographers—those without a political agenda—call ethnic attrition. If your grandparents came from Mexico, your parents were born in Arizona, you were born in Ohio, you married someone born in Ohio, and you have two kids born in Ohio, you are unlikely to identify your-self as Hispanic, and your kids even less so. Unless, perhaps, you've been told that your ethnic background makes you a victim deserving of compensatory justice.

Progressive activists seek to prevent the "marginalized" from ever leaving the margins and identifying as Americans. This is why, when asked how it was possible that Republicans had captured the vote of a third of the group known as Hispanics in the 2018 congressional election, Univision anchor Jorge Ramos could think of nothing else but to blurt out the truth: it was the fault of Hispanics "who identify completely with this country."[11] This was a vote, mind you, to elect leg-islators in the United States, and Ramos was chiding those who voted in America while identifying as Americans. In 2016, after the presi-dential election, Ramos reproved those same voters as "immigrants or the children of immigrants who have forgotten their origins." If he had said "their place" it couldn't have been better.

The Census and Its Discontents

Teixeira and the many other policy minds on the Left base their assumptions—and their plans—on numbers that the Census Bureau provides. In fact, the decennial census is key to all this. The ancient Greeks and Romans employed the census to get a count and an accu-rate picture of the populace, the *demos*. According to Claude Nicolet, a historian of ancient Rome, the Indo-European root of the word "cen-sus" means "to evoke in speech, almost to call a thing into existence by naming it."[12] Today, advocates of identity politics want to use the census to make sure the demos is divided.

According to the sociologist Richard Alba, who has done extensive work on immigration and assimilation, the Census Bureau's way of classifying people "produces the smallest possible estimate of the size of the non-Hispanic white population. Whenever there is ambigu-ity about ethnoracial identity, the statistics publicized by the bureau count an individual as a minority." Alba rightly compares this to the segregationist "one-drop" rule, which held that "one drop" of black blood made a person black. "A great deal of evidence shows, however," writes Alba, that many children growing up today in mixed families are integrating into a still largely white mainstream society and likely to think of themselves as part of that mainstream, rather than as minorities excluded from it." Another reason "to be skeptical about the excited talk about the end of a white majority is that it ignores the potential for blurring the boundary between mainstream and minority," he says. "The United States has previously seen excluded minorities such as the Irish, Italians, and Jews assimilate into the mainstream. Although the channels of assimilation are narrower today because of heightened inequality, many recent immigrant families seem to be on the same path as their predecessors." The mainstream is therefore likely to grow, which will "alter the circumstances under which individuals are seen as belonging to marginalized minorities."[13] Leaving aside Alba's questionable claim as to "heightened inequality," he is correct to observe that changing circumstances are likely to reduce feelings of marginalization.

The Census Bureau, indeed, does everything within its power to extend the one-drop rule. Julie Dowling, a Latina/Latino studies professor and vice chair of bureau's National Advisory Committee on Race, made that crystal clear at the committee's November 2018 meeting: Responding to a question on whether someone with a mix of ethnic backgrounds could tick the Hispanic box, she replied, "If you have Latino ancestry, you can be a yes."[14] In fact, the bureau does more than let you tick the box—it does it for you, as Edwin Meese III and I explained in a 2018 op-ed: "If you don't think of yourself" as one of the races listed on the census form, "there's a box on the census for 'some other race,' but the bureau explains: 'When Census 2010 data were edited to produce the estimates base, respondents who selected the Some Other Race category alone were assigned to one of the OMB-mandated categories.' For people who tick multiple boxes—permissible since 2000—OMB has instructed the Census Bureau to 'allocate' responses that 'combine one minority race and white' to 'the minority race.'"[15] Thus, as David Hollinger notes, "the federal government quietly reinserted into the tabulation of the census the principle of hypo-descent"—in plainer terms, the one-drop rule—"that the opportunity to mark 'more than one' was publicly said to repudiate."[16]

The Census Bureau acts in this manner because its racial counting system is in the clutches of grievance studies professors and the racial advocacy lobby. That has been the case for decades. Alice Robbin notes that "between 1988 and 1997, cultural, multiracial and multiethnic, advocacy, and minority population interest groups were a visible presence in congressional and OMB hearings and in the public comments to the OMB's review of Statistical Policy Directive 15" (the impact of which is described later in this chapter). As a result, Robbin observes, "minority interest groups… became an enduring part of American political life."[17] For progressive activists, the worst result would be that "longstanding processes of assimilation [would] produce a white-dominated mainstream at the national level and in many regions for the foreseeable future."[18]

For his heresies, Alba was taken to task by Cristina Mora and Michael Rodríguez-Muñiz. In a reply to his article, these two academics argued that Alba had naively forgotten that census racial categories have "become instituted through political efforts" and "for specific political reasons." Putting the matter plainly, they stated that, "in effect, rather than reflecting an existing reality, all census racial categories emerge, or are negotiated, in such a political fashion—none exists in nature."[19]

It can be said of many academics on the Left that they do not write to be understood. But some, like Mora, simply lay it all out. This may be because they don't believe any conservative will ever read their articles and books. In this instance, Mora and Rodríguez-Muñiz candidly admit that the census is not about counting what is there, but rather about counting what is needed politically. Some postmodern lingo does creep in: "In response to Alba, we bring politics to the fore, specifically as it relates to knowledge construction and the issue of racial incorporation." Their aim is to demonstrate "how politics, rather than simply demographic inevitability or the dynamics of social mobility, will also ultimately determine the country's future and the status of its ethnic and racial populations." After enumerating the ways that official racial categories can be used for political and "social projects," they argue that "evaluating census statistics with these overt political criteria reveals the limitations of Alba's suggestion that some Latinos and mixed-race individuals would be more accurately classified as white." Yes, "people of color can become more upwardly mobile and gain access to spaces that have historically excluded them," as Alba emphasizes in his essay. And yes, "many Asians and other minorities now constitute a larger part of the upper class." But, despite "growing rates of inter-marriage among some Latinos and mixed-raced persons," Mora and Rodríguez-Muñiz reject "analyses that are quick to link mobility and marriage patterns to blanket statements inferring white boundary blurring."[20] The boundaries, they make clear, must stay firmly drawn.

From this perspective, the fact that many Mexican Americans tick the box for white in the census form is nothing more than a cry for help against racist America. Mora and Rodríguez-Muñiz write:

> Scholars who see the growing number of Latinos selecting "white" on the census as straightforward evidence of Latinos becoming white rarely contextualize such data within political history or current social dynamics. To be sure, some Latinos understand themselves as racially white. This identification may be interpreted as aspirational—a kind of racial passing—but it does not necessarily provide blanket evidence for the inevitable social inclusion of Latinos in the white-dominant mainstream. In fact, Professor Julie Dowling of the University of Illinois shows that Mexican Americans identify as "white" on the census not because they are accepted as white or even because they see themselves as white. Rather, by reframing the borders of whiteness to include them, Mexican Americans resist racial "othering," in an effort to be accepted as fully American.

It's hard to say what's more heavy-handed here—the condescension to Alba, who has dared to deviate from the PC consensus, or the condescension to Mexican Americans. Either way, the passage betrays a certain desperation to prevent assimilation and ethnic attrition, or even an intellectual discussion of them. The Left knows it must concentrate its effort to thwart what would happen naturally. The economists Brian Duncan and Stephen Trejo, who have done extensive work on ethnic attrition, write: "As of 2000, more than a third of married, U.S.-born Mexicans have non-Mexican spouses, with the overwhelming majority of these non-Mexican spouses being U.S.-born, non-Hispanic whites." In fact, the "proclivity for intermarriage by second-generation Mexicans today is similar to what was observed for second-generation Italians in the early 1900s." Citing Richard Alba, they continue: "This argument has potentially provocative implications for ethnic attachment among future generations of Mexican Americans, because intermarriage became so commonplace for subsequent generations of Italian Americans that Alba (1986) characterized this group as entering the 'twilight of ethnicity.'"[21]

The twilight of ethnicity would really bum out the purveyors of Hispanic identity politics, so the language employed must be constantly reshaped, and the concepts "reified," to use a Marxian word beloved of the academic Left. For example, the terms "person of color" and "minority," and qualifiers like "marginalized," like the very term "Hispanic" itself, were created and put to use in order to manufacture the demography the Left needs.

New Groups, New Terms

The definition of the word "minority" as it is used today in the sociopolitical context did not appear in a dictionary until 1961.[22] Prior to that, the term had referred either, in the political sense, to those factions who were numerically inferior in an electorate or legislature (that is how Madison and other founders used it), or, later on, to the ethnic minorities in Europe between the world wars. The sociologist Philip Gleason, in the most comprehensive account of the development of the minority concept that I have seen, notes that there were mentions in the press in 1929 of "disgruntled minorities," such as "growling Ruthenians" and "scowling Macedonians," suggesting that "Americans found the spectacle of national minority bickering distasteful."[23]

Louis Wirth, a German-born American sociologist and urbanist, defined the term in the modern American meaning for the first time in 1945, in a foundational essay in which he also praised Stalin's nationalities policy in the Soviet Union (a few short years after the massacres in the Ukraine). A member of the Frankfurt School's advisory committee, Wirth discussed the minorities in the former Habsburg, Ottoman, and Russian empires, stating: "We may define a minority as a group of people who, because of their physical or cultural characteristics, are singled out by the others in the society in which they live for differential and unequal treatment, and who therefore regard themselves as objects of collective discrimination. The existence of a minority in a society implies the existence of a corresponding dominant group enjoying higher social status and greater privileges." He cited "the Negro, the Indian, and the Oriental," and "the Catholics, Jews, and Mormons" as examples of minorities in the United States.[24]

As we saw in chapter 1, in the first part of the twentieth century, few Mexicans saw themselves as objects of collective discrimination—that was a consciousness that had to be created for them. In the late 1940s, some began to speak of Mexicans as a minority, not coincidentally when Alinsky began to focus on Los Angeles as a theater of operation. "Disgruntled," of course, metamorphosed into "aggrieved" or "marginalized." For that to happen, the element of victimhood had to be included in the definition of the term minority. Gleason quotes the sociologists Arnold and Caroline Rose as writing in the late 1940s that "the mere fact of being generally hated because of religious, racial, or nationality background is what defines a minority group."[25] The expectation, at this time, continued to be that the best outcome for minorities would be to assimilate into mainstream society as their members were accepted on an equal basis with everyone else and ethnic attrition took its course. But in the 1960s groups emerged claiming minority status for themselves to bolster their moral and political leverage. "Because minorities are by definition victims of unequal treatment, their complaints enjoy *prima facie* justification and their claims for redress gain an automatic moral legitimacy,"[26] writes Gleason. The civil rights movement consolidated these understandings. With affirmative action, membership in a designated minority acquired legal status, and, of course, with membership came benefits.

Government began to give its imprimatur to designated minorities in the 1960s. In 1966, the Equal Employment Opportunity Commission (EEOC) began the practice of asking firms with more than a hundred employees to collect information through its EEO-1 form on "Negro, American Indian, Oriental and Spanish-surnamed" employees. As Meese and I wrote, "What began as an effort to track how policies affected people thought to be disadvantaged easily but tragically slid into government-sanctioned promotion of victimhood and racial preferences. The goal of the Civil Rights Act of 1964, to prohibit racial discrimination, was turned on its head."[27] John Skrentny notes that the "the EEO-1 was a public, if implicit, federal declaration of the nation's minorities. Being listed on the EEO-1 was a crucial prerequisite for benefiting from a difference-conscious justice." There was almost a frantic effort by bureaucrats, under pressure from the then nascent racial preference organizations (financed by the Ford Foundation) to analogize other groups to blacks. "Without much thought given to what they were doing, [policy makers] created and legitimized for civil society a new discourse of race, group difference and rights. This discourse mirrored racist talk."[28] The Department of Labor's Office of Federal Contract Compliance (mentioned in chapter 4) then started to require that government contractors meet a few conditions to show that they employed members of designated minority groups, in keeping with the ethnic and racial composition in the immediate labor area.

The Office of Management and Budget finished the job in 1977 with Policy Directive No. 15, directing the Census Bureau and all other agencies to employ the ethnoracial pentagon of white, black, Hispanic, Asian, and Native American. This had enormous consequences because, as Nathan Glazer once wrote, "One encourages what one recognizes and dissuades what one does not."[29] The ethnic advocacy organizations had insisted on the official government stamp, and especially census boxes, for a reason: it creates groups. This is why they have fought so hard to control the census process. And once the formal racial, ethnic, and sexual/gender categories were created, they were etched in stone. As Alice Robbin puts it, "The stance of the American Indian, Hispanic, and black interest groups throughout nearly all this period was that the classification system could not be altered or the gains they had made over the last two decades would be jeopardized." Prior to OMB's Policy Directive No.

15, Robbin writes, "national population statistics were, as a research analyst for the National Coalition of La Raza noted during a 1975 congressional hearing, 'the sole property and prerogative of the traditionally recognized academic and research community.' Advocacy and political mobilization would be critical for obtaining legitimacy in the development of national statistics on minority populations."[30] That "advocacy and political mobilization" by the Ford-created La Raza was what Tom Wolfe wrote about in the second part of his 1970 classic, *Radical Chic & Mau-Mauing the Flak Catchers*, an incisive take on how perhaps well-intended government programs fed the pockets of the race hustling organizations whose job it was to foment resentment on the part of blacks, Mexican Americans, Filipinos, and so on.

The term "diversity" also began to be employed in the last century and is now so ubiquitous as to have become an empty slogan. So many corporations claim to be committed to diversity in hiring that the concept has degenerated into coercive group proportionalism. In fact, some committed multiculturalists are starting to suspect that this is just another marketing ploy.[31] And as we have seen in the admissions fiasco at Harvard, diversity may sound "inclusive"—another word the multiculturalists love—but it can be used to exclude certain groups, like Asian Americans. In race-class-gender–obsessed academia and in much of the woke corporate world, diversity emphatically does not mean diversity of opinion, a much more important contributor to a well-rounded education or the success of an organization than diversity of skin color or background.

The newest term deployed to further identity politics is "person of color." Gleason speculates that it "owes part of its appeal to its implicit restriction of the special status accorded 'designated minorities' to those distinguished by a racially linked phenotypical feature." The term, which, in keeping with Gleason's comment, has a faux scientific quality to it, is convenient in that anyone can describe himself or herself as a person of color, and no one else can challenge that person's self-designation.

If the crafting of minority groups had truly been based on discrimination and other types of unfair treatment, then such a schema of groups would have recognized Italian Americans, Jews, Armenians, Greeks, and others who can also sometimes be phenotypically identifiable and have certainly been victims of discrimination. Advocacy organizations representing some of these groups had filed amicus briefs with the Supreme Court during its consideration of *Regents of the University of California v. Bakke*, the landmark 1978 case on racial preferences in university admissions. The amici argued that these preferences "relied on a pernicious quota system that wrongly treated Whites as a homogeneous group," as Rachel F. Moran notes. White ethnic groups "had suffered their own histories of discrimination and therefore should not be subject to reverse discrimination. B'nai B'rith and other Jewish organizations pointed to the harms that they had experienced as members of a discrete and insular minority." Further, "the Sons of Italy offered statistics on the underrepresentation of Italian Americans in the professions, and the Polish American Congress suggested that there was no substantial difference between the term 'Pollack' and other racial epithets."[32]

Justice Lewis Powell, who wrote the controlling opinion in the *Bakke* case, drew the decidedly Marcusian line that has persisted to this day:

> The concepts of "majority" and "minority" necessarily reflect temporary arrangements and political judgments.... [T]he white "majority" itself is composed of various minority groups, most of which can lay claim to a history of prior discrimination at the hands of the State and private individuals. Not all of these groups can receive preferential treatment and corresponding judicial tolerance of distinctions drawn in terms of race and nationality, for then the only "majority" left would be a new minority of white Anglo-Saxon Protestants. There is no principled basis for deciding which groups would merit "heightened judicial solicitude" and which would not.[33]

Although "[r]acial and ethnic classifications of any sort are inherently suspect," he wrote, "and call for the most exacting judicial scrutiny," "the goal of achieving a diverse student body is sufficiently compelling to justify consideration of race in admissions decisions under certain circumstances."[34] The Court agreed that there were "educational benefits" to be derived from being in a classroom with members of minority groups—but ever since *Bakke*, the problem has remained of defining exactly who is a minority in need of preferences.

The Foundations of Identity Politics

In a separate opinion concurring with Powell, Justice Harry Blackmun doubled down. He wrote,

> I suspect that it would be impossible to arrange an affirmative action program in a racially neutral way and have it successful. To ask that this be so is to demand the impossible. In order to get beyond racism, we must first take account of race. There is no other way. And in order to treat some persons equally, we must treat them differently. We cannot—we dare not—let the Equal Protection Clause perpetuate racial supremacy.[35]

The third sentence quoted here, including its inherent contradiction, was taken almost verbatim from an *Atlantic* article about the *Bakke* case by the very influential head of the Ford Foundation, McGeorge Bundy: "Precisely because it is not yet 'racially neutral' to be black in America, a racially neutral standard will not lead to equal opportunity. To get past racism, we must here take account of race."[36] In the 2003 *Grutter v. Bollinger* decision, Justice Sandra Day O'Connor reaffirmed racial preferences in college admissions, but she did so on the assumption that over time such preferences would no longer be needed: "It has been 25 years since Justice Powell first approved the use of race to further an interest in student body diversity in the context of public higher education. Since that time, the number of minority applicants with high grades and test scores has indeed increased.... We expect that 25 years from now, the use of racial preferences will no longer be necessary to further the interest approved today."[37] Seventeen of those twenty-five years later, admissions officers are still adamant about retaining racial preferences.

To Bundy and his officers at the Ford Foundation back in the 1960s and 1970s, a system of racial preferences wasn't enough. Only after a period of ethnic separation, they somehow reasoned, could assimilation take place at some time in the future. This staggering stratagem, called "developmental separatism" by one of the Foundation's top historians, is what convinced them that not only racial preferences but balkanization was needed. Thus was planted the seed of identity politics. In her history of the foundation's early years, Karen Ferguson notes that in 1969 the foundation's Social Development Program was making "grant proposals directed at increasing the group identity and power of minorities." Their goal, she explains, was to promote "a balkanizing ethic for the black urban poor that emphasized the need for the continuing isolation of minority communities so that they could experience a cultural revitalization that would lead to what Bundy called 'social development' and eventual assimilation into the mainstream American political economy."[38]

Ferguson, who is sympathetic to the foundation's goals, is nonetheless clear-eyed about the borderline arrogance of an Ivy League–educated Boston Brahmin, surrounded at the foundation by men equally removed from the ghettos they were trying to fix, making the consequential decisions we live with to this day. She is equally clear that the foundation's activities reduced the matter to a "psycho-cultural and therapeutic issue of black identity without having to deal with the structural and material issues that initially fostered the call for black self-determination." Still, she gives credit to Bundy and the foundation for the transition from the urban unrest of the 1960s to the "mediated conflicts of public-interest judicial activism of the 1970s." Evidently, the price we had to pay to end the riots was the agency-capturing mau-mauing as described by Robbin and skewered by Wolfe.[39]

This purchased peace can be attributed, Ferguson writes, to such actions as the founding of the Mexican American and Puerto Rican Legal Defense Funds, "both created out of whole cloth by the Foundation as Latino versions of the NAACP LDF. The Foundation founded these organizations, which had no grassroots membership.... They acted on behalf but not with their respective racial communities in the courts, not the streets, to achieve their public policy victories."[40]

As revealed in the foundation's annual report for 1968, the foundation endowed the Mexican American Graduate Studies Program at Notre Dame (which was headed by Julian Samora) with the goal of intellectually buttressing La Raza's activism. The annual report explains that a grant was made to help establish the Southwest Council of La Raza and adds that, "to provide the council with a factual base for its policy positions, the Foundation assisted historical and sociological studies by a research team at the University of Notre Dame."[41] La Raza received $630,000 and Notre Dame $140,000. In today's dollars, the combined sum would be $5.4 million.

But why did the foundation go to such lengths to add all the other groups? Why create Hispanics, Asian Americans, and so on, or make an analogy to the black experience that just did not exist? The foundation's actions were "an effort to help organize Hispanics into what Foundation officers considered a 'recognizable' interest group in the black mold,"[42] writes Ferguson, adding that "as late as 1977, Bundy would still 'shorten matters,' as he put it, by making 'black' synonymous with 'minority.'" Skrentny (like others who have studied the period) has pointed in amazement to the way in which Hispanics became an entity, and one that won victory after victory on such issues as bilingual education and redistricting, despite having "small numbers, weak organization, and inconsistent demands."[43] The official Hispanic category was "called into existence by naming it" because others believed it was politically expedient to do so.

At the time of these efforts, the Immigration and Naturalization Act of 1965—which overturned the 1924 law that had put the emphasis on immigrants from northwestern Europe, to the detriment of those seeking entry from other parts of Europe, Asia, and Africa—had yet to have any impact on America's demography. The Ford Foundation started to make grants to foster "group identity," creating La Raza and MALDEF, in 1968, a year when the foreign-born among the population numbered just over 5 percent and was declining; in 1974, when the foreign-born stood at 4.7 percent, perhaps the lowest in history, the Census Bureau created the first National Advisory Committee on Race. OMB created the ethnoracial pentagon in 1977, when the rate had started to rise, but was still hovering around 5 percent. America's divisions—its present demographic makeup, in fact—was thus not the result of a clamor from aggrieved sectors of the population. As Skrentny writes, "the images of the minority rights revolution are mostly of mainstream Euro-American males and minority advocates, wearing suits, sitting at desks, firing off memos, and meeting in government buildings to discuss new policy directions."[44]

The balkanization of America, and the identity politics it produced, were thus a social-engineering plan crafted by those at the highest echelons of institutional success panicking about the black riots that had consumed America in the late 1960s. These establishment figures were coping with their own "anxiety in [the] face of rioting that, escalating between 1965 and 1968, hit dozens of cities, cost hundreds of lives, and laid waste to hundreds of millions of dollars in property,"[45] writes Ferguson. Another historian of the time, Hugh Davis Graham, writes that the fact that the race riots took place only in northern and western cities demonstrates that the civil rights era had brought perceptible benefits only in the South, leaving policy makers scrambling to pacify blacks in the rest of the country. The movement had won a "massive payoff for black southerners. It brought Jim Crow crashing down.... Southern blacks thus had no incentive to riot. But outside the South, the Civil Rights Act and Voting Rights Act had produced few tangible benefits for inner-city blacks."[46] Frightened federal officials reacted by going beyond the promise of color-blind justice and proffering race-consciousness benefits to blacks. When activists then pressed them to treat other groups as they were treating blacks, the bureaucrats agreed without giving the matter too much thought, either to buy peace or because some of them, too, agreed that the constituency for affirmative action had to be broadened. Once the project to carve out minority set-asides began, the courts went along with it. Justice Thurgood Marshall had stated in *Bakke* that "[t]he experiences of Negroes in America has been different in kind, not just in degree, from that of any other ethnic group. It is not merely the history of slavery alone, but also that a whole people were marked as inferior by the law."[47] But this the purveyors of the new identity politics ignored.

Interestingly, the same process appears to have taken place in the United Kingdom a couple of decades later, when British officials responded to the same stimulus. British academic Kenan Malik writes that, following inner-city riots in the 1980s, British officials picked leaders and organizations to represent the interests of the rioters. "At its heart, the approach [they took] redefined the concept of racism and equality. Racism now meant not simply the denial of equal rights but also the denial of the right to be different. And equality not only entailed possessing rights that transcend race, ethnicity, culture and faith; it meant asserting different rights because of them."[48] Malik makes the point that these were demands made by political elites, not the immigrants themselves or their children, who were simply, and justly, asking for equal treatment. "What troubled them was not a desire to be treated differently but the fact that they were treated differently." In the United States, the civil rights movement was turned on its head, indeed betrayed, while across the Atlantic a similar development played out.

Although Bundy's plan was for a temporary ethnoracial dispensation, we now know that it has become entrenched. In fact, it is a threat to our body politic more dangerous than the violence that begat it, as we will see in the next chapter. Bundy exercised terrible judgment as national security advisor for Kennedy and later Johnson during the Vietnam War. His advice to Johnson that "the good intentions and works of the Americans would overcome the nationalist appeal of the Viet Cong, and that building the capacity of the South Vietnamese to rule and fight for themselves would allow U.S. troop withdrawal,"[49] disastrously misunderstood Hanoi's ruthless intentions and the catastrophic consequences of withdrawal. Similarly, Bundy exercised terrible judgment—or perhaps just naiveté—regarding minority groups, failing to see that people opposed to assimilation would take advantage of those groups to create Marcusian revolutionary bases in order to manipulate American demographics.

None of this is to deny that Mexican Americans, Chinese Americans, Indian Americans, and others have faced cruel discrimination. They still do to this day. We are never going to get rid of stupid people; prejudice will always be with us. What is important is that, whereas before 1964 discrimination and racism were legally enforced, we have made it illegal to discriminate in employment, housing, education, hiring, and the use of public accommodations. That is an enormous achievement, yet we are not supposed to celebrate it. This is because the purveyors of identity politics want you to believe in structural racism, unconscious racism, implicit bias, and so on. They insist that a root-and-branch reform is needed because "racism is embedded in our thought processes and social structures."[50]

Abandoning the assimilationist ethic in favor of its opposite, group formation, is a political project with a political end. Not only was Marshall right that the experiences of black Americans were unique, but it is also the case that the experiences of other groups were extremely similar to those of past immigrants from Europe. And those immigrants did not arrive with demands for entitlements. As Linda Chavez wrote in *Out of the Barrio* in 1991, "The history of American ethnic groups is one of overcoming disadvantage, of competing with those who were already here and proving themselves as competent as any who came before. Their fight was always to be treated the same as other Americans, never to be treated as special, certainly not to turn the temporary disadvantages they suffered into the basis for permanent entitlement."[51]

Earlier Immigrations

One of the oddities of the present moment is the sense that minority groups are competing for the honor of being the most aggrieved. But over the course of immigration history, newcomers of various ethnic origins have been thought of as inferiors, facing discrimination in employment and housing, and bigotry in the form of taunts and violence, however they were classified. For example, as Shana Bernstein writes about the period of the 1940s and 1950s, "like Mexicans, Jews were legally white, but still outsiders socially and politically."[52] Through it all, most immigrants viewed assimilation into the mainstream as a positive goal, and they worked hard to succeed. There are two groups that are so completely assimilated today that they are mostly indistinguishable from white Anglo-Saxon Protestants but who were very much the outsiders in their day: the Scots-Irish and the Germans.

The Scots-Irish were among the earliest groups of immigrants, and their experience is instructive. Not to put too fine a point on it, they were not welcomed anywhere. From Boston to Pennsylvania to Virginia, they were either met with riots or were told they could not practice their Presbyterianism. After having invited them to create a buffer zone between Indians and Quakers, the provincial secretary James Logan later wrote to a friend that "the settlement of five families from Ireland gives me more trouble than fifty of any other people."[53] As late as 2008, author Michael Hirsh saw fit to write in *Newsweek* that the outcome of that settlement "was that a substantial portion of the new nation developed, over many generations, a rather savage, unsophisticated set of mores." The Scots-Irish, in this writer's view, brought a "coarsened sensibility" that is now animating "our national dialogue."[54]

The story of German immigrants is also instructive, not least because those who came in the nineteenth century were also a group that ideologues tried to use to promote socialist ideas in America. The German immigration to America can be divided into those who immigrated to Pennsylvania in the late 1600s and early 1700s in pursuit of religious freedom, those who started to come in after the 1830s for economic reasons. Of the former, Benjamin Franklin wrote in 1755, "Why should the Palatine Boors be suffered to swarm into our Settlements, and by herding together establish their Language and Manners to the Exclusion of ours? Why should Pennsylvania, founded by the English, become a Colony of Aliens, who will shortly be so numerous as to Germanize us instead of our Anglifying them, and will never adopt our Language or Customs, any more than they can acquire our Complexion."[55] As the Irish Catholics were to be later, the Germans in Pennsylvania were hated because of their political heft. In a 1753 letter to the botanist Peter Collinson, Franklin wrote: "I remember when they modestly declined intermeddling in our Elections, but now they come in droves, and carry all before them, except in one or two Counties."[56]

The Germans who came to America starting in the 1830s seeking economic opportunity did not receive better treatment. Though discussion of the rise of anti-immigrant nativism in the 1840s tends to focus on the Irish Catholics, "more immigrants came to the United

States form Germany between 1800 and 1900 than from any other source" and were more evenly distributed, according to Duncan Moench. They were mostly Roman Catholic, and nativists feared that "Catholics had an inseparable predisposition toward despotic politics and therefore threatened the foundations of the liberal society Protestants had built, socially and politically." But the animus wasn't just generally anti-Catholic, it was specifically anti-German. "In total," writes Moench, "Anglo-American nativists saw German Catholics, Lutherans, and especially social-democratic rationalists as threatening the stability of the nation's predominantly Anglo, liberal and mainline Protestant political culture."[57]

The Germans who immigrated for economic reasons in the nineteenth century also sought political influence. Many of their leaders were socialists who fled here after the failed revolutions that convulsed Europe in 1848 (they are known as the "Forty-Eighters"), and they strived to accomplish in America what they had failed to do in their native land: push it ever leftward. In America that meant away from its Lockean attachment to liberalism, to the point that, as Moench admits, they "gave nativists good cause" to suspect them. The German Social Democratic Association of Richmond "called for the abolition of the presidency and the Senate and 'the right of the people to change the Constitution when they like." They also wanted public schools to teach in German and to work under a "prohibition of all clerical influence."[58]

One might even say they were an early Frankfurt School. The so-called Louisville Platform, issued after a meeting of Forty-Eighters in that city in 1854, made many of the same demands and, worse, called for a radical overhaul, if not the rejection, of the concept of private property so cherished by liberalism. It called for the "abolition of the land monopoly," stating that "to occupy the natural soil, as exclusive property" was something "no individual has a right to do." Instead, the platform called for an arrangement that brings to mind the Mexican *ejido* system: land was to be incorporated into a "common principal fund" for those "willing to cultivate it."[59] The platform, really an attempt to form a German American Social Democratic Party, "expressed a deep dissatisfaction with what was seen as the broken promises of the American Declaration of Independence," according to Mikkel Thorup. Karl Heinzen, another well-known Forty-Eighter and one of the organizers of the Louisville Platform, even advocated revolutionary mass murder. In a speech he gave on Independence Day in 1876, Thorup writes, he called for a complete overhaul of the US government, replacing the presidency and the Senate with "an assembly of agents and deputies of the people, in permanent session."[60]

As Moench puts it—in something of an understatement—"the demands of mid-nineteenth century German-American activists of the time did not go over well." Once these ideas became better known, the feeling grew quickly that the growing German presence in the United States threatened Americans' "hard-won Republican way of life."[61] The nativist Know-Nothing Party took off, winning elections on a platform that called for immigrants to have to wait twenty-one years before becoming eligible for citizenship and the vote. Violence erupted in several places, as when Protestant mobs in Louisville attacked German Americans on Election Day and prevented them from voting. As Meredith Mason Brown notes, that day, August 6, 1855, became known in the city as "Bloody Monday," and "on the same day, Know-Nothings set fire to a number of houses of German Americans and a brewery in Louisville's East End, killing 10 German Americans."[62] Cincinnati, where many Germans also had settled, also saw large riots that year.

Anti-German hatred extended into the first two decades of the twentieth century, and reached its height with the onset of World War I. In a speech on Flag Day in 1917, Woodrow Wilson declared: "The military masters of Germany denied us the right to be neutral. They filled our unsuspecting communities with vicious spies and conspirators and sought to corrupt the opinion of our people in their own behalf." These people, Wilson went on, "seek to undermine the Government with false professions of loyalty to its principles."[63] Teddy Roosevelt, as a former president, was even freer to demonize German Americans. "The Huns within our gates," Roosevelt said, had to abandon German practices, otherwise they were "traitors who have no right any longer to be treated as American citizens."[64]

Three-fourths of the states eventually restricted the teaching of the German language in some way. "Some states even tried to outlaw the German language's general use, including over the telephone," writes Moench, who cites the German history scholar Don Heinrich Tolzmann for a statistic of 17,903 people found guilty of speaking German. "The federal government labeled German language publications a potential organ of the enemy and required them to submit costly translations of every article printed, driving out of business a once-mighty ethnic press. Those caught reading German publications in public were spat on.... In at least 13 states, mobs of these 'superpatriots' tarred and feathered or violently beat German-Americans."[65]

Interestingly, the left-wing militants who set the table for these anti-German feelings represented but a small minority—less than 1 percent, according to Moench—of German Americans in the mid- and later nineteenth century. And yet, that minority was very successful. Well into the first decade of the twentieth century, "socialism was perceived by the Anglo-American mainstream as Germanic in origin." As we saw in the previous chapter, that assessment was not far off the mark. It wasn't seen that way just by WASPs in America. Socialists in Europe grew frustrated with the failure of socialism to take hold in America after 1848, and after Marx's writings grew in circulation, and pinned their hopes on German Americans. "Many in the international left at this time believed it was actually the duty of the German American population to lead the rest of the United States to a state of Marxist class consciousness," writes Moench.[66]

If the actual militants were such a small minority, why did socialism become so identified with the entire community in the 1800s, inside and outside the United States? The "small numbers...betrayed their steady impact on the growth of a radical left-wing political culture inside German-American communities in the second half of the nineteenth century and well into the 1910s," explains Moench.[67] Again, essentially, what we had with German American communities in the nineteenth century was a vanguard leading a revolutionary base with the goal of changing America. As we saw in chapter 1, a similar process happened with Mexican Americans, a very large group that leftists today want to use to induce America to shed its Anglo-Scottish Enlightenment legacy of limited government and adopt the Continental version that embraces a powerful state. In the case of the German Americans, it seemed both to politicians and intellectuals that assimilation to American ways was the only option. Thus, in 1894 future president Theodore Roosevelt published an essay in which he approvingly quoted the German-born Wisconsin congressman Richard Guenther, who said: "After passing through the crucible of naturalization we are no longer Germans; we are Americans.... America first, last, and all the time. America against Germany; America against the world; America right or wrong; Always America."[68] A Mexican American politician saying that today would be the target of a well-coordinated attack from the Left.

In the case of Mexican Americans, by the late 1960s that vanguard included the Chicano movement, which was very influential though it reflected the views of only a small percentage of Mexican Americans when it first emerged. As David Gutiérrez points out, "though many Mexican-Americans were alienated by the Chicano militants' ideology and rhetoric, the young activists helped to change the political landscape by raising demands for social justice in aggressive new terms.... In the process Chicano militants also helped to stimulate a far-reaching debate among Mexican-Americans over complex issues concerning their own sense of ethnic identity...and the logic, potential efficacy, and desirability of a strident, ethnically based politics for the Mexican-American minority at large."[69]

One important difference today is that very politically savvy people were able to use the crucial moment of the civil rights movement to create Marcusian vanguards everywhere. The foundation for the entire infrastructure was laid at that dramatic point for the nation. Preferential programs proliferated in an atmosphere of racial crisis with little unifying vision beyond the perceived need for action.[70] Through analogies between blacks and Mexicans, blacks and women, and so on, programs originally intended to ameliorate the condition of the descendants of slaves were extended to others. And then came the Gramscian view that these marginalized groups of people must abstain from adopting the nation's norms, because when they incorporate into their thinking the hegemonic metanarrative of the privileged, they participate in their own oppression. To even consider assimilation, let alone teach or promote it, is to participate in false consciousness. It is with such views that a project to change a nation from within begins.

We will see in the next chapter how the push to bring in Continental (Kantian, Hegelian, Marxian) ideas continues today, and why it is so important to fight back and defend the Anglo-American model. To conclude this chapter and prepare for the next one, here is an exchange between Judis and Teixeira from the *Talking Points Memo* interview, which appeared under the heading "There Is No Alternative to the Left":

> **Judis:** Countries are sometime structurally unable to do what is in their best interest. In the U.S., we have this strong anti-statist tradition going back to the revolution that seems to get in the way every time we want to do something like what you are proposing. It is possible that contrary to Hegel, the rational won't turn out to be the real.
>
> **Teixeira:** Of course it is possible, but if you look at the history of the United States, despite the anti-statist bias and despite all the other political problems, the way the country has evolved over time is toward a larger government that does more and provides more for people. And we obviously have evolved tremendously in the social realm as well. Governments don't do what is rational in the short term, at least rational in the sense you are describing it, but political systems evolve over time in a way that is consistent with the values and priorities of the left, and I expect that to continue over time.[71]

CHAPTER 7

★ ★ ★

Why It Matters

Richard Carranza, the chancellor of the New York City Department of Education, is in charge of the largest public school system not just in the United States but in the world. More than 1.1 million children are taught at the city's 1,800 public schools. Carranza oversees an annual budget of $25 billion. That makes Carranza extraordinarily powerful, and potentially dangerous. Having drunk deep of the witches' brew of identity politics, he now gets to use his position to impose his views on a staff of 135,000, including seventy-five thousand educators, and, of course, the most impressionable one-eighth of the Big Apple's population. In an example of what he can do and in fact does, in early 2019 Carranza ordered that principals, central office supervisors, and superintendents undergo mandatory training to root out the "white supremacy culture" and the "implicit bias" that is supposedly rampant in New York schools.[1] With an almost religious zeal, Carranza says, "It's good work. It's hard work. And I would hope that anybody that feels that somehow that process is not beneficial to them, I would very respectfully say they are the ones that need to reflect even harder upon what they believe." Matt Gonzales, an outside adviser on Carranza's school diversity task force and director of New York Appleseed, an advocacy group, states the obvious when he says of the reeducation camps, "it requires discomfort." That pain is supposed to be felt by the educators, and that is bad enough; but they are adults who can walk away and seek other employment.

What the consciousness-raising struggle sessions aim to do among the students is much worse. In order to root out "white-supremacy culture," teachers are drilled on stamping out "individualism," "objectivity," "perfectionism," either/or thinking," a "sense of urgency," and "worship of the written word." Readers who have reached this chapter will recognize all this as an attempt to replace the hegemonic narrative of America and the West with a counternarrative that sees reason, logic, truth, and objectivity as instruments to universalize patriarchal Western oppression. This is critical theory and postmodernist deconstruction turned into a multimillion-dollar industry of outside consultants. Even worse, in this case, it is hurting children. As I wrote in the *New York Post*, "perfectionism and love of reading are human traits, as evidenced by the fact we have all perfected our way from the Stone Age and now read on hand-held tablets. All of these traits contribute to academic and lifetime success. Without striving for perfection, a person will accept shoddy work; love of reading will lead to learning; linear thinking makes a person try to work through contradictions."[2] Carranza's identity politics will thus not just waste scarce resources and cause discomfort among educators, it will seriously imperil the future chances of a generation of schoolchildren, many of whom already face difficult odds.

For all these reasons, Carranza is the face of the damage that identity politics perpetrates on the nation, day by day, and why it is so urgent that our citizens understand its nature and force their policy makers to do something about it. Unless identity politics is confronted and ceased, there will be Commissar Carranzas in every school district and every HR department at every company in America.

Diversity seminars such as the one Carranza forces on his staff are not contradictory by happenstance. The designers of these struggle sessions do understand that children need to read and write, and thus need to appreciate the written word; they know that objectivity is essential to solving quadratic equations; they are aware that individualism incentivizes hard work. They know the achievement gap in education that they say they are trying to fix is a serious problem. Their object is not the children (who are just collateral damage, the eggs broken on the way to making the social-engineered omelet), and they understand that they are not offering a better pedagogy. What they want to do is destroy the free-enterprise, liberal system that best offers protection for man's natural rights. Whether one believes these rights come from God or nature does not matter; what matters is that our rights are under attack. The seminar designers do not hide their intentions, and they justify the complete systemic overhaul they seek on the claim that racism is deeply ingrained in America's very social framework. They attempt to intimidate and shame their critics into joining the fight against "white supremacy."

They are slightly less forthcoming about what they want to replace capitalism and democracy with. Nobody comes out and says, "We are rooting out individualism, objectivity, and perfectionism from the classroom because we want to introduce socialism." But the mask slips often enough, and they have "you can't handle the truth!" moments. What they want is socialism—a large Kantian, Hegelian, and Marxian state that will force people to behave in ways they have defined as good. This goes against the grain of the American system.

Critical Race Theory and the End of Natural Rights

Seminars such as the ones Carranza required are the product of critical race theory, the smorgasbord of half-baked ideas at the center of identity politics. Critical race theory is the mutant child of critical theory and owes its birth to a workshop held in a convent, of all places, outside of Madison, Wisconsin, in 1989. "Unlike traditional civil rights discourse, which stresses incrementalism and step by step progress, critical race theory questions the very foundations of the liberal order, including equality theory, legal reasoning, Enlightenment rationalism, and neutral principles of constitutional law," write Richard Delgado and Jean Stefancic in their primer on the subject. Unless we do something drastic, "something inherent in the nature of our capitalist system [that] ineluctably produces poverty and class segregation...will continue to create and chew up victims." The alternative? "The free enterprise system, which is built on the idea of winners and losers, will continue to produce new ones every day."[3]

In this way, the victimization and oppressor–oppressed narratives become handy justifications for the ever-growing involvement of government and diminution of our rights. Equality, the core principle of the Declaration of Independence that is central to the American way of life, is dropped in exchange for its functional opposite, what critical theorists (or "crits") call "equity." Equity requires unequal treatment, by the schools, corporations, even the law. Whereas equality is understood to mean equality of opportunity, equity focuses on equality of outcome, which requires the redistribution of resources to those deemed to have a victim status—whatever their real socioeconomic status actually is! "If I had a poor white male student and I had a middle-class black boy, I would actually put my equitable strategies and interventions into that middle-class black boy because over the course of his lifetime he will have less access and less opportunities than that poor white boy. That's what racial equity is," training consultant Darnisa Amante said at one of Carranza's workshops.[4] One of the top critical theorists, Iris Marion Young, succinctly described the new dogma when she wrote that, in America, "racism, as well as other group oppressions...condition the lives of most or all Blacks, Latinos, Asians, American Indians and Semitic peoples." Therefore, she adds, what is required is "different treatment for oppressed and disadvantaged groups. To promote social justice, I argue, social policy should sometimes accord special treatment to groups."[5]

The Constitution, with its persnickety equal treatment clauses, is to be ignored, again, because racism is structural. "Color blindness can be admirable," write Delgado and Stefancic. "But it can be perverse, for example, when it stands in the way of taking account of difference in order to help people in need...." Therefore, "if racism is embedded in our thought processes and social structures as deeply as many crits believe, then the 'ordinary business' of society—the routines, practices and institutions that we rely on to do the world's work—will keep minorities in subordinate positions. Only aggressive, color-conscious efforts to change the way things are will do much to ameliorate misery."[6] There are many aspects of America that require improvement, to be sure, but it is possible to achieve these outcomes while treating everybody equally.

Critical theorists also seek to sweep away freedom of conscience, which often gets in the way of their social experiment with sex. In 2013, when an Oregon bakery refused to bake a cake for a lesbian couple's wedding because it violated the bakers' religious beliefs to do so, the couple took them to court. Responding to that case, Isaac West wrote in the journal *First Amendment Studies*: "When we privilege religious freedom as a frame for understanding these controversies, we do so at the expense of a fuller commitment to equality." The Supreme Court eventually sided with the bakers, throwing out the $135,000 penalty imposed by the state, which had forced the bakers to close their shop. West, of Vanderbilt University, argues that because the United States is without a common ethnic, racial, or religious heritage, it depends on the idea of law as a binding cultural agent; but the law, in his view, is an "incoherent conglomeration" of competing ideas. Thus, "fluctuating allegiances to freedom and equality riddle American figurations of the law. When these abstract principles are made concrete by persons claiming them as a right in a specific situation, freedom and equality often are less compatible discourses than previously imagined."[7] On whether doctors have a right to refuse to perform certain procedures, such as abortion or administering euthanasia drugs, Julian Savulescu (a chaired professor of ethics at Oxford University) and Udo Schuklenk have called for "removing a right to conscientious objection," praising the atheist Richard Dawkins for getting it "right" when he said, "religion is not simply vicars giving tea parties. There are evil consequences."[8]

In the pages of the *New York Times*, free speech is now described as having been "weaponized" by conservatives. The *Times*'s legal correspondent quotes Georgetown law professor Louis Michael Seidman: "It's a mistake to think of free speech as an effective means to accomplish a more just society." And radical feminist Catharine A. MacKinnon is quoted as observing that the First Amendment "has mainly become a weapon of the powerful."[9] The attack on free speech is partly a result of postmodernist thinking. If truth is constructed by competing discourses, and the existing hegemonic narrative must be crushed and replaced with a counterhegemonic narrative, then any defense of the present dominant hegemony must be made illegal, or at the very least toxic. The key here is to crush and banish; the "marketplace of ideas" won't do. As Delgado and Stefancic explain, "The idea that one can use words to undo the meaning that others attach to these very same words is to commit the empathic fallacy—the belief that one can change a narrative by merely another better one."[10]

Seidman—again, a professor at one of the country's most prestigious law schools—pins his attack on free speech on the need to dismantle the present power structure. Free speech simply cannot coexist with the social-justice goals of the progressive agenda, which Seidman defines as "favoring an activist government that strives to achieve the public good, including the correction of unjust distributions produced by the market and the dismantling of power hierarchies based on traits like race, nationality, gender, class, and sexual orientation." Free speech, a natural right upon which the American republic is based, is on the chopping block because capitalism has a distribution problem. "Speech must occur somewhere and, under modern conditions, must use some things for purposes of amplification. In any capitalist economy, most of these places and things are privately owned, and in our capitalist economy, they are distributed in dramatically inegalitarian fashion," says Seidman. "The connection between property and speech posed a problem for a progressive version of the speech right. Because speech opportunities reflect current property distributions, free speech inherently favors people at the top of the power hierarchy."[11]

This last part of Seidman's argument brings us to another natural right that identity politics seeks to suppress: the right to private property. As we know from previous chapters, this is the greatest bugaboo of all socialists, as they believe it ineluctably leads to inequality. To be fair, this is a logical deduction; talents are not distributed equally, and in a free society in which men are not slaves but get to keep the product of their own labors, inequality in property will arise. In his *Second Treatise of Government*, which some call the foundational text of liberalism (not in the narrow modern political sense but in the classical sense of pluralism and individual rights), John Locke anticipates that the new system will lead to inequality but will produce far more wealth for all, including those at the bottom. The founders believed that it was the principal job of government to protect our talents.

Madison wrote in *Federalist* No. 10 that there is a "diversity in the faculties of men, from which the rights of property originate," and that "[from] the protection of different and unequal faculties of acquiring property, the possession of different degrees and kinds of property immediately results."[12] But as Joshua Mitchell, also a Georgetown professor, puts it, "because identity politics supposes that we *are* our identities, politics does not consist in the speech, argument, and persuasion of normal politics, but instead in the calculation of resource distribution based on identity—what in Democratic parlance is called 'social justice.'"[13] Neither property nor opportunity are allocated by a market, with the most efficient and productive receiving the greater share; they are available to people based on their degree of assigned group victimhood (no matter how successful the individual member of a group might be).

Rather than just enumerate the rights we take for granted but that are under attack by critical race theorists, we must understand that the very *concept* of rights is under attack. "Crits are suspicious of another liberal mainstay, namely rights," Delgado and Stefancic write. Some CRT scholars

> believe that moral and legal rights are apt to do the right holder much less good than we like to think. In our system rights are almost always procedural (for example, to a fair process) rather than substantive (for example, to food, housing or education). Think how that system applauds affording everyone equality of opportunity but resist programs that assure equality of results, such as affirmative action at an elite college or university or efforts to equalize public school funding among districts in a region. . . . Moreover, rights are said to be alienating. They separate people from each other—"stay away I've got my rights"—rather than encouraging them to form close, respectful communities.[14]

The Fight to Retain Rights

The denial of the natural rights on which the country was founded, the natural law that grants the legitimate authority for our government, is not just a theoretical matter but has real-life consequences. Simply put, the attack on natural rights is making us less free. It has given us campuses where Marcuse's repressive tolerance is put into effect to snuff out conservative ideas, through violent means if necessary. It has given us social-media mobs, "doxxing," and the shutting down of conservative views by the very companies that run social media. It has given us hate-speech laws and politically correct standards that make a mockery of the First Amendment. The mostly white woke minority we discussed in chapter 6, today's revolutionary vanguard, has accrued formidable power, which it puts to use in a "cancel culture" that allows it to destroy the lives of those who step out of line. "In today's American culture, wokeness is privilege," writes the pop culture writer Art Tavana. The new hierarchical shaming system "is how the woke minority ensures that they remain majority shareholders in the grand enterprise of the arts."[15] Panicked company executives and administrators will fire people on the spot.

Take the case of James Damore, who lost his job at Google simply because he wrote a memo in which he noted, based on research, that women may be less interested than men in pursuing a tech career (to counter the idea that women are being discriminated against in the tech workplace). He's just a well-known example out of many. Others are avoiding getting fired because they practice self-censorship, do not exercise their First Amendment rights, agree to put the "I'm An Ally" sign on their desks, as HR suggests, join their ethnically assigned after-hours activities group at the office, and generally engage in Soviet double-think in the land of the free. One of the biggest fears a breadwinner has is to be accused of racism, homophobia, misogyny, or transphobia. It is the equivalent of being accused of heresy prior to the Modern Age, which is why postmodernism should more rightly be called premodernism. It is to this age that we are at risk of returning unless we take action.

The charge that conservatives, when they do stand up for the rights our country is founded on, are "weaponizing" these rights has become all too common on the Left. Justice Elena Kagan did so in June 2018, when she strongly dissented in *Janus v. American Federation* by reading from the bench that the majority was "weaponizing the First

Amendment, in a way that unleashes judges, now and in the future, to intervene in economic and regulatory policy."[16] The curiously named People for the American Way Foundation did as well in 2016 when it asked "Who Is Weaponizing Religious Liberty?"[17] This leaves the impression that it is somehow improper to stand up for one's rights when they are under unrelenting attack. But a very interesting, and happy, development has been that identity politics' attacks on liberalism—its entire continuum, from Locke in the seventeenth century, through Mill in the nineteenth, through classical liberalism and welfare-state liberalism in twentieth-century America—has finally convinced many liberal intellectuals and commentators to denounce it and come to the defense of liberal ideals. Mark Lilla at Columbia, Steven Pinker at Harvard, William Galston at the Brookings Institution, Francis Fukuyama at Stanford, Andrew Sullivan at *New York Magazine*, Claire Lehmann at Quillette, and the triple threat of the scholars Helen Pluckrose, James A. Lindsay, and Peter Boghossian, to name some prominent examples, have dared to speak out and have braved the criticism they knew would come their way.

In a 2018 interview with the *Washington Examiner*, Pinker demolished point by point many of the arguments made by the critical theorists. "Identity politics is the syndrome in which people's beliefs and interests are assumed to be determined by their membership in groups, particularly their sex, race, sexual orientation, and disability status," Pinker told Adam Rubenstein. Pinker allowed that certain disadvantaged groups do have some cause to form a coalition with common interests, giving the example of Jews and the Anti-Defamation League.

> But when it spreads beyond the target of combatting discrimination and oppression, it is an enemy of reason and Enlightenment values, including, ironically, the pursuit of justice for oppressed groups. For one thing, reason depends on there being an objective reality and universal standards of logic. As Chekhov said, there is no national multiplication table, and there is no racial or LGBT one either.... Even the aspect of identity politics with a grain of justification— that a man cannot truly experience what it is like to be a woman,

or a white person an African American—can subvert the cause of equality and harmony if it is taken too far, because it undermines one of the greatest epiphanies of the Enlightenment: that people are equipped with a capacity for sympathetic imagination, which allows them to appreciate the suffering of sentient beings unlike them. In this regard nothing could be more asinine than outrage against 'cultural appropriation.'

And when empathy is not enough, added Pinker, there is also another Enlightenment principle: "people can appreciate principles of universal rights that can bridge even the gaps that empathy cannot span. Any hopes for human improvement are better served by encouraging a recognition of universal human interests than by pitting group against group in zero-sum competition."[18]

Conversely, on the right, there has been a surge of conservative condemnation of the concept of universal human interests, the market economy, and of classical liberalism itself. A prominent group of conservative intellectuals are, rather, emphasizing the localism and incipient historicism (the idea that concepts such as rights have to be considered within a historical context) of Edmund Burke, the eighteenth-century Anglo-Irish politician considered the father of modern conservatism. To this group belong conservative intellectuals such as Patrick Deneen, Yoram Hazony, and Oren Cass. To one degree or another (and this is a very heterogeneous group) they share the critical theorists' disdain for liberalism and its emphasis on "individual autonomy," consumerism, and free markets, especially global capitalism, and some are willing to accept state intervention. Cass, for example, advocates for a national industrial policy. Deneen and Hazony challenge aspects of the American founding. Hazony, more lightheartedly, allows that "it is not the Constitution itself that is the problem, nor even…Enlightenment-rationalist phrases in the Declaration of Independence. The actual problem is the fact that many judges [interpret] the world from within the intellectual straitjacket of the liberal axiom system."[19] Deneen, on the other hand, comes closer to Howard Zinn in bitterly describing the founding as an ultimately doomed experiment by men with ulterior motives. Inequality, equally for Zinn and Deneen, was baked into the liberal system spawned by the Enlightenment.

By emphasizing a civic nationalism (or in Deneen's case, local communitarianism) that promotes color-blind solidarity among all compatriots, the nationalist conservatives (NatCons) are trying to provide an antidote to identity politics. For that, they should be lauded. Hazony, for example, offers a sophisticated explanation of nation-states being birthed when component tribes and clans decide to coalesce— precisely what identity politics tries to prevent.

Questions remain, however. First, how long can the NatCons stave off the effort of some to turn their undertaking from civic into ethnic nationalism? What, after all, unifies the civic American nation, if not the founding and the Enlightenment views on natural rights on which it was based? Most of them might say culture, and Deneen some sort of local attachment mixed with Burkean little platoons. But absent the Declaration and its creed of all men being created equal, localism would not unite Texas, Massachusetts, Oregon, and Hawaii (and arguably culture wouldn't either). Second, will they fall for the siren song of statism and support big government? Cass, Mitt Romney's domestic policy director during the 2012 presidential campaign, already foresees the government directing decisions to a greater degree than most conservatives have for decades. Third, because the NatCons are allergic to Enlightenment claims on universal natural rights, could they form a league with a new iteration of the Left that throws out identity groups and replaces them with civic nationalism? Though at the moment it's admittedly hard to see any 2020 Democratic presidential candidate doing so, it remains a fact that a socialist like Bernie Sanders, or a statist like Elizabeth Warren, are clearly old economic Marxists with little use for subnational group identities, whatever Warren's pretense to Indian ancestry and the lip service they must pay to group identities. Or, conversely, some NatCons could potentially come to accept a balkanized America provided all groups received benefits.

It is easy to recognize more than mere hints of the anti-Enlightenment case made by critical race theorists in Deneen's 2018 book *Why Liberalism Failed*: "Nearly every one of the promises that were made by the architects and creators of liberalism has been shattered....

The only rights that seem secure today belong to those with sufficient wealth and position to protect them." Deneen is not wrong when he points out the glaring signs of unhappiness in America, including the astonishing 70 percent of Americans who believe that their country is moving in the wrong direction, or the half who think America's best days are behind it. The political system is broken and the social fabric is fraying, Deneen argues. If liberalism made Americans a contented lot of consumerists in the postwar period, today everyone is a great deal more disgruntled (the ghosts of Horkheimer and Adorno would approve!). Moreover, according to Deneen and other conservative critics of the Enlightenment, what we have today is not a glitch but a feature. "Liberalism has failed—not because it fell short, but because it was true to itself," he writes. The radical individualism that grew out of the Enlightenment ignored that man is a creature that requires "a thick set of constitutive bonds" such as family, community, and church. "Statism arose as a violent reaction against this feeling of atomization," writes Deneen, which is why he states that "individualism and statism advance together."[20]

In a 2018 interview with the leftist publication *The Nation* (which the interviewer saw as "an effort to determine whether common ground can, or should, be found between factions of the left and right against liberalism"), Deneen admitted that "there's a certain overlapping consensus in the left's critique of global capitalism and my own. But we probably part in some of the ways we seek to address the problem." The difference is not small, and it exposes another problem with identity politics—its borderless utopianism—a stance that nationalist conservatives not only do not share but make a point of criticizing. As Deneen explained, "I tend to favor less-global political solutions, which is I think where the left tends to go. According to the left, the way to address the injustices of global capitalism is to move toward a more comprehensive global political structure."[21] This opposition to transnationalism is a reminder that, whatever the problems with the new NatCons—one of the top ones being their inability to see that the primacy of culture in determining societal outcomes is not mutually exclusive with the concepts of universal rights or common humanity—their analysis is of value today.

But their criticism of universal natural rights and the social contract directly questions the philosophical basis of America. This makes it all the more important that old-time liberals like Pinker are taking up the cudgel against identity politics in the name of rights that apply to all humanity, even if many governments violate them and some national cultures are much better than others at defending them. Acknowledging that all humans, qua humans, are born with certain rights is not to give in to utopian universalism, much less the dangerous transnational governance that multiculturalism abets. In this regard, some liberals have come to the defense of sovereignty. William Galston, for example, in a 2018 *Wall Street Journal* op-ed, recommended to his fellow liberals to "make peace with national sovereignty. Nations can put their interests first without threatening liberal democratic institutions and norms. Defenders of liberal democracy should acknowledge that controlling borders is a legitimate exercise of sovereignty."[22]

Old-time liberals who oppose identity politics are also just as wary as conservatives of the dangerous idea that individuals *are* their assigned identities, that their thoughts and actions inhere in their group membership. They spot an old enemy of civilization in comments like those made by Massachusetts representative Ayanna Pressley at a 2019 Netroots convention in Philadelphia: "From whatever lived experience or identity you represent, if you are not prepared to come to the table and represent that voice, don't come. Because we don't need any more brown faces that don't want to be a brown voice; we don't need any more black faces that don't want to be a black voice. We don't need Muslims that don't want to be a Muslim voice. We don't need queers that don't want to be a queer voice." To the impeccably liberal George Packer, writing in the impeccably liberal *Atlantic*, Rep. Pressley's worldview "sets up a new hierarchy that inverts the old, discredited one—a new moral caste system that ranks people by the oppression of their group identity. It makes race, which is a dubious and sinister social construct, an essence that defines individuals regardless of agency or circumstance." The importance of people such as Packer, Pinker, and Galston coming around to the view that, as Packer puts it, "the new progressivism, for all its up-to-the-minuteness,

carries a whiff of the 17th century, with heresy hunts and denunciations of sin and displays of self-mortification," cannot be overstated.
"The atmosphere of mental constriction in progressive milieus, the
self-censorship and fear of public shaming, the intolerance of dissent—these are qualities of an illiberal politics.... It took me a long
time to see that the new progressivism didn't just carry my own politics
further than I liked. It was actually hostile to principles without which
I don't believe democracy can survive."[23]

Old-style liberals who care about liberty, lastly, may be taking up
the fight against identity politics because they grasp that it is a betrayal
of one of modern liberalism's greatest achievements, the Civil Rights
Act of 1964, as it resegregates America. Setting up subnational "protected" groups with unequal rights is nothing less than a backdoor
return to the era introduced by the *Plessy v. Ferguson* decision in 1896,
which created the "separate but equal" doctrine. The one-drop rule
that identity politics is trying to bring back first made its way into
southern jurisprudence in the era that followed *Plessy*. Until identity
politics and critical race theory made their appearance, those fighting
for racial justice abided by the dissent of Justice John Marshall Harlan
in *Plessy* that,

> [i]n view of the Constitution, in the eye of the law, there is in this
> country no superior, dominant, ruling class of citizens. There is no
> caste here. Our Constitution is color-blind and neither knows nor
> tolerates classes among citizens. In respect of civil rights, all citi-
> zens are equal before the law. The humblest is the peer of the most
> powerful. The law regards man as man and takes no account of his
> surroundings or of his color when his civil rights as guaranteed by
> the supreme law of the land are involved.[24]

The civil rights movement tried to put the Harlan standard of
color-blindness into effect, starting with the *Brown* decision in 1954.
The goal was to stop having the government making decisions based
on race, not doubling down on that foul practice. We know this
from the 1963 speech Martin Luther King Jr. gave on the steps of the
Lincoln Memorial, where he said, "I have a dream that my four little

children will one day live in a nation where they will not be judged by the color of their skin but by the content of their character." There was Sen. Hubert Humphrey's promise in a debate on the Senate floor that Title VII of the Civil Rights Act, prohibiting discrimination by race in hiring, would not turn into racial preferences. "It the Senator can find in Title VII ... any language which provides that an employer will have to hire on the basis of percentage or quota related to color, race, religion, or national origin, I will start eating the pages one after another, because it is not in there,"[25] Humphrey said, in response to Sen. Willis Robertson's contention that quotas would appear. As we saw in the previous chapter, the group-conscious balkanization that did indeed follow was the consequence of a mix of related factors, including the perhaps well-intentioned but grievously wrongheaded strategy by Ford Foundation officers to institute temporary "developmental separatism," the cynical opportunism of those who sought to build a revolutionary base to refashion the country from within, and the surrender to race-based preferences by panicked bureaucrats. Not least, identity politics betrays the civil rights movement by inciting a new and emboldened form of identity politics, the egregious white supremacy movement.

Not Just for the Left

White supremacists are numerically small and have little to no impact on policy or politics. A 2017 *Washington Post* poll found that only 9 percent of Americans said it was acceptable to hold "neo-Nazi or white supremacist views," while 83 percent of Americans found it unacceptable, 72 percent strongly so.[26] And note that's a question of whether it's acceptable to hold those views, not those who support those views, which would be much, much smaller. I abhor communism, for example, but, of course, I believe it is acceptable for Americans to believe that government should order every aspect of their lives, and I would politely speak to or debate a communist (as in fact I did in late 2019, with the editors of *Jacobin*). White supremacists, however, have been given a prominence by the press that has elevated their influence in the culture in an effort to taint President Trump and bolster the charge that America is structurally racist. This dangerous supply of oxygen to their ideas, along with the unrelenting discussion of "whiteness" by the grievance industry that surrounds us, bears watching.

At best crackpots and at worst murderous psychopaths, the only useful function of white supremacists is to demonstrate that, contra critical race theory, a good message does drive out a bad one. All one need do is read racist material or hear a racist speak to quickly grasp that, whatever they are, they aren't superior. This is no doubt why, despite the mainstream media's best efforts to portray them as some sort of large and menacing force, their numbers remain infinitesimally small. As a wry joke has it, with white supremacists, media demand definitely outstrips supply.

There is a danger, however, that recent events involving white supremacists, such as the 2016 rally in Charlottesville, Virginia, or the August 3, 2019, shooting in El Paso, Texas, portend a future surrender to identity politics by the entire country. That outcome, a permanent "cultural divide," was what Huntington warned against in his 2004 book *Who Are We?*

The always astute Heather Mac Donald of the Manhattan Institute echoes those fears. While there have always been white supremacists, not just in America but all over the world, the recent upsurge is tied to related elements in the culture. "Identity politics," Mac Donald says, "celebrates the racial and ethnic identities of designated victim groups while consigning whites—especially heterosexual white men—to scapegoat status. But its advocates should be careful what they wish for. If 'whiteness' is a legitimate topic of academic and political discourse, some individuals are going to embrace 'white identity' proudly." She rightly pins such violence as the El Paso shooting by a white supremacist targeting Latinos on the pathologies that have been created by identity politics: "the dominant culture is creating a group of social pariahs, a very small percentage of whom—already unmoored from traditional sources of meaning and stability, such as family—are taking their revenge through stomach-churning mayhem. Overcoming racial divisiveness will be difficult. But the primary responsibility rests with its main propagators: the academic left and its imitators in politics and mass media."[27]

Overcoming such bitter division is indeed made all the more difficult by the turn our culture has taken, fueling grievances among some, making social pariahs out of others, leaving nothing but frustration and anger in its wake. In *The Disuniting of America*, Arthur Schlesinger, the court intellectual at Kennedy's Camelot, worried that, "If separatist tendencies go on unchecked, the result can only be the fragmentation, resegregation, and tribalization of American life." Such worries prompted him to ask, "In the century darkly ahead, civilization faces a critical question: *What is it that holds a nation together?*"[28]

Culture of Victimhood

To hear sociologists Bradley Campbell and Jason Manning tell it, the organizing system that now holds us together as a nation of disgruntled group members is not the sense of common purposes that Schlesinger and Huntington sought, but something entirely new. Grievance mongering has created for all groups, and all American institutions, what the two sociologists call "a culture of victimhood." This new dispensation has several features worth enumerating: All perceived grievances, even the most minor and inadvertent (microaggressions) have to be carefully catalogued and publicized, in order to make the case for structural oppression; administrative authority mushrooms to deal with what is then seen as an epidemic of racism and oppression, with a consequent rise in the cost of university; the people making claims of microaggressions and demanding victimhood status will tend to be affluent (and those most likely to become diversity administrators and reap the material rewards of the new system); victimhood, not ability, becomes the new way to acquire moral status; and finally, the condition of victimhood attracts not just recognition and esteem, but also material rewards.

As was to be expected, rewarding victimhood in this manner has only increased the number of people claiming to be victims (you get more of what you reward and less of what you tax). As Campbell and Manning wrote in a 2014 paper, "the aggrieved actively seek to attract and mobilize the support of third parties." Victimization thus becomes "a way of attracting sympathy, so rather than emphasize either their strength or inner worth, the aggrieved emphasize their oppression and social marginalization.... People increasingly demand help from others, and advertise their oppression as evidence that they deserve respect and assistance."[29] Microaggressions must thus be carefully curated in order to demonstrate a larger pattern of domination, inequality, and marginalization—the purported structural, deeply ingrained racism in every aspect of American life that is then used by Carranza and his ilk to justify an all-out attack on liberalism. "The core of much of modern activism, from protest rallies to leaflet campaigns to publicizing offenses on websites, appears to be concerned with rallying enough public support to convince authorities to act," write Manning and Campbell. Quoting from a blog called "Oberlin Microaggressions," they note that "its purpose is to show that 'racist, heterosexist/homophobic, anti-Semitic, classist, ableist, sexist/cissexist speech etc.' are 'not simply isolated incidents, but rather part of structural inequalities.'" These offenses are "a repeated pattern of oppression said to contribute to the marginalization of entire collectivities."[30]

It is in the nature of microaggression complaints that the only ones that matter are those with the identity politics stamp of approval. Thus they must concern preconceived notions of oppression and exclusion. People have grievances about many things—co-workers not pulling their weight, a neighbor repeatedly playing loud music—but unless a grievance can be used as evidence of oppression or exclusion, it's of no interest to identity politics. Also, it's important to note that demands for support of the oppressed "do not necessarily emanate from the lowest reaches of society.... Rather, such forms of micro-aggression complaints and protest demonstrations appear to flourish among the relatively educated populations of American colleges and universities." It is the most fortunate among us who are complaining the loudest about victimization. As Tavana says, "the woke minority" are in fact the ones with the privilege, which they wield angrily against the unwoke in the name of victimhood.

One of the notable social effects of identity politics concerns the moral status of offenders and the offended. It used to be that a person who committed a moral infraction saw their moral status go down, but now not only is that true but the moral status of the victim goes up.

Naturally, "This only increases the incentive to publicize grievances, and it means aggrieved parties are especially likely to highlight their identity as victims, emphasizing their own suffering and innocence. Their adversaries are privileged and blameworthy, but they themselves are pitiable and blameless."[31] Thus do victims and grievances multiply, with a seemingly limitless supply of villains.

This stands in complete contrast to the America of the recent past, when stoicism, strength, and a can-do approach were the admired traits, and displays of self-pity were considered petulant. Now we have what many on the right call the victimhood Olympics, which stands in stark contrast to the culture of honor and culture of dignity that social scientists recognize as having once characterized American society and other Western societies. In the former, one's honor bestows moral status. In the latter, the dignity that inheres in all persons accords moral status that an insult cannot alienate.

Perhaps the national sense that "we're all in this together" breaks down when we relentlessly instill a consciousness of group grievances, not to mention when we teach students that the founding was a massive conspiracy by men who intended to maintain their privilege. Victimhood culture applies only on an intergroup basis and only when it serves the interest of leftist goals. All individuals must submit to group formation even if said group does not correspond to their aspirations. "The goals of a 'unified' group may not reflect exactly those of certain factions within it," Delgado and Stefancic observe, "yet the larger group benefits because of the increased numbers they bring."[32] To clarify this point, it may not suit Argentinian Americans to be counted as Hispanics, or Chinese Americans to be counted as part of an amorphous group called Asian Americans, but the collectivities are thought to benefit, so they have to lump it.

Social Division

The cultural homogeneity that once characterized America is no longer holding us together, and the coalition building that precedes the creation of a nation, as Hazony has argued, is stunted, taking place at the subnational level only. Identity politics, by its very nature, is concerned with the interests of specific, designated groups, and not with the larger polity. But constitutional republicanism can exist only through the active participation of a united people working within the confines of the nation-state, debating among themselves but coming together to agree on principles. The sharing of a common culture and language creates the trust quotient that is necessary to succeed. It permits and encourages the economic competition needed to improve our standard of living because it allows it to proceed as harmoniously as possible within the boundaries of social cooperation.

The best we can hope for without the unity that comes when the tribes unite is an agreement by different identity groups to engage in power sharing in the public sphere, while returning to their respective primal attachments at night. But America would cease to be our home then, and become simply a guesthouse where we all live. Can a free society long endure that arrangement? John Stuart Mill, observing the multicultural, polyglot Habsburg Empire of his day, did not think so. "Free institutions are next to impossible in a country made up of different nationalities," he said. "Among a people without fellow-feeling, especially if they read and speak different languages, the united public opinion, necessary to the working of representative government, cannot exist."[33]

Social scientists like Robert Putnam—who wrote in "*E Pluribus Unum*: Diversity and Community in the Twenty-first Century" (2007) that diversity was divisive and made people in communities turn inward and mistrustful of each other—have pointed out the pitfalls of a disunited society. In 2002 a working paper titled "Fractionalization," which was produced by a team of social scientists led by Alberto Alesina for the National Bureau of Economic Research and is considered the gold standard in the field, found that "ethnic and linguistic fractionalization are associated with negative outcomes in terms of quality of government." Ethnic fractionalization "is highly negatively correlated with GDP per capita growth, schooling and telephones per capita,... financial depth, [and] fiscal surplus." In terms of social solidarity (and in a statement nobody will find surprising in the America of the early twenty-first century), the authors also found that "It seems that governments have a much more difficult task achieving consensus for redistribution to the needy in a fractionalized society." Unscrupulous politicians can play havoc with a society made up of fixed groups. As the authors of the NBER paper observe, "When people persistently identify with a particular group, they form potential interest groups that can be manipulated by political leaders, who often choose to mobilize some coalition of ethnic groups ('us') to the exclusion of others ('them'). Politicians can mobilize support by singling out some groups for persecution, where hatred of the minority group is complementary to some policy the politician wishes to pursue."[34]

A Nation of Commissars

Is this what America wants? A nation in which commissars like Richard Carranza put us through Maoist struggle sessions, suppressing the rights and freedoms that have been America's hallmark from its very beginnings? Will we acquiesce in becoming substantially less free, fearing to speak up lest we lose our jobs? Do we want a country where the promise of the civil rights movement has been betrayed and we are going back to the *Plessy* era of "separate but equal" and the one-drop rule? Do we want multiplying grievance claims by pampered individuals styling themselves as victims, a culture that fetishizes neediness instead of celebrating success? Are we going to accept the end of social solidarity, fueling the actions ugly white supremacists, and the growth of distrust?

Since the mid-1800s, America has taken in over 100 million immigrants. In the past they managed to hang on to their grandparents' stories, cooking, and music while acquiring the common creed and norms of their new adopted land. Over time, assimilation and ethnic attrition took its natural course and people became "Heinz 57" Americans, a bit German, a bit Italian, Croatian, Welsh, Armenian— but 100 percent American. The answer to Samuel Huntington's question—whether America "should be a nation of individuals with equal rights and a common culture and creed, or an association of racial, ethnic, and cultural subnational groups held together by the hopes for the material gains that can be provided by a healthy economy and a compliant government"[35]—remain unresolved. An association of groups, as we have seen in this chapter, does not work. In the following and final chapter, we will explore what changes are needed to get us back to a common culture.

CHAPTER 8

★ ★ ★

Now What?

We don't have to accept any of this. In fact, we must fight all of it. There are not thirty-one genders; sex is an anatomical reality, and except for extremely rare cases of people born with physical manifestations of both, there are two sexes. People are one or the other. It is a scandal that there are some municipalities where saying this earns Americans a fine, or corporations where the long hand of HR will get you for it. There is no "Hispanic" race, nor is there any "Hispanic music" or "Hispanic cuisine." Millennials who think they enjoy either have been misled. We should never give anyone preferential treatment because of the group to which he or she has been assigned, just as we should not penalize anyone for their race, national origin, or sex. That our government does this on a regular basis is a disgrace. We should never allow impertinent martinets like Richard Carranza to have any impact on what any child not his own learns, let alone 1.1 million of them. Knowledge does not inhere in ethnicity, especially a synthetic one cooked up in the cubicles of the Office of Management and Budget. That is a dangerous idea, as the history of the twentieth century will attest. Giving these and other falsehoods the imprimatur of government writ, enforcing them, suppressing or banning their denial under the specious rules of "hate speech," has been a political project from the start, one meant to transform the country, upend the culture, abolish the family, and replace it all with a totalitarian system that eliminates the individual, his agency and his rights. It is not just a rejection of the Enlightenment, it is an outright return to the Dark Ages, its stratified estates and its prohibitions on free thought.

Some Americans will wonder what transforming society means, and why it's even bad. After all, the only constant in life is change. That is a good conservative principle recognized as such by Burke in the eighteenth century, but improvement while conserving what is good in a culture is not what the Left has in mind. No. They mean 1917 Russia or 1959 Cuba. They mean wholesale. Very little of the previous era survives into the next. The geography of a country remains, but that's about it.

I came to this country just after turning fourteen. During the twelve years I lived in Cuba, I had already witnessed (i.e., suffered under) communist totalitarianism, and in the two years I spent in Franco's Spain, soft fascism ("soft" in the sense that people were not persecuted for their race and there was religious liberty—I myself attended a Protestant evangelical school in seventh grade). The United States had me at hello. I lived happily with my extended Cuban family in Queens, among teeming masses of Irish, Italians, Jews, Chinese, blacks, Puerto Ricans, Greeks, and so on (though not a WASP in sight). America gave me my first taste of freedom, and has never since disappointed. I feel a responsibility to expose the ideologies I witnessed before arriving here, and those I have seen in other lands during my fifteen years overseas as an American journalist and later, after leaving journalism, in my many travels abroad as a fellow at a think tank. Communism and fascism both stoke resentment, then feed on it when it spreads. They are ideologies that crush the individual as if he were a bug, for the sake and great glory of the state, which their adherents see as the only rational distributive agent. In the language of the Left—and Alinsky does teach us to borrow the language of our opponents—my "lived experience" has allowed me to compare and contrast.

In Carranza and his minions, I can see the Cuban principal who once bullied me when I was eight because I would not join the communist student group.[1] In the plot to transform America's culture, I recognize the extinguishing of Cuba's pre-1959 essence. In today's struggle sessions I discern the attempts to make Che Guevara's "New

Man," who lives today in true servitude to the state, roaming the streets and fields of Cuba. And in the growing lack of trust, the hunkering down brought about by balkanization, I remember Franco's Spain, where city dwellers and villagers alike regarded each other with mistrust because an intrusive authoritarian state had snuffed out civil society. I choose to use my lived experience to try to keep America free. How could I do otherwise? I am optimistic we can do so. I agree with Samuel Huntington that "all societies face recurring threats to their existence... yet, some societies, even when so threatened, are capable of postponing their demise by halting and reversing the processes of decline and renewing their vitality and identity."[2] I believe that America is at the point, with so many conservatives and liberals alike questioning what is happening with identity, of being able to reverse decline.

To do that, there are many things all of us, and our leaders, can do. The identity politics that those who would transform America have employed relies on an interplay of category making, grievance stoking, and benefit granting under the guise of compensatory justice. As is usually the case, the way out is the way in.

From the evidence presented in this book, a pattern emerges. We see people desiring to be classified as white when that conferred real privileges, such as the ability to immigrate, become naturalized, get married, buy land, enter one's chosen profession, and so. Then activists changed the privilege scheme and set out to convince those very same people—Mexicans, Indians, Middle Easterners, and so on—to, in effect, change their race and the way they thought of themselves. They would henceforth have to, in Louis Wirth's definition, "regard themselves as objects of collective discrimination." So collectives needed to be created, and a sense of victimhood and grievances implanted. To the politicians and the all-important administrative state, the activists drew a false analogy with the historical plight of African Americans. Implicit, and sometimes explicit, in the bargain was the demand for people to separate themselves from the mainstream, to cease assimilating, to no longer think of themselves as belonging to one large American nation with common purposes, but as members of a tribe under Ottoman-style millets.

Obviously, to save America from this fate does not mean a return to the imperfections of the past; our goal must be to complete the promise of the civil rights movement before it was betrayed by Bundy, Samora, Marcuse, Alinsky, and others of similar mind. Our struggle is to realize the promise of a color-blind America, where no one either benefits from or is persecuted for their real or attributed traits, and to cease creating the impression that people are victims without personal agency. What we need is to confront whatever racial discrimination and social injustice persist in America with a new civil rights movement—a civil rights movement 2.0. We need to say no to both *Plessy* 1.0 and 2.0.

I should add in passing at this point that lumping together the people discussed in this book tends to obscure very real differences between them. We have every reason to believe that McGeorge Bundy loved America; he just thought he had come up with a formula to fix America at a time when he feared it was about to break. He then hubristically employed the billions at his disposal to put his blueprint in place, with consequences worthy of a Greek tragedy. The same cannot be said of Herbert Marcuse or his mentee Angela Davis. Marcuse made clear again and again that only under communism could man realize his dreams. If he loved America, he had an odd way of showing it. Davis proclaims herself a communist and has never missed an opportunity to attribute evil to the United States. But all three—indeed, all the people this book has looked at—promoted group identities, group resentment, and group-based justice. The path of reason and objective truth will take us toward policies that can start healing America's real historical wounds as well as the new ones inflicted since the 1960s. The goal is to regain the social cohesion that so bothered Marcuse.

Our Old "Fixed, Dogmatic Liberalism"

What was the nature of the liberal consensus that so rankled all those clamoring to transform America? What was John Judis talking about when he complained to his friend Ruy Teixeira that "in the U.S., we have this strong anti-statist tradition going back to the revolution that seems to get in the way every time we want to do something"?

From its founding, America was the product of a commonsensical marriage between the Enlightenment idea that humans have certain natural rights and a belief that universal principles are shaped and affected by local conditions and traditions. "America's constitutional liberalism was certainly informed by the ideas of Locke and other theorists of natural rights, but the U.S. Constitution is much more than reification of Lockean liberalism," writes Kim Holmes.[3] The result was a particular culture shaped from the start by the Anglo-Scottish Enlightenment of John Locke and Adam Smith, the American colonial experience with common law, and the dissenting form of Protestant Christianity.

This last part is a strong component of America's identity that often goes overlooked. Edmund Burke spoke of this phenomenon in a speech to the House of Commons in 1775, when he noted that the American colonists

> are Protestants, and of that kind which is the most adverse to all implicit submission of mind and opinion. . . . All Protestantism, even the most cold and passive, is a sort of dissent. But the religion most prevalent in our northern colonies is a refinement of the principle of resistance: it is the dissidence of dissent, and the Protestantism of the Protestant religion. . . . The colonists left England when this spirit was high, and in the emigrants highest of all; and even that stream of foreigners which has been constantly flowing into these colonies has, for the greatest part, been composed of dissenters from the establishments of their several countries, and have brought with them a temper and character far from alien to that of the people with whom they mixed.[4]

All this combined to produce an attachment to liberty unlike that of any other people on earth, said Burke. "In this character of the Americans, a love of freedom is the predominating feature which marks and distinguishes the whole. . . . This fierce spirit of liberty is stronger in the English colonies probably than in any other people of the earth."[5] This ethos thrived despite massive immigration because immigrants of all religions did not just accommodate themselves to this particular Christian ethic; self-selection contributed to a virtuous circle of liberty and enterprise. As Thomas Archdeacon has observed, "Members of foreign ethnic groups were entitled to citizenship and the full range of civic privileges, but English political forms and economic practices remained the norm, and success fell to those best able to conform to them."[6]

Even before its very birth, then, America was already a land uniquely committed to liberty. The United States was unlike Europe, with its history of feudalism and rigid class hierarchies; there, the reaction took the form of socialism on one hand and blood-and-soil conservatism on the other. The United States was also unlike its neighbor Mexico, with its *ejido* system of communally owned, inalienable land, and its other neighbor, Canada, which had remained attached to Britain for far longer and had thus borrowed its Fabianism.[7] In terms of political culture, America was more like an island, and a remote one at that.

It was the American liberal consensus on freedom and natural rights that so rankled Horkheimer, Adorno, and Marcuse. Marcuse left an intellectual legacy that severely damaged that consensus, but he wasn't the first to try. He built on the foundation that had been laid by American Progressives at the turn of the twentieth century. He and the thinkers he influenced were far more successful than the early Progressives because of the panic among the establishment sparked by the race riots of the 1960s.

Follow the Money—and Cut It Off

While the heirs of Marcuse carried out the transformation of the American university, Lyndon B. Johnson's Great Society, with massive government expenditures on social programs, carried out the Progressive agenda in Washington. Activists' eyes lit up when they saw the pot of gold to be spent on affirmative action, contract quotas, and electoral redistricting that would be dangled as the wages of minoritization.

The husband-and-wife duo of sociologists Frances Fox Piven and Richard A. Cloward wrote in *The Nation* in 1966: "Whereas America's poor have not been moved in any number by radical

political ideologies, they have sometimes been moved by their economic interest. Since radical movements in America had rarely been
able to provide visible economic incentives, they had usually failed to
secure mass participation of any kind."[8] The duo proposed to so flood
the public welfare system with demands for benefits that it would
collapse, forcing the government to take direct action to end poverty.
Thus would the elites engineer a mass movement among the unsuspecting underclass. Cloward had conducted research in 1960 with his
colleague Lloyd Ohlin that led to the idea that local neighborhood
organizations had to be created to organize individuals. That study
was then used by the Ford Foundation in what became known as its
Gray Areas project, founded by Paul Ylvisaker. And the Gray Areas
project served as a blueprint for Johnson's Great Society.

To start dismantling identity politics, then, and begin the civil
rights movement 2.0, we need to stop the government from handing
out benefits to those with a claim of victimhood simply because of
membership in a protected group. Race- and group-conscious programs only entice people to subdivide, conjure up or invent instances
of victimization, and encourage them to feel damaged. For example,
preferential contracting programs require that owners seek certification as a "disadvantaged business enterprise" (DBE). To get such
certification, the owner must be a member of one of the designated
groups and swear an affidavit that he or she has been "subjected to
ethnic prejudice or cultural bias." The fact that such an owner may
have overcome those obstacles does not matter. George La Noue draws
the logical conclusion: "Thus, social disadvantage is, as a practical
matter, established at birth, and cannot be challenged by evidence of
a successful life."[9]

That is the crux of the problem. The government is unremit-
tingly sending us the message that lower status is established at birth
and is inexpungable. Programs that encourage such feelings are the
lifeblood of identity politics, and fomenting a culture of victimhood
and birth castes is the last thing a government that wants to create
a healthy society should be doing. These programs contradict other
ideals, and laws, of the United States. The protections afforded by
the Constitution, specifically by the Reconstruction Amendments,

are meant for individuals, not groups. Title VI of the Civil Rights Act of 1964 prohibits discrimination in any program or activity that receives federal funds or financial assistance, while Title VII prohibits employment discrimination on the basis of an individual's "race, color, religion, sex, or national origin." Johnson's Executive Order 11246, prohibiting federal contractors with more than $10,000 in government contracts from "discriminating in employment decisions on the basis of race, color, religion, sex, or national origin" and requiring that contractors take "affirmative action to ensure that applicants are employed…without regard to their race, color, sex or national origin," was twisted into precisely the opposite. The result is that today the federal government has a panoply of programs that contravene our ideals and laws, and provide the economic incentives that Cloward and Piven rightly foresaw would reshape society in ways that would benefit radical political ideologies.

In 2011 the Congressional Research Service (CRS) issued a report that catalogued nearly three hundred federal statutes that "specifically refer to race, gender, or ethnicity as factors to be considered in the administration of federal programs." The report's authors said they sought to be "as comprehensive as possible," but that their report still was "by no means exhaustive." Included in the massive sweep were "all variants of the following words or phrases: underrepresented, affirmative action, minority, woman, disadvantage, race, and gender." All in all, there were twelve government-wide statues and 264 agency-specific ones that called for the use of discriminatory preferences. These programs make "noncompetitive awards," which means that we are fostering the divisions of identity politics on the backs of the American taxpayers, the vast majority of whom, as we saw in chapter 6, have no time for any of this. A typical such statute, 15 U.S.C. 637, authorizes agencies to "restrict competition for any contract for the procurement of goods and services by the Federal Government, to small business concerns owned and controlled by women."[10]

The hundreds of federal programs that spend money on such efforts to prevent or redress discrimination extend to all of the government's vast activities. In 2011, the leading areas were Health and Human Services, with fifty-three programs, followed by the Departments of

Education and Agriculture with forty-one and thirty-two, respectively. Even the Department of Defense had a whopping eighteen programs, and Homeland Security 8, which means these programs do not just render us poorer, but also less safe. While the 2011 paper is the most recent the CRS has done (originally, this was an effort requested by Senator Bob Dole), the total of 276 set-aside and preference programs and grants marked a 60 percent increase over a similar survey conducted in 1995. There is very little question that in the years since 2011, including six years of the Obama administration, the number has grown even larger.

What we need now, then, is for the government to conduct this survey again, but this time not by the CRS but more thoroughly at the executive level. My colleague Hans von Spakovsky and I called for such a probe in a 2018 paper, including in our report a proposed executive order to that effect drafted by Roger Clegg, president of the Center for Equal Opportunity.[11] In such an order, the president, whoever he or she might be, and of whichever party, should command each agency to "examine its regulations and relevant statutes to determine if any of them contain such requirements or permitting of discrimination or preference. Where such regulations are found, the agency shall prepare…an amendment to such regulation ending the requirement." Agencies would be required to amend statutes that call for racial discrimination.

Under a civil rights movement 2.0, Congress could also return America to its goal of not judging people "by the color of their skin, but by the content of their character" by enacting nothing less than a new Civil Rights Act, this one eliminating all the distortions of the 1964 act. Clegg, Elizabeth Slattery, and von Spakovsky, in a separate 2014 paper, laid out in fine detail the various forms such legislation could take.[12] All of them should stipulate clearly that no agency of the federal government can grant preferences based on race, ethnicity and national origin for purposes of education, employment, or contracting. I would add to that preferences based on sex, gender, or sexual orientation. The law should extend this injunction to the states and to individuals for whom it is already unlawful to discriminate on the basis of those traits. Lastly, states and individual Americans can take

matters into their own hands. Nine states already ban racial preferences known as affirmative action. Citizens of other states should press
to introduce such ballot initiatives to amend their states' constitution
to bar preferences in education, employment and contracting by all
private and public entities.

As for universities that take federal funding (nearly all, the notable
exceptions being Hillsdale College and Grove City College, both
conservative institutions), the approach can be similar. Institutions
such as Harvard, for example, take half a billion dollars a year in taxpayer funds of one sort or another—more than Harvard takes in in
tuition. Congress can require that they disclose their racial preference
practices. In reality, however, as we saw with the Students for Fair
Admissions case (representing mostly Chinese American students)
against Harvard in 2018–19, universities are very good at conceal-
ing how they implement affirmative action. But that case and many
others give hope that once one of them reaches the Supreme Court,
the justices will finally end an unseemly practice that since the *Bakke*
decision in the 1970s has twisted them into jurisprudential pretzels.
Eliminating racial preferences in admissions is one of the most important things that can be done to prevent further social splintering. It is
the "gateway drug" of identity politics. It grabs adolescents at a critical time, when they are filling out college applications and searching
for what is known as the "it factor" that will make a difference to an
admissions officer. It thus entices them to tick a box and stick with it.
The very principle enshrined in *Bakke* that "diversity" in the classroom
confers educational benefits implies that the students who are there
as a result of this process are ambassadors of their group—that such
group knowledge inheres in their DNA.

No true campaign to end the explicit discrimination of preferences
can leave the doctrine of disparate impact in place. First blessed by the
Supreme Court in *Griggs v. Duke Power Company* in 1971, disparate
impact concerns actions by employers or schools that have a disproportionately negative effect on certain groups. An action with disparate
impact can be held to be discriminatory even when the action is neutral
on its face and there was no discriminatory intent. Disparate impact
extends discriminatory preferences by category to housing and lending.

But law professor Gail L. Heriot, a member of the US Commission on Civil Rights, has argued that disparate impact was clearly not intended by Congress when it passed the Civil Rights Act of 1964. It is also incoherent because all actions have a disparate impact on some group; through the theory of disparate impact, government agencies (i.e., the state) have acquired unlimited discretion in a way that makes a sham of the concept of limited government. Heriot calls for a "disparate impact inventory" by the federal government. The attorney general would send a letter to all the heads of agencies that enforce any antidiscrimination statute, regulation, or policy asking four questions: "1. Do you consider your statute, regulation or policy to impose liability for disparate impact? 2. If so, what is the legal basis for that view? 3. How does disparate impact liability work under that statute, regulation or policy... and what is the agency's legal basis for thinking so? 4. Finally, why does the agency believe disparate impact liability will survive strict scrutiny?"[13] Heriot thinks this approach would free us of disparate impact analyses because few of the agencies would be able to articulate a compelling state interest in the policies, or that they have been narrowly tailored, requirements necessary to survive the high "strict scrutiny" standard that the Court deems necessary in matters of race.

Heriot's solution is ingenious. In their 2014 paper, von Spakovsky, Slattery, and Clegg propose a related strategy that is likewise direct and democratic: amending all the different acts, titles, statutes, regulations, and so on that permit a disparate impact analysis in a manner that explicitly states that what is prohibited is "disparate *treatment*." Discrimination without intent is an oxymoron, after all. Either way, these two approaches would require uniform and widespread action throughout the government. The Trump administration, to its credit, has moved on disparate impact in some instances. Secretary of Education Betsy DeVos, for example, rescinded an Obama-era "Dear Colleague" letter telling schools that they could lose federal funding if they enforced neutral disciplinary policies that penalized African American students at a higher rate than other students. But it is doubtful that such a piecemeal approach will eradicate a deeply entrenched doctrine that enlists the government and all its agencies in the balkanization of the nation.

Leave the Balkans in Europe

Cutting off the money and benefit supply is a sine qua non of any solution, and any of the strategies outlined above would go a long way toward doing just that. But, to paraphrase Chief Justice John Roberts, to end balkanization, we must end balkanization. The government simply has to get out of category creation. Racial preferences and racial categorization are joined at the hip. If government at all levels and the courts call for racial preferences in employment, contracting, education, and housing (practically all the areas that matter to a person), then dividing the population by race is a must. There are several good reasons to stop government from creating categories in the first place, and from then gathering data on them.

As we saw in chapter 6, the census gives the all-important state recognition and legal remit for category creation. It brings categories inside every household every ten years. The census, moreover, extends racial preference into a further domain that affects our democracy directly: redistricting for the purposes of apportioning legislative and other elective seats.

Every year after the decennial census is conducted, state legislatures use the data garnered to see whether they need to redraw electoral boundaries. Because Congress has amended, and the Supreme Court has interpreted, the Voting Rights Act of 1965 in various ways, redistricting now aims at creating racially compact districts in which members of a group form a majority. The original intent of the law was to prevent racist practices against blacks, such as redistricting in the South that was aimed at denying blacks their right to vote. But persuaded by the Ford Foundation–created MALDEF, Congress in 1975 expanded the right to a compact district to four "language minority groups" comprised of Alaska Natives, Asian Americans, Indians, and "persons of Spanish heritage." And in 1982, Congress compounded the problem by applying the disparate impact standards to Justice Department oversight of redistricting, making "discriminatory result" rather than "intent" the condition on which a district could be challenged in court. The fact that a member of a particular group was not elected was all that was needed to prove discrimination. As a result, members of racial and ethnic categories have been given what American Enterprise Institute scholar Abigail Thernstrom has called "a new entitlement," the right to elect a member of Congress of their race or ethnicity.[14] While this may sound at first like a good thing, what it does is promulgate the heinous idea that we can only be truly represented by members of our group; it is destructive of the principle that we're all Americans, and it limits the urge to reach across racial lines.

Racial categorization also gets the United States dangerously close to a proportional representation system, which in fact is a goal of the Left.[15] That would change the character of America, making it something more akin to Lebanon, where Shiite and Sunni Muslims, and Christians, have constitutionally assigned offices. There are potentially darker, more sinister consequences when the state creates groups by fiat. In the previous chapter, we saw warnings in the "Fractionalization" paper for NEBR that unscrupulous politicians can manipulate hatred of one group or another for policy reasons. In that paper the authors cite the example of Somalia, which prior to its 1991 civil war was seen as homogeneous, with 85 percent of the population ethnic Somalis; during and after the war, clans emerged as the "dominant dimension of ethnic cleavage."[16]

Gaming of the system is another constant problem. The OMB's formal categories are so incongruous as to have led to unseemly rent seeking, a scramble for government benefits based on claims of victimhood. Law professor Sean Pager tells the tragicomic story of Rocco Luiere, who one evening in February 2004 "went to sleep Hispanic and woke up white." As Pager recounts, Luiere's maternal grandparents were born in Spain, and that lucky accident qualified his construction business as a "minority-owned business enterprise" (MBE). For fifteen years, Luiere's company benefited from racial set-asides in contracting in New York City. The state, however, changed the definition of "Hispanic" overnight, leaving Luiere's business out in the cold. He went to court to challenge the change in status, but eventually the system left Iberians out of the coveted "victim" category. Luiere had to lay off one-third of his workers and sell 30 percent of his equipment.[17] Of many other similar examples, one of the most familiar is the case of the Fanjul brothers in Florida, who despite a net worth of hundreds of millions continue to qualify for minority set-asides because of their origins in Cuba. In 2019 the city of St. Louis removed five firms from its list of certified minority-owned firms, but only after they had already won city contracts because they claimed to be owned by members of the Cherokee Nation. But these firms are less than 10 percent of the 550 St. Louis firms certified as MBEs.[18]

The categories are opaque on purpose. Cristina Mora writes that "government officials, activists, and media executives never precisely defined who Hispanics actually were." Why? Purely for reasons of politics and power. "Ambiguity was important because it allowed stakeholders to bend the definition of Hispanic panethnicity and use the notion instrumentally—as a means to an end."[19] Ambiguity also helped supporters of racial preferences in the Supreme Court, which has remained agnostic as to who's in and who's out of this profitable victim racket. Pager thinks that a factor in Supreme Court interpretations is the justices' knowledge that to press "the ambiguities of race would expose the normative incoherence of affirmative action in a way that would prove politically untenable. The Court therefore deflects the Who Question to preserve the status quo." Playing ostrich on the all-important question of who qualifies as Hispanic or Asian is thus "the price of our continued commitment to [race-conscious] affirmative action."[20] The lower courts and the administrators do not always have that luxury, of course, and struggle to find an answer.

What obtains, however, is that for both "Hispanics" and "Asians"— and it would have been the case for "MENA" as well—chaos can reign, with real-life consequences for people like Luiere. The cities of Baltimore and Miami, and the Small Business Administration, treat Spaniards, Portuguese, and Latin Americans as Hispanics, and thus their businesses can be certified as DBE and benefit from set-asides. Stanford University's racial preferences, on the other hand, don't apply to Spaniards, Portuguese, or any Latin American who is not of Mexican or Puerto Rican descent. The state of Ohio, too, ran into a raft of litigation when it decided that contractors of Indian and Lebanese descent no longer qualified for MBE programs. Heriot believes that the Supreme Court is only delaying the day of reckoning, as the high standards of strict scrutiny will eventually catch up with it.

The whole thing cries out for wholesale change. As we saw in chapter 6, the introduction of these formal categories gathered pace starting in the late 1960s and became official in 1977 when the OMB's Policy Directive No. 15 made the standard categories we have today of black, white, Hispanic, Asian, and American Indian mandatory for all agencies that gather statistics. The ethnoracial pentagon then entered the next census, in 1980. The government acted under pressure from ethnic affinity organizations that had no ties to the grassroots—and were in fact often acting against grassroots interests and desires—but were responsive to Ford Foundation officers seeking temporary "developmental separatism." The way to end these practices, therefore, is to get the government out of the category-creating business.

The president has the power to end this madness by rescinding both the 1977 policy directive and its 1997 revision (it must be both). By executive order, the president can then direct all agencies of the executive branch to stop collecting data on all false ethnicities created by government in the first place. Wherever there is a need for data collection, as for epidemiological research, it can be conducted, but of course, that would have to rely on science, not synthetic government categories (which would be of zero use). Such executive orders are exempt from the Administrative Procedure Act, the tool used by President Trump's opponents to stop him from including a question on citizenship in the decennial census, which makes things administratively easier. Politically, it is another matter. It is, of course, clear that any president who proceeded to take this all-important action would come under withering criticism from the race-hustling industry. Any president, let alone Donald Trump, must explain the reason for these actions clearly and passionately, leaving no doubt that this is truly the inclusive approach.

Critics will say that the problems with racial preferences can be fixed with better data. This is what activists are already trying to do with the Asian American category—disaggregate it to tease out the Cambodian and Laotian Americans, and others, who are underrepresented in elite schools, and extend the preferences to them, not to Chinese or Indian Americans, who are overrepresented. It speaks volumes that left-of-center Asian American affinity organizations like

AJCC have taken this approach, to the dismay of Chinese Americans. What is needed is not better data, but to end the use of data to give people of one race benefits that are denied to people of other races. We must recall Justice Antonin Scalia's dictum: "In the eyes of the government, we are just one race here. It is American."[21] The idea that government at all levels today uses race to allocate resources is what should outrage all Americans; the fact that the Supreme Court continues to permit racial preferences without deciding formally who is a member of the victims category is but a powerful symptom of the underlying disease. Americans never voted for these arrangements, and politicians were never forthcoming about what was being done. Echoing Skrentny, Mora, and many other historians who have looked at the era of category formation, Pager reminds us that, despite such tangible stakes, "the construction of racial identities has been mediated through obscure bureaucratic processes operating largely outside the public eye."[22] We have every reason to believe that if these decisions had been put to the American voter in a clear manner, the entire plan would have been overwhelmingly defeated.

But getting rid of the categories and the benefits that seduce people to wear the mantle of victimhood would not, by itself, be sufficient. We now live with a segment of the population, usually on the young side, that has been made to feel deeply aggrieved because of a political project carried out by other people with ulterior motives. To promote feelings in others of having been damaged, to instill grievances and resentment, purposely to take away a sense of individual empowerment or agency—this, I believe, is the devil's work. And again, not for nothing did Saul Alinsky dedicate his work to Satan. But we are here now, and the question is, what do we do? While we may not be able to undo the damage that has been done to millennials and others—we should not advocate for "our" version of consciousness-raising struggle sessions—we must stop the indoctrination of the present generation of students, and future ones, into hatred of their country and into seeing society as made up of groups that are constantly caught up in power relations. We must do all we can to put victimhood culture in the rearview mirror so that within two decades we will look back aghast and ask ourselves, what on earth was that about? Competitive victimhood is a heck of thing to teach a child, especially in the "everyone gets a trophy" age when competition for real achievements is disparaged. It must be made clear that flaunting one's sense of being aggrieved is not the proper way to receive attention, respect, or dignity from society—or benefits from the government or the private sector.

Fire the Grievance Industry

Getting there won't be easy. The United States has 13,600 school districts (according to the National Center for Education Statistics) and fifty million students, 90 percent of whom attend more than 98,000 public schools.[23] And the indoctrination of our youth does not stop at high school graduation—hardly. Our universities and colleges—some thirty thousand four-year institutions, and 1,500 two-year ones—have become madrassas in the Woke Jihad.[24]

The task, in other words, is enormous. It is made all the more daunting by the fact that it is part of the hard left's plan to have a centralized education policy for K–12. That enables radical "reformers" to implement a national strategy, using the Department of Education to impose its will across the country through policy ukases. Those who care about individual liberty and limited government should not copy this approach but instead seek to return America to the days when decisions on curricula were made at the local level, which is as the founders intended. The Department of Education, created by Congress in 1979, during the Carter presidency, is already overly involved in choices that should remain local, closer to the parents, so they can have a voice. The wanton use of "Dear Colleague" letters in the Obama administration as tools to impose policy decisions has done damage that we must work to reverse; in fact there are at least three federal laws barring the Department of Education from getting involved in curricula or standards, and they should be used to stop federal fiat.

There have been several key elements in the radicals' multipronged approach to use universities to transform society. One has been the introduction of critical theory content into the syllabuses of many of the nation's 1,206 education schools, the schools that teach future teachers—a game plan that helps corrupt the young minds in K–12 classrooms. Another has been the embedding of race, ethnic, and gender studies departments in universities across the country, a strategy that corrupts not just the schools and their students but many other parts of American life, not least corporate America. Graduates with degrees in the various "studies" departments become the future consultants, task force leaders, HR officials, and so on who impose the "diversity" regime.

As we saw in chapter 5, Angela Davis advertises the fact that the "studies" departments now entrenched in the universities are "the intellectual arm of the revolution." She is not exaggerating. A long report by Jay Schalin at the James G. Martin Center for Academic Renewal detailed in 2019 the frightening success of the activists who have sought to transform America by undertaking a long march through our universities. Following the landmark 1954 *Brown v. Board of Education* decision, which finally desegregated schools and ended the *Plessy* era (briefly, anyway), there was a brief attempt to foster "positive interracial contact," an approach called intergroup education that was led primarily, and to their credit, by white liberal educators. "But intergroup's dominance was short-lived," writes Schalin. Soon, Marcuse's ideological brethren began creating what has mushroomed today into a veritable grievance industry. Citing a history of the creation of the nation's first black studies department at San Francisco State College in 1969, Schalin notes that the purpose of this new field was to counter "white values" and provide alternatives to "white attitudinal courses." Thus, from the start, these departments were "based on grievances and radical politics rather than a well-planned program for expanding knowledge using objective scholarly standards."[25] Gender studies departments were created for similar reasons. Kate Millett's first job with NOW in 1968 was as chair of the organization's education committee, a position she used to promote the creation of women's studies departments at the nation's colleges and universities. And when McGeorge Bundy wanted to give La Raza intellectual ballast, he used Henry Ford's legacy funds to endow a Mexican American (later Hispanic) studies program at Notre Dame.

Schalin conducted a study of three leading schools of education and concluded that the textbooks being used overwhelmingly take a critical theory approach. "Faculty and authors who are on the fringes of political thought . . . and who advocate that the purpose of education is to transform society according to their radical vision are the most frequently assigned writers in the most prominent schools of education,"[26] he writes. Not for nothing did the former terrorist Bill Ayers decide, after coming out of hiding in the 1980s, that the thing to do was to earn multiple degrees from Columbia's Teachers College and in time join the faculty at the College of Education at the University of Illinois at Chicago.

As we enter the third decade of this century, the attempt to poison students' minds continues apace. The *New York Times* has launched the latest effort with its *1619 Project*, named for the year the first slave arrived in what would become America.[27] The *Times*—of course—has prepared this project as a curriculum for use in our schools. Following Marcuse to a T, the project is replete with essays that present slavery as the central issue of the American founding and subsequent history, and indicting the "brutal" free-market system for perpetuating slavery. That the history it tells is riddled with errors and distortions will likely not hurt its chances of being adopted by the nation's school districts, unless valiant efforts by eminent historians to expose the project's errors have any effect.[28] Decades after it was first published, Howard Zinn's *A People's History of the United States* retains top rankings on Amazon and is used in schools across the country, including the College Board's coveted Advanced Placement courses that prepare the next generation of American leaders in politics, business, and the arts, even though it has been repeatedly debunked for its shoddy scholarship.[29]

The Left has also been very good at reinterpreting the meaning of civics, away from the traditional understanding of grounding school-children in the common historical, cultural, and political knowledge that all American must share (how was the country founded; why do we celebrate Thanksgiving; how does a bill become law?) and into the "action activism" of street demonstrations, boycotts, and cancel culture. This transformation mirrors the larger divide between those who want to preserve the valuable aspects of our heritage, and improve on them as conditions change, and those who seek to overhaul completely what they see as a racist and unjust country. One of the preferred courses of action for those in the latter group who seek revolutionary change is to make use of so-called service learning, which takes students out of the classroom and turns them into community activists earning academic credit for doing free labor for radical groups. College students now are hopping buses, traveling across state lines, and holding signs at demonstrations on the Supreme Court's steps, but only in support of liberal causes, of course.

When they're in the classroom, they're not learning the content that all educated Americans mastered at one point, because, in the thinking that prevails these days, that would just deepen the institutional racism that favors the oppressor class. Little thought is given to how much this actually deepens the type of cultural disparity that turns into economic inequality. Children raised by well-off parents will very likely learn the cultural references and norms at home, while the poor of any race will be left bereft. In other words, this is not, in fact, strictly a race issue, but a social and economic issue, as J. D. Vance's memoir, *Hillbilly Elegy*, makes clear. As someone who'd been raised in difficult circumstances in Ohio, by grandparents from Appalachia, Vance, who is white, felt isolated and out of place among his fellow students at Yale Law School, so many of whom had been raised in upper-middle-class households.

Even as common cultural literacy is being lost, K–12 schools across the country are now using "critical" pedagogies whose hidden agenda is to further introduce the divisions and grievances of identity politics into the minds of children. One such pedagogy is Culturally Responsive Teaching (CRT), which is supposed to be a cure-all for the very real racial achievement gap in education. How does CRT purport to do that? By teaching students all subjects, even math, according to their racial or ethnic identities. From any sane perspective, CRT is an egregious offense against American education. Its proponents are cruelly convincing school systems to spend scarce resources to fix a real problem with something that is pedagogic snake oil. It begs for ridicule. In this way, it actually shows us that one way to fight the grievance industry is to treat it with open scorn. CRT is premised on the idea that the race of the child (or the ethnic group in which OMB has dropped her), predicts how she learns, and should have an impact on *what* she learns. Along the way, it makes cringeworthy generalizations. Mexican American children, according to the Association for Supervision and Curriculum Development, "are comfortable with cognitive generalities and patterns" and prefer "broad concepts than component facts and specifics." Native American children, meanwhile, "generally value and develop acute visual discrimination and skills in the use of imagery, perceive globally, have reflective thinking patterns, and generally value and develop acute visual discrimination and skills in the use of imagery."[30] The stereotyping is over the top.

CRT's ostensible raison d'être is to close the racial achievement gap that sees black children fall behind whites in math and English in tests administered in the fourth and eighth grades. But it fails miserably at that. Studies showing that CRT has had any impact are lacking on the National Center for Education Evaluation's What Works Clearinghouse (WWC) page. That could be because there have been no WWC interventions in the more than twenty years this so-called pedagogy has been around, or it could be that none has passed muster. Nor am I aware of any controlled, randomized trials to judge the impact of this approach. But because it divides us, CRT has a chance of succeeding at its real agenda of transforming America by first transforming the children. CRT's purveyors are often only too happy to draw back the curtain on their real agenda, as did two leading academics when they wrote, "part of this social justice commitment must include a critique of liberalism, neutrality, objectivity, color-blindness, and meritocracy as a camouflage for the self-interests of powerful entities of society. Only aggressive, color-conscious efforts to change the way things are done do much to ameliorate misery."[31] CRT, in other words, is part of the ideological project that Richard Carranza peddles in New York; it fails miserably to deliver answers to struggling students and parents, but if left in place it would succeed at sowing even more division in our country.

Denouncing the waste and outright evil of pedagogies such as CRT is one way to fight it. Carranza's antibias training boondoggle came with a hefty price tag of $23 million, which is three-quarters of the city's funding for a program to boost literacy.[32] With regard to what schools of education are doing, it may be too late to save many of them, but state legislatures have to start weighing in. As Schalin writes, legislators and governors "appoint members of governing boards, who in turn appoint the top administrators. They control the purse strings for universities, and have ultimate control over the K–12 curriculum. They can alter certification procedures and standards, encourage partnerships with innovators, and more. They can even change education school governance and personnel practices—a drastic step, perhaps, but one that may be necessary if real reform is to occur."[33]

We need new schools. Rigorous studies indicate statistically significant positive effects of school choice or private schooling on the teaching of civic values, with public schools falling short.[34] This suggests two things: the first is that public schools need to do a better job at instilling civic values, and the second is that policy makers should increase school-choice options for families—charter schools, cottage classes, private schools that can steer these ideas without the heavy hand of government. Charter schools are the fastest-growing segment of public school enrollment. Their charters include their own mission statements and curriculum and a separate school board. We should be encouraging the growing number of civically minded charter schools.

American leaders at all levels should also make the case that schoolchildren, native-born or otherwise, should not be taught to hate the country to which so many immigrants want to come. This will not be easy, as witnessed by the invective hurled at Mitch Daniels when, as governor of Indiana in 2010, he suggested that schools stop teaching Howard Zinn's version of American history. Daniels described his book as a "truly execrable, anti-factual piece of disinformation that misstates American history on every page."[35] Our leaders should rhetorically support parents who demand from their local school boards that American principles be taught.

Americans must wage a crusade for classrooms to teach the content that will help children grow into confident, knowledgeable adults. The conundrum is that we have to fight for shared national knowledge, for a sense of civics that unites us from coast to coast, in 13,600 school districts across fifty states, without advocating for a national curriculum or relying on the federal government. This is doable, and it is in fact the only way to do it. We have no choice. As Reagan's secretary of education, William Bennett, said in a 2019 talk, if we don't, "the vacuum cedes the field to the other side, who knows very well what it intends to do."[36] The education expert Robert Pondiscio echoes this view, writing that, "where conservatives have grown wary and suspicious of meddling in curricula, activists and advocates on the Left have demonstrated far less reticence about imposing their views, moving further from the unifying impulse undergirding the entire purpose of public education."[37]

Bennett argues that we can lead a state-based campaign for inclusion in curriculum and textbooks of the things a civically engaged American population requires. We can reach a liberal–conservative consensus that every American kid should have some knowledge of—to give a very partial list—the Declaration of Independence, the Constitution, and the *Federalist Papers*; the speeches of Abraham Lincoln; great works of American literature like *Huckleberry Finn* and of world literature like the *Iliad*; and have at least a secular understanding of both the Hebrew and Christian bibles. If a district or a state wants to add the Quran or Confucius to that, without subtracting from the Western, Anglo-American canon, that is hardly a hill to die on. Neither of those traditions contributed in even a modest manner to the American creed, but knowledge of them is a good thing in itself. Our future generations need to have a solid grounding in what made their country what it is, so they can then confidently deal with the world in the pursuit of the national interest.

To do the above we don't need 13,600 different strategies, but one that is adapted to fifty realities. The public must be informed of the work of education experts who understand what is at stake so that they can demand that political leaders support sound education policies. As Bennett told his audience, "What a state can do is say 'you should be…familiar with the following concepts, facts, ideas and dates.' So you don't get fake history, you get real history…. Then districts have to apply it." Common learning is "critical if you want to be one country, if you want to talk about the *Unum* [in the U.S. motto of *E Pluribus Unum*]…. We lost the sense of a common core of knowledge, ideas, books, notions that we can share.... If we're all Americans there has to be some commonality of understanding."[38]

And the fight, wearying as it is, cannot stop at grade twelve. Our universities have become what Arthur Milikh calls "the Left's research and development headquarters," and the "dissemination point for the political and moral transformation of the nation, especially seen in the rolling sexual revolution and the identity politics revolution."[39] It was our universities that launched Ichioka, Samora, and Millett. The Department of Education obviously cannot and should not mandate what private universities teach, even if they take public money. But state legislatures can and should demand that there be diversity of opinion among the professoriate. The faculty lounge has to become a less ideologically repressive place, or funding can be cut. States can pass laws that enforce First Amendment rights on campuses; they're not, like embassies, foreign territory. That conservative thinkers such as Charles Murray and Heather Mac Donald, or liberals with unfashionable views like Christina Hoff Sommers, are shouted down or face violence when they speak on campus is a disgrace, and no taxpayer should have to support it.

Conclusion

For any of this to happen—for the elimination of categories, the culture of victimhood and expectations of benefits, the grievance mongering—the public must become aware of what has happened and get involved. Our political leaders at the federal, state, and local levels simply won't get there by themselves. It is not that they lack the courage, but that the incentives are not there at the moment for them to do the right thing. We must remember Milton Friedman's words: "The important thing is to make it politically profitable for the wrong people to do the right thing. If it is not politically profitable for the wrong people to do the right thing, the right people will not do the right thing either."[40]

We must create the environment that makes it not just possible but necessary for a politician to go to his constituents and present the case that categories such as Hispanics and Asians start as way stations but soon become terminal points; that preferences only stigmatize real achievement—when you are suspected of having attained your position because of your last name, that diminishes your success in the eyes of others and thus takes away your ability to enjoy the fruits of your labor; that harping constantly on grievances sours everyone's life, including not just those accused of oppression but obviously those feeling aggrieved. Our national leaders can make the rational case that so-called antibias training does not work and is only a tax on businesses imposed by litigators. They should be able, very easily, to denounce CRT as a witches' brew that embarrasses us all. Only if voters and opinion leaders voice these views will we finally see politicians take on this task. The politician who would do this can draw on an American advantage that is unique in the world. The *Hidden Tribes* study cited in an earlier chapter—not a conservative exercise by any means—puts it this way:

> America has one great asset unrivalled in the world: a powerful story of national identity that, at its core, is idealistic, hopeful and inclusive. It is a story that calls the nation and its people to act with virtue and against division; that speaks to the better angels of our nature. America today needs a renewed sense of national identity, one that fosters a common vision for a future in which every American can feel that they belong and are respected. National identity can be the force that unifies people to overcome…polarization.[41]

This civil rights movement 2.0 won't be easy. Those who have benefited from the regime of identity politics—not the intended beneficiaries, but the leaders of affinity organizations and the race-hustling politicians in racially gerrymandered districts—will not suddenly throw up their hands and abdicate their privileges. They have become used to winning and thus they think they are entitled to it. They really believe they can drain this country of its true character and replace it with their own vision of how things ought to be. But a switch has been flipped in America's subconscious. No matter what happens in future elections, the upheaval of 2016 happened for a reason.

And that brings you, the reader, back into the spotlight. Reading this book has exposed you to an understanding of what has transpired, and to ideas for what we can do about it. What you do with this information is now up to you. I have kept faith with the country that kept faith with me. Now what are you going to do?

Acknowledgments

When an author writes a book, that's all he or she does. That's why this book was written and constantly revised not just at my home and office, but also in hotels and airports in New York, Boston, El Paso, Bethany, Toronto, Kyiv, Cherkasy, Riga, Prague, Munich, Amsterdam, and so on. This is also why all authors eventually cheat their spouses and children out of vacation time, as well as some weekends and evenings. I therefore must first thank my wife Siobhan and my children for their sufferance and apologize for shows not watched, footballs not thrown, dinners not shared, and while I'm at it, any other inadequacy.

I must also thank the many other people who, in many different ways, contributed to *The Plot to Change America*. We are all busy, so we know what a service is rendered when a colleague reads a chapter and offers suggestions. I therefore want to thank Kay Cole James, Kim Holmes, James Jay Carafano for letting me take time to write the book, supporting the project and then reading parts of it, and offering their ideas. I have greatly benefited, too, from Caesar Arredondo's advice and friendship, for which I want to thank him. I also want to thank my Heritage Foundation colleagues, who helped me think through the ideas in this book, specifically Bridgett Wagner, Genevieve Wood, Emilie Kao, Lindsey Burke, Michael Howell, Lili Serna, Ryan Anderson, Helena Ramirez Richardson, Michael May, Alex Morales, Maiya Clark, Angela Sailor, Hans von Spakovsky, Christopher Byrnes, Joseph Natali and Laura VanderPloeg. Their kind attention to this project will never be forgotten. Outside of Heritage, I benefited from the help of such scholars as Joshua Trevino, Chelsea Michta, John Fonte, and Roger Clegg, whom I also thank. Of course, I also very much need to thank my editor Jessica Evans.

I want to beg the forgiveness of those who helped me, but whose names I have forgotten. And, of course, I would like to add that the inclusion of any of these names in no way indicates that they endorse all or any of the opinions expressed in this book.

Notes

INTRODUCTION

1 For a good explanation of how the demise of the family has contributed to identity politics, see Mary Eberstadt, *Primal Screams: How the Sexual Revolution Created Identity Politics* (West Conshohocken, PA: Templeton Press, 2019). For an exposition of how the erosion of social capital has contributed to identity politics, see Patrick T. Brown, "The Dark Side of Social Capital," *National Affairs* 41 (Summer 2019), https://www .nationalaffairs.com/publications/detail/the-dark-side-of-social-capital. For a perspective on how the fall of the Soviet Union and the end of the Cold War contributed to identity politics, see Francis Fukuyama, "Against Identity Politics: The New Tribalism and the Crisis of Democracy," *Foreign Affairs* 97, no. 5 (2018), https://www.foreignaffairs.com/articles/ americas/2018-08-14/against-identity-politics-tribalism-francis-fukuyama.

2 Adam Rubenstein, "Steven Pinker: Identity Politics Is 'an Enemy of Reason and Enlightenment Values,'" *The Weekly Standard*, February 15, 2018, https://www.weeklystandard.com/adam-rubenstein/steven-pinker-identity -politics-is-an-enemy-of-reason-and-enlightenment-values.

3 Uri Harris, "Is the 'Intellectual Dark Web' Politically Diverse?," *Quillette*, April 17, 2019, https://quillette.com/2019/04/17/ is-the-intellectual-dark-web-politically-diverse/.

4 Peter Skerry, *Mexican Americans: The Ambivalent Minority* (New York: Free Press, 1993), 319.

5 For this quote I rely on the research of Carmen Samora (Julian Samora's daughter), "Los Tres Grandes—Herman Gallegos, Ernesto Galarza, Julian Samora: Rooted in Community, Guided by Friendship, Cultivating Leadership" (PhD diss., University of New Mexico, 2011).

6 Yoram Hazony, *The Virtue of Nationalism* (New York: Basic Books, 2018).

7 Mario T. García, *Mexican Americans: Leadership, Ideology, and Identity, 1930–1960* (New Haven, CT: Yale University Press, 1989), 146.

8 "Playboy Interview: Saul Alinsky, A Candid Conversation with the Feisty Radical Organizer," *Playboy*, March 1972, http://documents.theblackvault .com/documents/fbifiles/100-BA-30057.pdf.

9 Herbert Marcuse, *One-Dimensional Man: Studies in the Ideology of Advanced Industrial Society* (Boston: Beacon Press, 1991), 9.

10 Marcuse, *One-Dimensional Man*, 256–57.

11 Bradley Campbell and Jason Manning, "Microaggression and Moral Cultures," *Comparative Sociology* 13, no. 6 (2014): 716.

12 John David Skrentny, *The Minority Rights Revolution* (Cambridge, MA: Belknap Press of Harvard University Press, 2004), 110.

13 Frances Fox Piven and Richard Cloward, "The Weight of the Poor: A Strategy to End Poverty," *The Nation*, May 2, 1966.

14 See Marshall's dissent on the part of the decision that states that the university's admissions program violated the Constitution, in *Regents of the University of California v. Bakke*, 438 U.S. 265 at 400 (1978), https://www.law.cornell.edu/supremecourt/text/438/265.

15 Paul Freedman, "The Early Middle Ages: Barbarian Kingdoms," Yale Courses, from 14:15, https://www.youtube.com/watch?v=YAVUS-QUe_c&feature=youtu.be.

CHAPTER 1

1 For this exchange between Sánchez and Samora, I rely on Benjamin Francis-Fallon, "Minority Reports: The Emergence of Pan-Hispanic Politics, 1945–1980," (PhD diss., Georgetown University, 2012), 1, https://repository.library.georgetown.edu/bitstream/handle/10822/557625/FrancisFallon_georgetown_0076D_11925.pdf?sequence=1&isAllowed=y. Francis-Fallon quotes from the Julian Samora Papers in the Benson Latin American Collection, University Libraries, the University of Texas at Austin. Some of the quotes in this chapter were also used in an essay I wrote on Mexican Americans for the Claremont Review of Books, "The Invention of Hispanics," which was published in the fall 2019 edition.

2 Francis-Fallon, "Minority Reports," 2.

3 Francis-Fallon, "Minority Reports," 3.

4 Francis-Fallon, "Minority Reports," 2–3.

5 Francis-Fallon, "Minority Reports," 3.

6 Carmen Samora, "Los Tres Grandes."

7 Ronnie Dugger, "Integration Hero and Education Legend George I. Sanchez Gets a New Biography," *Texas Observer*, March 18, 2015, https://www.texasobserver.org/george-i-sanchez-biography/.

8 Julian Samora, "Minority Leadership in a Bi-Cultural Community" (PhD diss., Washington University, 1953).

9 Skerry, *Mexican-Americans*, 319.

10 Benjamin Márquez, *LULAC: The Evolution of a Mexican American Political Organization* (Austin: University of Texas Press, 1993), 33.

11 *Mendez, et al., v. Westminster School District, et al.*, 64 F.Supp. 544 (C.D. Cal. 1946), aff'd, 161 F.2d 774 (9th Cir. 1947), https://www.tolerance.org/classroom-resources/texts/mendez-v-westminster.

12 See Toni Robinson and Greg Robinson, "*Méndez v. Westminster:*

Asian-Latino Coalition Triumphant?," *Asian Law Journal* 10, no. 161 (2003): 161–83, https://scholarship.law.berkeley.edu/cgi/viewcontent .cgi?article=1012&context=aalj.

13 Michael Omi and Howard Winant, *Racial Formation in the United States* (New York: Routledge and Kegan Paul, 1986), 64.

14 G. Cristina Mora, *Making Hispanics: How Activists, Bureaucrats, and Media Constructed a New American* (Chicago: University of Chicago Press, 2014), 63.

15 Skerry, *Mexican-Americans*, 320.

16 Philip Gleason, "Minorities (Almost) All: The Minority Concept in American Social Thought," *American Quarterly* 43, no. 3 (1991): 392.

17 Mora, *Making Hispanics*, 4.

18 Victoria-Maria MacDonald, "Demanding Their Rights: The Latino Struggle for Educational Access and Equity," in *American Latinos and the Making of the United States: A Theme Study* (Washington, DC: National Park System Advisory Board, 2013), https://www.nps.gov/articles/latinothemeeducation .htm).

19 Moses Y. Beach, *New York Sun*, November 20, 1847, quoted in Frederick Merk and Lois Bannister Merk, *Manifest Destiny and Mission in American History: A Reinterpretation* (Cambridge, MA: Harvard University Press, 1995), 122.

20 Quoted in David G. Gutiérrez, *Walls and Mirrors: Mexican Americans, Mexican Immigrants, and the Politics of Ethnicity* (Berkeley: University of California Press, 1995), 4.

21 John C. Calhoun, *The Works of John C. Calhoun*, vol. 4, ed. Richard K. Crallé (New York: Appleton, 1854), 325.

22 Quoted in Gutiérrez, *Walls and Mirrors*, 174.

23 Another example of how the present echoes the past is the insistence by today's Left that African Americans did not participate in the founding, which is the same case that Justice Roger Taney made in his majority opinion in the abominable *Dred Scott* decision. Abraham Lincoln debunked this idea in his June 26, 1857, speech on that decision: "Chief Justice Taney … insists at great length that negroes were no part of the people who made, or for whom was made, the Declaration of Independence, or the Constitution of the United States. On the contrary, Judge Curtis, in his dissenting opinion, shows that in five of the then thirteen states … free negroes were voters, and, in proportion to their numbers, had the same part in making the Constitution that the white people had." See https://teachingamericanhistory.org/library/document/ speech-on-the-dred-scott-decision/.

24 *Annals of Congress*, 8th Cong., 1st sess. (1803–4), 1061.

25 *Annals of Congress*, 8th Cong., 1st sess. (1803–4), 480.

26 Peter J. Kastor, *The Nation's Crucible: The Louisiana Purchase and the Creation of America* (New Haven, CT: Yale University Press, 2012), 57.

27 Gutiérrez, *Walls and Mirrors*, 59.

28 Gutiérrez, *Walls and Mirrors*, 59.

29 Quoted in Gutiérrez, *Walls and Mirrors*, 138, 143.

30 Gutiérrez, *Walls and Mirrors*, 145.

31 Kenneth C. Burt, "The Power of a Mobilized Citizenry and Coalition Politics: The 1949 Election of Edward R. Roybal to the Los Angeles City Council," *Southern California Quarterly* 85, no. 4 (2003): 413.

32 Carmen Samora, "Los Tres Grandes," 74.

33 Laura M. Westhoff, "Social Capital and Political Change in the Community Service Organization," in *Rethinking Social Capital: Global Contributions from Theory and Practice*, ed. Elisabeth Kapferer, Isabell Gstach, Andreas Koch, and Clemens Sedmak (Newcastle upon Tyne, UK: Cambridge Scholars Publishing, 2017), 194.

34 Burt, "The Power of a Mobilized Citizenry and Coalition Politics," 414.

35 Edward E. Telles and Vilma Ortiz, *Generations of Exclusion: Mexican Americans, Assimilation, and Race* (New York: Russell Sage Foundation, 2008), 278.

36 H.J. Res. 92, Pub. L. No. 94-311, 90 Stat. 688 (1976), http://uscode.house.gov/statutes/pl/94/311.pdf.

37 Ruben Rumbaut, "Pigments of Our Imagination: The Racialization of the Hispanic-Latino Category," Migration Policy Institute, April 27, 2011, https://www.migrationpolicy.org/article/pigments-our-imagination-racialization-hispanic-latino-category.

38 Interview with Dolores Huerta, June 9, 1995, Paradigm Transcripts, https://libraries.ucsd.edu/farmworkermovement/media/oral_history/ParadigmTranscripts/HuertaDoloresRecovered.pdf.

39 Carmen Samora, "Los Tres Grandes," 79.

40 Carmen Samora, "Los Tres Grandes," 83, 184, 184.

41 Matea Gold, "The No Longer 'Invisible Minority' 30 Years Later," *Los Angeles Times*, April 5, 1999, http://articles.latimes.com/1999/apr/05/local/me-24316.

42 Leo Grebler, Joan W. Moore, Ralph C. Guzman, *The Mexican-American People: The Nation's Second Largest Minority* (New York: Free Press, 1970), 5.

43 Grebler, Moore, and Guzman, *The Mexican-American People*, 389.

44 Grebler, Moore, and Guzman, *The Mexican-American People*, 390.

45 Matt M. Matthews, *The U.S. Army on the Mexican Border: A Historical Perspective* (Fort Leavenworth, KS: Combat Studies Institute Press, 2007), 65.

46 Ralph Edward Morales III, "Hijos de la Gran Guerra: The Creation of the Mexican American Identity in Texas, 1836–1929" (PhD diss., Texas A&M University, 2015), 90, https://pdfs.semanticscholar.org/d37e/b44e7de5cefc46cdb9a5efcd1563a93330a4.pdf.

47 Quoted in Morales, "Hijos de la Gran Guerra," 100.

48 Grebler, Moore, and Guzman, *The Mexican-American People*, 390.

49 Grebler, Moore, and Guzman, *The Mexican-American People*, 4, 577.

50 Grebler, Moore, and Guzman, *The Mexican-American People*, 569.

51 Grebler, Moore, and Guzman, *The Mexican-American People*, 390.

52 Grebler, Moore, and Guzman, *The Mexican-American People*, 576–77, citing Tamotsu Shibutani and Kian M. Kwan's 1965 work, *Ethnic Stratification*.

53 115 Cong. Rec., 9952–53 (1969) (Rep. González), http://www.historymuse .net/readings/GonzalezCongressionalRecord1969.htm.

54 Skerry, *Mexican-Americans*, 221, 319.

55 115 Cong. Rec., 9953.

56 Quoted in Gutiérrez, *Walls and Mirrors*, 174.

57 Quoted in Miguel Pendás, *Chicano Liberation and Socialism* (Atlanta, GA: Pathfinder Press, 1976), 3.

58 Gutiérrez, *Walls and Mirrors*, 175.

59 Mora, *Making Hispanics*, 52.

60 *Cisneros v. Corpus Christi Independent School District*, 324 F. Supp. 599 (S.D. Tex. 1970)

61 Grace Flores-Hughes, The Origin of the Term Hispanic, Harvard Journal of Hispanic Policy, Vol. 18 2005-2006, 81, http://hjhp.hkspublications.org/ wp-content/uploads/sites/15/2015/02/HJHP-Volume-18.pdf#page=91.

62 Mora, *Making Hispanics*, 64.

63 Quoted in Mora, *Making Hispanics*, 64.

64 Robert Reinhold, "Census Questions on Race Assailed as Political by Population Experts," *New York Times*, May 14, 1978, https://www.nytimes .com/1978/05/14/archives/census-questions-on-race-assailed-as-political -by-population.html.

65 Campbell and Manning, "Microaggression and Moral Cultures," 32.

66 Mora, *Making Hispanics*, 63.

67 Mora, *Making Hispanics*, 9; quoted in Mora, 92.

68 Quoted in Mora, *Making Hispanics*, 34.

69 Office of Management and Budget Directive No. 15: Race and Ethnic Standards for Federal Statistics and Administrative Reporting (as adopted May 12, 1977), https://wonder.cdc.gov/wonder/help/populations/bridged-race/directive15.html.

70 Pew Research Center, "National Labels Used Most Often among Latinos to Describe Their Identity," December 18, 2017, based on the Pew Research Center 2015 National Survey of Latinos, https:// www.pewresearch.org/hispanic/2017/12/20/hispanic-identity-fades-across-generations-as-immigrant-connections-fall-away/ ph_2017-12-20_hispanic-identity_04/.

71 Tom Wolfe, *Back to Blood* (New York: Little, Brown, 2012), 29.

72 Yessenia Funes, "Forget About 'Latino'—Why I'm All for 'Latinx' and You Should Be, Too," *Salon*, October 7, 2017, https://www.salon.com/2017/10/07/ forget-about-latino-why-im-all-for-latinx-and-you-should-be-too/.

73 Mora, *Making Hispanics*, 159.

CHAPTER 2

1 Mike Gonzalez, "Affirmative Action in Education Looks a Lot Like Bigotry—Especially to Asian Americans," *The Hill*, May 1, 2018, https://thehill.com/opinion/education/385687-affirmative-action-in-education-looks-an-awful-lot-like-bigotry-especially.

2 Wesley Yang, "Asian Americans Can Blow Up America's Racial Quota System. Will They?," *Tablet*, March 13, 2018, https://www.tabletmag.com/jewish-news-and-politics/257250/asian-americans-racial-quota-system.

3 A phrase used by Frank Chin in his novel *Gunga Din Highway* (Minneapolis, MN: Coffee House Press, 1994), 313.

4 Daryl J. Maeda, "Black Panthers, Red Guards, and Chinamen: Constructing Asian American Identity through Performing Blackness, 1969–1972," *American Quarterly* 57, no. 4 (2005), reprinted in *Works and Days* 24, nos. 1–2 (2006): 119, 125–26, https://www.marxists.org/history/erol/ncm-1a/maeda.pdf.

5 Maeda, "Black Panthers, Red Guards, and Chinamen," 127.

4 Maeda, quoting Studs Terkel's interview with Frank Chin in the 1992 book *Race*, "Black Panthers, Red Guards, and Chinamen," 124.

5 Daryl Joji Maeda, *Rethinking the Asian American Movement* (New York: Routledge, 2012), 1, 5.

6 Maeda, *Rethinking the Asian American Movement*, 12.

7 Yen Le Espiritu, *Asian American Panethnicity: Bridging Institutions and Identities* (Philadelphia, PA: Temple University Press, 1992), 34.

8 Maeda, *Rethinking the Asian American Movement*, 11.

9 Espiritu, *Asian American Panethnicity*, 35.

10 "Asian-American Political Alliance," confidential FBI memo, 1970, Internet Archive, https://archive.org/stream/AsianAmericanPoliticalAlliance/DOCID-32549242_djvu.txt.

11 Madeline Yuan-yin Hsu, *Asian-American History: A Very Short Introduction* (New York: Oxford University Press, 2017).

12 Reihan Salam, "The Utility of White-Bashing," *Atlantic*, August 6, 2018, https://www.theatlantic.com/ideas/archive/2018/08/the-utility-of-white-bashing/566846/.

13 William McGurn, "An Asian-American Awakening," *Wall Street Journal*, June 11, 2018, https://www.wsj.com/articles/an-asian-american-awakening-1528755635.

14 "'Howdy Modi': Thousands of Indian Americans Attend Trump Rally," *Guardian*, September 22, 2019, https://www.theguardian.com/world/2019/sep/22/thousands-of-indian-americans-expected-at-modi-rally-in-houston.

15 US Bureau of the Census, Table no. 24: "Population, by Race and Sex, 1930 to 1950, and Urban and Rural, 1950" in *Statistical Abstract of the United States: 1960*, 81st edition (Washington, DC, 1960), 28.

16 US Census Bureau, Table: "Asian Alone or in Any Combination by Selected Groups," https://factfinder.census.gov/faces/tableservices/jsf/pages/

productview.xhtml?pid=ACS_15_1YR_B02018&prodType=table.

17 US Census Bureau, Table: "Asian Alone or in Any Combination by Selected Groups," https://factfinder.census.gov/faces/tableservices/jsf/pages/ productview.xhtml?pid=ACS_15_1YR_B02018&prodType=table.

18 Taunya Lovell Banks, quoting *United States v. Dolla*, "Both Edges of the Margin: Blacks and Asians in *Mississippi Masala*, Barriers to Coalition Building," *Asian American Law Journal* 5, no. 7 (1998), https://scholarship .law.berkeley.edu/cgi/viewcontent.cgi?referer=https://www.google.com/&ht tpsredir=1&article=1039&context=aalj.

19 Vinay Harpalani, quoting *In re Mozumdar*, "DesiCrit: Theorizing the Racial Ambiguity of South Asian Americans," *New York University Annual Survey of American Law* 69, no. 1 (2013), https://annualsurveyofamericanlaw.org/ wp-content/uploads/2014/10/69-1_harpalani.pdf.

20 Espiritu, *Asian American Panethnicity*, 173.

21 Quoted in Ronald Takaki, *India in the West: South Asians in America*, ed. Rebecca Stefoff and Carol Takaki (New York: Chelsea House, 1995), 446–47.

22 Ann Morning, "The Racial Self-Identification of South Asians in the United States," *Journal of Ethnic and Migration Studies* 27, no. 1 (2001): 64.

23 Morning, "The Racial Self-Identification of South Asians in the United States," 65.

24 Valerie Wilson, "Digging into the 2017 ACS," Economic Policy Institute, September 14, 2018, https://www.epi.org/blog/digging-into-2017-acs -income-native-americans-asians/; "United States Median Household Income," American Community Survey 2013–2017, 5-year estimates, https:// www.census.gov/search-results.html?searchType=web&cssp=SERP&q=me dian%20income.

25 Pew Research Center, "The Rise of Asian Americans," June 19, 2012, https:// www.pewsocialtrends.org/2012/06/19/the-rise-of-asian-americans/.

26 Yang, "Asian Americans Can Blow Up America's Racial Quota System."

27 Samuel Leiter and William M. Leiter, *Affirmative Action in Antidiscrimination Law and Policy: An Overview and Synthesis*, 2nd ed. (Albany: State University of New York Press, 2011), 21.

28 Valerie Wilson, "Working Economics Blog," Economic Policy Institute, September 14, 2018, https://www.epi.org/blog/digging-into-2017-acs -income-native-americans-asians/.

29 Pew Research Center, "The Rise of Asian Americans," June 19, 2012, updated April 4, 2013, https://www.pewsocialtrends.org/2012/06/19/ the-rise-of-asian-americans/.

30 These figures are pulled from reports on political and social trends, including Pew Research Center's "Chinese in the U.S. Fact Sheet," 2000– 2015, https://www.pewsocialtrends.org/fact-sheet/asian-americans-chinese -in-the-u-s/, and AAPI Data's "The Asian American Vote in 2016: Record Gains, but Also Gaps," http://aapidata.com/blog/voting-gains-gaps/.

31 R. Kelly Raley, Megan M. Sweeney, and Danielle Wondra, "The Growing Racial and Ethnic Divide in U.S. Marriage Patterns," *Future of Children*

25, no. 2 (2015): 89–109, https://www.ncbi.nlm.nih.gov/pmc/articles/PMC4850739/.

32 Joyce Martin, Brady Hamilton, Michelle Osterman, and Anne Driscoll, "Births: Final Data for 2018," *National Vital Statistics Reports* 68, no. 13 (November 27, 2019): 5, https://www.cdc.gov/nchs/data/nvsr/nvsr68/nvsr68_13-508.pdf.

33 National Center for Education Statistics, Youth Indicators 2011, Table 35: Average Hours Spent on Homework, https://nces.ed.gov/pubs2012/2012026/tables/table_35.asp.

34 National Center for Education Statistics, *Status and Trends in the Education of Racial and Ethnic Groups 2016*, figures 16.1a and 16.2a, https://nces .ed.gov/pubs2016/2016007.pdf.

35 Akemi, "A History of Oppression, a Life of Privilege: What It's Like to Be 4th Generation Japanese American in the Movement for Social Justice," *Medium*, February 21, 2017, https://medium.com/@akemialchemy/as-a-fourth-generation-japanese-american-heres-where-i-fit-into-the-movement-for-social-justice-d969d739d127.

36 J. Burton, M. Farrell, F. Lord, and R. Lord, "A Brief History of Japanese American Relocation During World War II," in *Confinement and Ethnicity: An Overview of World War II Japanese American Relocation Sites*, National Park Service, Publications in Anthropology 74 (1999, rev. 2000), https://www.nps.gov/parkhistory/online_books/anthropology74/ce3.htm.

37 "The Harvard Plan That Failed Asian Americans," *Harvard Law Review* 131 (December 2017), https://harvardlawreview.org/2017/12/the-harvard -plan-that-failed-asian-americans/.

38 Plaintiff's Memorandum of Reasons in Support of Its Motion for Summary Judgment, filed June 5, 2018, in *Students for Fair Admissions v. President and Fellows of Harvard College*, https://int.nyt.com/data/documenthelper/43-sffa-memo-for-summary-judgement/1a7a4880cb6a662b3b51/optimized/full.pdf#page=1.

39 Plaintiff's Memorandum of Reasons in Support of Its Motion for Summary Judgment.

40 Plaintiff's Memorandum; see Mike Gonzalez, "Time for Racism at Harvard and Our American Education System to End," *The Hill*, June 18, 2018, https://thehill.com/opinion/education/392765-time-for-racism-at-harvard-and-our-american-education-system-to-end.

41 See the chapter "The New Jews," in Daniel Golden, *The Price of Admission: How America's Ruling Class Buys Its Way into Elite Colleges* (New York: Broadway Books, 2019), 201.

42 Mike Gonzalez, "Affirmative Action in Education Looks an Awful Lot Like Bigotry—Especially to Asian-Americans," *The Hill*, May 1, 2018, https://thehill.com/opinion/education/385687-affirmative-action-in-education-looks-an-awful-lot-like-bigotry-especially.

43 See my analysis of the decision, written with my Heritage colleague Elizabeth Slattery, "A Judge's Wrongheaded Ruling Saves Harvard's Non-Colorblind Admissions Policy," *Daily Signal*, October 3, 2019, https://www.

dailysignalcom/2019/10/03/a-judges-wrongheaded-ruling-saves
-harvards-non-colorblind-admission-policy/.

44 "Demographic Breakdown of New York City Public Schools," 2017–18
school year, New York City Council, https://council.nyc.gov/data/
school-diversity-in-nyc/.

45 Mike Gonzalez, "Why Politicians on the Left Can't Fix What Ails Public
Schools in New York City," *Daily Signal*, March 21, 2019, https://www
.dailysignal.com/2019/03/21/why-politicians-on-the-left-cant-fix-what-ails-
public-schools-in-new-york-city/.

46 Gonzalez, "Why Politicians on the Left Can't Fix What Ails Public Schools
in New York City."

47 Leslie Brody, "Parents Sue New York City Over Mayor's Plan to Diversify
Elite High Schools," *Wall Street Journal*, December 13, 2018, https://www
.wsj.com/articles/parents-sue-city-over-mayors-plan-to-diversify-elite-
high-schools-11544731339.

48 Mike Gonzalez, "'Race-Norming' in a Maryland Public-School District,"
National Review, May 8, 2019, https://www.nationalreview.com/2019/05/
maryland-public-school-district-race-norming-practices/.

49 Gonzalez, "'Race-Norming' in a Maryland Public-School District."

50 Shalini Shankar, "How Indian Americans Came to Dominate the National
Spelling Bee," *Los Angeles Times*, May 30, 2019, https://www.latimes.com/
opinion/op-ed/la-oe-shankar-national-spelling-bee-indian-americans-
20190530-story.html.

51 Yang, "Asian Americans Can Blow Up America's Racial Quota System."

52 Ford Foundation, Grants Database, https://www.fordfoundation.org/work/
our-grants/grants-database/grants-all?minyear=2006&maxyear=2019&pag
e=0&search=%26SearchText%3Dasian%20american%20advancing%
20justice.

53 Bernadette Lim, "'Model Minority' Seems Like a Compliment, but It Does
Great Harm," *New York Times*, October 16, 2015, https://www.nytimes.com
/roomfordebate/2015/10/16/the-effects-of-seeing-asian-americans-as-a
-model-minority/model-minority-seems-like-a-compliment-but-it-does
-great-harm.

54 Kat Chow, "'Model Minority' Myth Again Used as a Racial Wedge Between
Asians and Blacks," *NPR*, April 19, 2017, https://www.npr.org/sections/
codeswitch/2017/04/19/524571669/model-minority-myth-again-used-as-a-
racial-wedge-between-asians-and-blacks.

55 Andrew Sullivan, "Interesting Times" column, April 14, 2017, http://nymag
.com/intelligencer/2017/04/why-do-democrats-feel-sorry-for-hillary
-clinton.html?gtm=top.

CHAPTER 3

1 John Fonte and Mike Gonzalez, "Should Left Wing Activists Like
Linda Sarsour Be Allowed to Divide America through the Census?,"
Daily Signal, August 2, 2017, https://www.dailysignal.com/2017/08/02/
left-wing-activists-like-linda-sarsour-allowed-divide-america-census/.

2   Office of Management and Budget, "Standards for Maintaining, Collecting, and Presenting Federal Data on Race and Ethnicity," Regulations.gov, https://www.regulations.gov/document?D=OMB-2016-0002-0001.

3   For the many references in this chapter to the May 29, 2015, forum at the Census Bureau headquarters in Suitland, Maryland, I rely on the transcript created by the Heritage Foundation. The transcript is available at http://thf _media.s3.amazonaws.com/2017/CensusForumonMENATranscript.pdf (also hyperlinked in Fonte and Gonzalez, second paragraph; see note 1). The videos of the sessions, Forum on Ethnic Groups from the Middle East and North Africa, can be viewed at the website of the Census Bureau, https://www.census.gov/library/working-papers/2015/demo/2015-MENA -Experts.html.

4   Maryam Asi and Daniel Beaulieu, "Arab Households in the United States, 2006–2010," American Community Survey Brief, US Census Bureau, May 2013, https://www2.census.gov/library/publications/2013/acs /acsbr10-20.pdf.

5   Iranian Studies Group, "Iranian-American Community Survey Results," 2005, http://web.mit.edu/isg/survey.htm.

6   Asi and Beaulieu, "Arab Households in the United States, 2006–2010."

7   "A Beginner's Guide to Hijab," Vox, January 24, 2017, https://www.youtube .com/watch?v=DclppILcDcg&feature=youtu.be&t=1m13s&app=desktop.

8   National Iranian American Council, "MENA Category Rejected by Census Bureau Despite Clear Benefits," February 6, 2018, https://www.niacouncil .org/mena-category-rejected-census-bureau-despite-clear-benefits/.

9   Dunia El-Zobaidi, "How Significant Is Rejection of MENA Category from the 2020 US Census?" Arab Weekly, April 3, 2018, https://thearabweekly .com/how-significant-rejection-mena-category-2020-us-census.

10 Ali Harb, "US Census Fails to Add MENA Category: Arabs to Remain 'White' in Count," Middle East Eye, January 27, 2018, https://www .middleeasteye.net/news/us-census-fails-add-mena-category-arabs -remain-white-count.

11 Hansi Lo Wang, "No Middle Eastern or North African Category on 2020 Census, Bureau Says," NPR, January 29, 2018, https://www.npr.org/2018 /01/29/581541111/no-middle-eastern-or-north-african-category-on-2020 -census-bureau-says.

12 Samuel P. Huntington, Who Are We?: The Challenges to America's National Identity (New York: Simon & Schuster, 2004), 303.

13 Mike Gonzalez, "Obama's Last Play for Ethnic Identity Politics," National Review, December 6, 2016, https://www.nationalreview.com/2016/12/ethnic- racial-identity-politics-obama-administration-mena-office-management- budget/.

14 Mike Gonzalez, "Think of America as One People? The Census Begs to Differ," Washington Post, December 2, 2016, https://www.washingtonpost .com/opinions/think-of-america-as-one-people-the-census-begs -to-differ/2016/12/02/e6a93df4-b4eb-11e6-a677-b608fbb3aaf6_story. html?utm_term=.8e51f42fcdcd.

15 Mike Gonzalez, "There Is Time to Reverse Obama Census Proposal That Promotes Group Identity Politics," *Daily Signal,* April 20, 2017, https://www.dailysignal.com/2017/04/20/there-is-time-to-reverse-obama-census-proposal-that-promotes-group-identity-politics/.

16 Casey Kasem, "I Want My Son to Be Proud," Al-Hewar: The Center for Arab Culture and Dialogue, http://www.alhewar.com/CaseyKasem.htm.

17 Jeff Karoub, "Census Bureau May Count Arab-Americans for the First Time in 2020," *PBS NewsHour/*Associated Press, January 30, 2015, https://www.pbs.org/newshour/nation/census-bureau-considering-new-category-arab-americans-2020-count.

18 "History," *Arab American Stories,* http://www.arabamericanstories.org/arab-americans/history/, based on information in the *Arab American Almanac.*

19 See Sarah M. A. Gualtieri, *Between Arab and White: Race and Ethnicity in the Early Syrian American Diaspora* (Berkeley: University of California Press, 2009), 57–58.

20 Office of Management and Budget (OMB), Directive No. 15: Race and Ethnic Standards for Federal Statistics and Administrative Reporting, *Centers for Disease Control and Prevention,* May 12, 1977, https://wonder.cdc.gov/wonder/help/populations/bridged-race/directive15.html.

21 Edmund Burke, "Speech on Conciliation with the Colonies" (1775), in *Fundamental Documents,* chap. 1, doc. 2, *The Founders' Constitution,* http://press-pubs.uchicago.edu/founders/documents/v1ch1s2.html.

22 Alexis de Tocqueville, *Democracy in America,* edited and translated by Harvey C. Mansfield and Delba Winthrop (Chicago: University of Chicago Press, 2002), 2:405–6.

23 Burke, "Speech on Conciliation with the Colonies."

24 Huntington, *Who Are We?,* 94.

25 Huntington, *Who Are We?,* 62.

26 Thomas J. Archdeacon, *Becoming American: An Ethnic History* (New York: Free Press, 1983), 189.

27 Huntington, *Who Are We?,* 96.

28 John Quincy Adams, Letter to Moritz von Furstenwaerther, June 4, 1819, in *Niles' Register,* vol. 18 (April 29, 1820).

29 George Washington, "Letter to the Hebrew Congregation in Newport, Rhode Island," August 18, 1790, *Founders Online,* National Archives, https://founders.archives.gov/documents/Washington/05-06-02-0135.

CHAPTER 4

1 Mallory Millet, "Marxist Feminism's Ruined Lives," *Front Page Mag,* September 1, 2014, https://www.frontpagemag.com/fpm/240037/marxist-feminisms-ruined-lives-mallory-millett.

2 Scott Yenor, "Sex, Gender, and the Origin of the Culture Wars: An Intellectual History," Heritage Foundation report, June 30, 2017, https://www.heritage.org/gender/report/sex-gender-and-the-origin-the-culture-wars-intellectual-history.

3   Interview with Alice Schwarzer, quoted in Yenor, "Sex, Gender, and the Origin of the Culture Wars."

4   Sheila Tobias, *Faces of Feminism: An Activist's Reflections on the Women's Movement* (Boulder, CO: Westview, 1997).

5   Friedrich Engels, *Origin of the Family, Private Property, and the State* (1884), Marx/Engels Internet Archive, 39, 82, 76, 40, https://www.marxists.org/archive/marx/works/download/pdf/origin_family.pdf.

6   Parul Sehgal and Neil Genzlinger, "Kate Millett, Ground-Breaking Feminist Writer, Is Dead at 82," *New York Times*, September 6, 2017, https://www.nytimes.com/2017/09/06/obituaries/kate-millett-influential-feminist-writer-is-dead-at-82.html.

7   Kate Millett, *Sexual Politics* (Garden City, NY: Doubleday, 1970), 111, 120.

8   Millett, *Sexual Politics*, 121.

9   John D. Skrentny, *The Minority Rights Revolution* (Cambridge, MA: Belknap Press of Harvard University Press, 2002), 116, 117–18. In this section I have relied on the author's excellent analysis of the era.

10 Skrentny, *The Minority Rights Revolution*, 117, 118, 130.

11 Skrentny, *The Minority Rights Revolution*, 133, 137, 141. (Note: Skrentny appears to err in attributing the statement to George Shultz rather than to his successor at Labor, James Hodgson.)

12 Skrentny, *The Minority Rights Revolution*, 141, 131.

13 See Influence Watch, "National Organization for Women," 2019, https://www.influencewatch.org/non-profit/national-organization-for-women/.

14 See, e.g., Oren Cass, "The Wage Subsidy: A Better Way to Help the Poor," Manhattan Institute for Policy Research, Issue Brief no. 37, August 2015, https://media4.manhattan-institute.org/pdf/ib_37.pdf.

15 Pew Research Center, "The Decline of Marriage and Rise of New Families," November 18, 2018, https://www.pewsocialtrends.org/2010/11/18/ii-overview/.

16 Discover the Networks, "Karen Nussbaum," https://www.discoverthenetworks.org/individuals/karen-nussbaum/; interview with Karen Nussbaum by Kathleen Banks Nutter, *Voices of Feminism Oral History Project*, Sophia Smith Collection, Smith College, December 18–19, 2003, https://www.smith.edu/libraries/libs/ssc/vof/transcripts/Nussbaum.pdf.

17 Lynn Neary, "A Cup of Ambition and Endurance: 9 to 5 Unites Workers Across Decades," July 11, 2019, https://www.npr.org/2019/07/11/738587297/a-cup-of-ambition-and-endurance-9-to-5-unites-workers-across-decades.

18 Nussbaum interview, *Voices of Feminism Oral History Project*.

19 Yenor, "Sex, Gender, and the Origin of the Culture Wars."

20 Justin Lehmiller, "Gay People Make More Money Than Their Straight Peers," *Vice*, September 14, 2017, https://www.vice.com/en_us/article/59dm4q/gay-people-make-more-money-than-their-straight-peers.

21 Abdel Jimenez, "Cities Around the Country Are Helping LGBT Businesses Get Big-Money Government Contracts—and Chicago Could Be Next,"

Chicago Tribune, June 28, 2019, https://www.chicagotribune.com/business/
ct-biz-lgbt-business-looking-for-inclusion-supplier-program-20190628-
cayxetpwjbbu5n4ldpvx7hgyqm-story.html.

22 Jimenez, "Cities Around the Country Are Helping LGBT Businesses Get
Big-Money Government Contracts."

23 Simone de Beauvoir, *The Second Sex,* translated by H. M. Parshley (New
York: Vintage, 1989), 597.

24 Millett, *Sexual Politics,* 62.

25 Yenor, "Sex, Gender, and the Origin of the Culture Wars."

26 Ryan Anderson, *When Harry Became Sally: Responding to the Transgender
Moment* (New York: Encounter Books, 2018), 153.

27 John Money and Patricia Tucker, *Sexual Signatures: On Being a Man or a
Woman* (Boston: Little, Brown, 1976), 95.

28 Yenor, "Sex, Gender, and the Origin of the Culture Wars." The boy at the
center of Money's famous case, David Reimer, later committed suicide in
his thirties.

29 Anderson, *When Harry Became Sally,* 153.

30 Alexander Pease, "University Investigates Feminist Grad Student For Saying
Men Can't Become Women," *College Fix,* July 12, 2019, https://www
.thecollegefix.com/university-investigates-feminist-grad-student-for
-saying-men-cant-become-women/.

31 Laura Tanner@saltyfemst, Twitter, https://twitter.com/saltyfemst.

32 Ryan Anderson, "The Big Same-Sex Marriage Lie," *Daily News,* May 5, 2013,
https://www.nydailynews.com/opinion/big-same-sex--lie-article-1.1334665

33 Yenor, "Sex, Gender, and the Origin of the Culture Wars."

34 Susan B. Boyd, "Marriage Is More Than Just a Piece of Paper: Feminist
Critiques of Same Sex Marriage," *National Taiwan University Law Review* 8,
no. 2 (2013), 274, https://pdfs.semanticscholar.org/7227/2e445c5147352d1efd2
a595a439c318835f9.pdf.

35 Rachel Shteir, "A Last Interview with Kate Millett," *New Yorker,* September
13, 2017, https://www.newyorker.com/books/page-turner/a-last
-interview-with-kate-millett.

36 Ti-Grace Atkinson, "The Descent from Radical Feminism to
Postmodernism," presentation at the conference "A Revolutionary Moment:
Women's Liberation in the Late 1960s and the Early 1970s," Boston
University, March 27–29, 2014, https://www.bu.edu/wgs/files/2013/10/
Atkinson-The-Descent-from-Radical-Feminism-to-Postmodernism.pdf.

37 American Psychological Association, Division 44, Task Forces: Consensual
Non-Monogamy Task Force, https://www.apadivisions.org/division-44/
leadership/task-forces/.

CHAPTER 5

1 Friedrich Engels, introduction to the 1892 English edition of *Socialism,
Utopian and Scientific,* Marxists.org, https://www.marxists.org/archive/
marx/works/1880/soc-utop/int-hist.htm.

2 Quoted in Loren Balhorn, "Joschka Fischer's Long March," *Jacobin*, March, 23, 2018, https://www.jacobinmag.com/2018/05/joschka-fischers -long-march/.

3 Quoted in Joseph A. Buttigieg, "Subaltern Social Groups in Antonio Gramsci's *Prison Notebooks*," in *The Political Philosophies of Antonio Gramsci and B.R. Ambedkar*, ed. Cosimo Zene (New York: Routledge, 2013), 39.

4 Antonio Gramsci, "Socialism and Culture," in *The Gramsci Reader: Selected Writings 1916–1935*, ed. David Forgacs (New York: New York University Press, 2000), 58, http://ouleft.org/wp-content/uploads/gramsci-reader.pdf.

5 Herbert Marcuse, "Repressive Tolerance," in *A Critique of Pure Tolerance*, by Robert Paul Wolff, Barrington Moore Jr., and Herbert Marcuse (Boston: Beacon Press, 1969), 95–137.

6 Richard Bernstein, "In Dispute on Bias, Stanford Is Likely to Alter Western Culture Program," *New York Times*, January 19, 1988.

7 Engels, "Origin of the Family, Private Property, and the State," 34.

8 Engels, "Origin of the Family, Private Property, and the State," 4, 35, 31.

9 Lauren Kaminsky, "Utopian Visions of Family Life in the Stalin-Era Soviet Union," *Central European History* 44, no. 1 (2011): 63, https://scholar .harvard.edu/files/kaminsky/files/kaminsky_ceh_article.pdf.

10 Anon. [A Woman Resident in Russia], "The Russian Effort to Abolish Marriage," *Atlantic*, July 1926, https://www.theatlantic.com/magazine/ archive/1926/07/the-russian-effort-to-abolish-marriage/306295/.

11 Karl Marx to Sigfrid Meyer and August Vogt, in *Letters of Karl Marx* (1870), https://www.marxists.org/archive/marx/works/1870/letters/70_04_09.htm. (Italics in the original.)

12 John Fonte, "Why There Is a Culture War," *Policy Review*, December 1, 2000, https://www.hoover.org/research/why-there-culture-war.

13 E. J. Hobsbawm, Introduction, in *The Gramsci Reader*, 13.

14 See the "Chronological Outline" in *The Gramsci Reader*, 21.

15 Gramsci, "Political Ideologies," in *The Gramsci Reader*, 196.

16 Gramsci, "Ethical or Cultural State," in *The Gramsci Reader*, 234.

17 Gramsci, "Some Theoretical and Practical Aspects of 'Economism,'" in *The Gramsci Reader*, 211.

18 Gramsci, "Notes for an Introduction and an Approach to the Study of Philosophy and the History of Culture," in *The Gramsci Reader*, 334.

19 Gramsci, Letter to the Central Committee of the Soviet Communist Party, in *The Gramsci Reader*, 170.

20 Gramsci, "Internationalism and National Policy," in *The Gramsci Reader*, 231.

21 David Forgacs, "Introduction to the Art and Science of Politics," in *The Gramsci Reader*, 223–24.

22 Antonio Gramsci, *Pre-Prison Writings*, ed. Richard Bellamy (Cambridge: Cambridge University Press, 1994), xvi, 10.

23 Gramsci, "Note for an Introduction and an Approach to the Study of Philosophy and the History of Culture," in *The Gramsci Reader*, 325.

24 Fonte, "Why There Is a Culture War."

25 Martin Jay, *The Dialectical Imagination: A History of the Frankfurt School and the Institute of Social Research, 1923–1950* (Berkeley: University of California Press, 1996), 3.

26 Max Horkheimer, quoted in *Foundations of the Frankfurt School of Social Research*, ed. Judith T. Marcus and Zoltan Tar (New Brunswick, NJ: Transaction Books, 1984), 74.

27 Jay, *The Dialectical* Imagination, 20.

28 Max Horkheimer and Theodor W. Adorno, *Dialectic of Enlightenment: Philosophical Fragments*, ed. Gunzelin Schmid Noerr, trans. Edmund Jephcott (Stanford, CA: Stanford University Press, 2002), 67.

29 Horkheimer and Adorno, *Dialectic of Enlightenment*, 126.

30 Horkheimer and Adorno, *Dialectic of Enlightenment*, 106.

31 Horkheimer and Adorno, *Dialectic of Enlightenment*, 110.

32 Marcuse, *One-Dimensional Man*, 9.

33 John Bew, review of *Secret Reports on Nazi Germany: The Frankfurt School Contribution to the War Effort,* by Franz Neumann, Herbert Marcuse, and Otto Kirchheimer, ed. Raffaele Laudani (Princeton, NJ: Princeton University Press, 2013), *New Statesman America*, August 22, 2013, https://www.newstatesman.com/culture/2013/08/secret-reports-nazi-germany-neumann-marcuse-and-kircheimer-possible-patterns-german-.

34 Gramsci, "The Problem of Political Leadership in the Formation and Development of the Modern State in Italy," in *The Gramsci Reader*, 258.

35 Roger Kimball, "Some Perils of Sexual Liberation," *New Criterion*, January 26, 2005, https://www.newcriterion.com/blogs/dispatch/some-perils-of-sexual-liberation.

36 Marcuse, *One-Dimensional Man*, 251–52.

37 Marcuse, *One-Dimensional Man*, 256.

38 Marcuse, *One-Dimensional Man*, 12.

39 Marcuse, *One-Dimensional Man*, 256–57.

40 Marcuse, *One-Dimensional Man*, 21.

41 Marcuse, *One-Dimensional Man*, 57.

42 Louis Hartz, *The Liberal Tradition in America: An Interpretation of American Political Thought Since the Revolution* (New York: Harcourt, Brace, 1955), 9.

43 Herbert Marcuse, *Eros and Civilization: A Philosophical Inquiry into Freud* (Boston: Beacon Press, 1955), xv.

44 Marcuse, *Eros and Civilization*, 201.

45 Victor Gaetan, "Presidential Election Was Major Setback for Cultural Marxism's Hegemony," *Washington Examiner*, December 6, 2016, https://www.washingtonexaminer.com/presidential-election-was-major-setback-for-cultural-marxisms-hegemony.

46 Marcuse, "Repressive Tolerance," 120.

47 Marcuse, "Repressive Tolerance," 120.

48 Bill Moyers, "Second Thoughts: Reflections on the Great Society," *New Perspectives Quarterly* 4 (Winter 1987).

49 "Angela Davis on Protest, 1968, and Her Old Teacher, Herbert Marcuse," *Literary Hub*, April 3, 2019, https://lithub.com/angela-davis-on-protest -1968-and-her-old-teacher-herbert-marcuse/.

50 Haley Smith, "Angela Davis Proclaims She's a 'Lifelong Communist,' Audience Erupts in Applause," *New Guard*, Young America's Foundation, May 31, 2016, https://www.yaf.org/news/angela-davis-speaks-at-csula/.

51 Quoted in Vijay Prashad, *Everybody Was Kung Fu Fighting: Afro-Asian Connections and the Myth of Cultural Politics* (Boston: Beacon Press, 2001), 63.

52 Kara Peters, "Civil Rights Activist Angela Davis Speaks at the Paramount Theater," *Cavalier Daily*, March 29, 2018, https://www .cavalierdaily.com/article/2018/03/civil-rights-activist-angela-davis-speaks -at-the-paramount-theater.

53 Marcuse, "Repressive Tolerance," 100.

54 "Rudi Dutschke and the German Student Movement in 1968," *Socialist Worker*, April 29, 2008, https://socialistworker.co.uk/art/14460/Rudi%20 Dutschke%20and%20the%20German%20student%20movement%20in%20 1968.

55 Herbert Marcuse, *Counterrevolution and Revolt* (Boston: Beacon Press, 1972), 55.

56 Herbert Marcuse, *Marxism, Revolution and Utopia*, vol. 6, *Collected Papers of Herbert Marcuse*, ed. Douglas Kellner and Clayton Pierce (Abingdon, Oxon, UK, and New York: Routledge, 2014), 336.

57 Charles Edward Merriam, *A History of American Political Theories* (New York: Macmillan, 1903), 305.

58 Merriam, *A History of American Political Theories*, 310, 313.

59 Peoria Project, "The Rise of Modern Progressivism: Charles Merriam's 'Recent Tendencies' in American Political Thought (1903)," https:// peoriaproject.com/progressivism/recent-tendencies/.

60 Kim R. Holmes, *The Closing of the Liberal Mind: How Groupthink and Intolerance Define the Left* (New York: Encounter Books, 2016), 225, 224.

61 Jay, *The Dialectical Imagination*, 44, 46, 42.

62 Friedrich Nietzsche, *The Genealogy of Morals* (Mineola, NY: Dover, 2003), 11.

63 Jay, *The Dialectical Imagination*, 63.

64 Helen Pluckrose, "How French 'Intellectuals' Ruined the West: Postmodernism and Its Impact, Explained," *Areo*, March 27, 2017, https:// areomagazine.com/2017/03/27/how-french-intellectuals-ruined-the-west -postmodernism-and-its-impact-explained/.

65 Jean-François Lyotard, *The Postmodern Condition: A Report on Knowledge*, translated by Geoff Bennington and Brian Massumi (Minneapolis: University of Minnesota Press, 1984), xxiv.

66 Jamelle Bouie, "The Enlightenment's Dark Side," *Slate*, June 6, 2018, https://slate.com/news-and-politics/2018/06/taking-the-enlightenment-seriously-requires-talking-about-race.html.

67 Alan Sokal and Jean Bricmont, *Fashionable Nonsense: Postmodern Intellectuals' Abuse of Science* (New York, Picador USA, 1998), 124.

68 Pluckrose, "How French 'Intellectuals' Ruined the West."

69 Pluckrose, "How French 'Intellectuals' Ruined the West."

70 Pluckrose, "How French 'Intellectuals' Ruined the West."

71 Holmes, *The Closing of the Liberal* Mind, 48. (Italics in the original.)

72 Holmes, *The Closing of the Liberal Mind*, 39.

73 Kimberlé Crenshaw, "Mapping the Margins: Intersectionality, Identity Politics, and Violence Against Women of Color," *Stanford Law Review* 43, no. 6 (1991): 1241–99.

74 Carmen Samora, "Los Tres Grandes."

75 Heather Mac Donald, "The Billions of Dollars that Made Things Worse," *City Journal* (Autumn 1996), https://www.city-journal.org/html/billions-dollars-made-things-worse-12159.html.

76 Letter of Resignation by Henry Ford II, Philanthropy Roundtable, https://www.philanthropyroundtable.org/home/resources/donor-intent/donor-intent-resource-library/when-philanthropy-goes-wrong/the-ford-foundation-and-safe-guarding-donor-intent/letter-of-resignation-by-henry-ford-ii.

77 Mario T. García, *Memories of Chicano History: The Life and Narrative of Bert Corona* (Berkeley: University of California Press, 1994), 126.

78 Burt, "The Power of a Mobilized Citizenry and Coalition Politics," 427, 431, 428.

79 García, *Mexican Americans*, 146.

80 "Playboy Interview: Saul Alinsky."

81 Shana Bernstein, *Bridges of Reform: Interracial Civil Rights Activism in Twentieth-Century Los Angeles* (Oxford: Oxford University Press, 2011), 158.

CHAPTER 6

1 John B. Judis and Ruy Teixeira, *The Emerging Democratic Majority* (New York: Scribner, 2002), 2.

2 Judis and Teixeira, *The Emerging Democratic Majority,* 59.

3 John Judis, "Why the Left Will (Eventually) Triumph: An Interview with Ruy Teixeira," *Talking Points Memo*, April 28, 2017, https://talkingpointsmemo.com/cafe/why-left-will-eventually-win-ruy-teixeira.

4 Ruy Teixeira, "Could America's Democrats be 'Corbynised'?," *UnHerd*, October 8, 2018, https://unherd.com/2018/10/americas-democrats-corbynised/.

5 Rob Griffin, William H. Frey, and Ruy Teixeira, "States of Change: How Demographic Change Is Transforming the Republican and Democratic Parties," June 2019, https://www.americanprogress.org/issues/democracy/reports/2019/06/27/471487/states-of-change-3/.

6 Griffin, Frey, and Teixeira, "States of Change."

7 Griffin, Frey, and Teixeira, "States of Change."

8 Ruy Teixeira, "The Emerging Democratic Majority Turns 10," *Atlantic*, November 9, 2012, https://www.theatlantic.com/politics/archive/2012/11/the-emerging-democratic-majority-turns-10/265005/.

9 Stephen Hawkins, Daniel Yudkin, Miriam Juan-Torres, and Tim Dixon, *Hidden Tribes: A Study of America's Polarized Landscape* (New York: More in Common, 2018), 10, https://hiddentribes.us/pdf/hidden_tribes_report.pdf.

10 Hawkins et al., *Hidden Tribes*, 30.

11 "Jorge Ramos Denuncia Hispanos 'Totalmente Identifiicados' con EEUU," *MRC NewsBusters*, November 21, 2018, https://www.newsbusters.org/blogs/latino/mrc-latino-staff/2018/11/21/jorge-ramos-denuncia-hispanos-totalmente-identificados-con.

12 Claude Nicolet, *The World of the Citizen in Republican Rome*, translated by P. S. Falla (Berkeley: University of California Press, 1980), 50.

13 Richard Alba, "The Likely Persistence of a White Majority: How Census Bureau Statistics Have Misled Thinking about the American Future," *American Prospect* (Winter 2016), https://prospect.org/civil-rights/likely-persistence-white-majority/.

14 National Advisory Committee on Racial, Ethnic and Other Populations Fall Meeting, November 1–2, 2018, https://www.census.gov/about/cac/nac/meetings/2018-11-meeting.html.

15 Edwin Meese III and Mike Gonzalez, "Trump Can Help Overcome Identity Politics," *Wall Street Journal*, February 27, 2018, https://www.wsj.com/articles/trump-can-help-overcome-identity-politics-1519772254.

16 David A. Hollinger, *Postethnic America: Beyond Multiculturalism*, 10th anniversary ed. (New York: Basic Books, 2005), 235.

17 Alice Robbin, "The Politics of Representation in the US National Statistical System: Origins of Minority Population Interest Group Participation," *Journal of Government Information* 27, no. 4 (2000): 443, 446, https://repository.arizona.edu/bitstream/handle/10150/105405/RobbinPoliticsOfRepresentationJGI2000.pdf?sequence=1&isAllowed=y.

18 Alba, The Likely Persistence of a White Majority."

19 G. Cristina Mora and Michael Rodríguez-Muñiz, "A Response to Richard Alba's 'The Likely Persistence of a White Majority,'" *New Labor Forum*, April 2017, https://newlaborforum.cuny.edu/2017/04/28/a-response-to-richard-albas-the-likely-persistence-of-a-white-majority/.

20 Mora and Rodríguez-Muñiz, "A Response to Richard Alba's 'The Likely Persistence of a White Majority.'"

21 Brian Duncan and Stephen J. Trejo, "Who Remains Mexican? Selective Ethnic Attrition and the Intergenerational Progress of Mexican Americans," in *Latinos and the Economy: Integration and Impact in Schools, Labor Markets, and Beyond*, ed. David L. Leal and Stephen J. Trejo (New York: Springer, 2011), 291.

22 Gleason, "Minorities (Almost) All," 392.

23 Gleason, "Minorities (Almost) All."

24 Louis Wirth, "The Problem of Minority Groups," in *The Science of Man in the World Crisis*, ed. Ralph Linton (New York: Columbia University Press, 1945), 347, 353.

25 Gleason, "Minorities (Almost) All," 399.

26 Gleason, "Minorities (Almost) All," 403.

27 Meese and Gonzalez, "Trump Can Help Overcome Identity Politics."

28 Skrentny, *The Minority Rights Revolution*, 353.

29 Nathan Glazer, "Reflections on Race, Hispanicity, and Ancestry in the U.S. Census," in *The New Race Question: How the Census Counts Multiracial Individuals*, ed. Joel Perlmann and Mary C. Waters (New York: Russell Sage Foundation, 2002), 319.

30 Robbin, "The Politics of Representation in the US National Statistical System," 433.

31 For an example of this type of grousing, see Anna Holmes, "Has 'Diversity' Lost Its Meaning?," *New York Times Magazine*, October 27, 2015, https://www.nytimes.com/2015/11/01/magazine/has-diversity-lost-its-meaning.html, in which she writes, "It's almost as if cheerfully and frequently uttering the word 'diversity' is the equivalent of doing the work of actually making it a reality."

32 Rachel F. Moran, "*Bakke*'s Lasting Legacy: Redefining the Landscape of Equality and Liberty in Civil Rights Law," *UC Davis Law Review* 52 (2019): 2585, https://lawreview.law.ucdavis.edu/issues/52/5/Symposium/52-5_Moran.pdf.

33 *Bakke*, 438 U.S. at 295–96.

34 *Bakke* 438 U.S. at 267.

35 *Bakke* 438 U.S. at 407.

36 McGeorge Bundy, "The Issue Before the Court: Who Gets Ahead in America?," *Atlantic*, November 1977, https://www.theatlantic.com/past/docs/unbound/flashbks/affact/bundyf.htm.

37 *Grutter v. Bollinger*, 539 U.S. 306, at 343 (2003), https://www.law.cornell.edu/supct/html/02-241.ZO.html.

38 Karen Ferguson, *Top Down: The Ford Foundation, Black Power, and the Reinvention of Racial Liberalism* (Philadelphia: University of Pennsylvania Press, 2013), 80, 7.

39 It is worth noting that Bundy was not alone in reacting this way. In the wake of the Detroit riots, Governor George Romney co-founded a new organization called "New Detroit," which funded black nationalists and other radicals with extremely little support among black Americans—seemingly as a form of "riot insurance." According to research by Jake Klein of the Capital Research Center, New Detroit produced a school curriculum that contained for the first time the notion that racism had to include both prejudice and power.

40 Ferguson, *Top Down*, 81, 82.

41 Ford Foundation, Annual Report, 1968, 6, https://www.fordfoundation.org/media/2438/1968-annual-report.pdf.

42 Ferguson, *Top Down*, 18.

43 Skrentny, *The Minority Rights Revolution*, 5.

44 Skrentny, *The Minority Rights Revolution*, 5.

45 Ferguson, *Top Down*, 69–70.

46 Hugh Davis Graham, *Collision Course: The Strange Convergence of Affirmative Action and Immigration Policy in America* (Oxford and New York: Oxford University Press, 2002), 31.

47 *Bakke* 438 U.S. at 400, separate opinion of Marshall.

48 Kenan Malik, "The Failure of Multiculturalism: Community Versus Society in Europe," *Foreign Affairs*, March/April 2015, https://www.foreignaffairs.com/articles/western-europe/2015-02-18/failure-multiculturalism.

49 Ferguson, *Top Down*, 78.

50 Richard Delgado and Jean Stefancic, *Critical Race Theory: An Introduction*, 3rd ed. (New York: New York University Press, 2017), 27.

51 Linda Chavez, *Out of the Barrio: Toward a New Politics of Hispanic Assimilation* (New York: Basic Books, 1991), 170.

52 Shana Bernstein, "Interracial Activism in the Los Angeles Community Service Organization: Linking the World War II and Civil Rights Eras," *Pacific Historical Review* 80, no. 2 (2011): 231–67.

53 Henry Jones Ford, *The Scotch-Irish in America* (Princeton, NJ: Princeton University Press, 1915), 291.

54 Michael Hirsh, "Southernism Triumphs in the National Dialogue," *Newsweek*, April 24, 2008, https://www.newsweek.com/southernism-triumphs-national-dialogue-85827.

55 Benjamin Franklin, *Autobiography and Other Writings*, ed. Ormond Seavey (Oxford and New York: Oxford University Press, 1999), 251–52.

56 Benjamin Franklin to Peter Collinson, May 9, 1753, *Founders Online*, National Archives, https://founders.archives.gov/documents/Franklin/01-04-02-0173.

57 Duncan Moench, "Anti-German Hysteria and the Making of the 'Liberal Society,'" *American Political Thought* 7, no. 1 (2018): 90, 92, 93, https://www.journals.uchicago.edu/doi/pdfplus/10.1086/695645.

58 Moench, "Anti-German Hysteria and the Making of the 'Liberal Society,'" 96.

59 Moench, "Anti-German Hysteria and the Making of the "'Liberal Society,'" 97.

60 Mikkel Thorup, *The Total Enemy: Six Chapters of a Violent Idea* (Eugene, OR: Pickwick, 2015), 28, 27.

61 Moench, "Anti-German Hysteria and the Making of the 'Liberal Society,'" 97.

62 Meredith Mason Brown, *Touching America's History: From the Pequot War through World War II* (Bloomington: Indiana University Press, 2013), 131.

63 Woodrow Wilson, Flag Day Address, June 14, 1917, in *Selected Addresses and Public Papers of Woodrow Wilson*, ed. Albert Hart (New York: Modern Library, 1918), 211, 216.

64 Moench, "Anti-German Hysteria and the Making of the 'Liberal Society,'" 112.

65 Moench, "Anti-German Hysteria and the Making of the 'Liberal Society,'" 86.

66 Moench, "Anti-German Hysteria and the Making of the 'Liberal Society,'" 104.

67 Moench, "Anti-German Hysteria and the Making of the 'Liberal Society,'" 105.

68 Quoted in Theodore Roosevelt, "True Americanism," *The Forum*, April 1894, Teaching American History, http://teachingamericanhistory.org/library/document/true-americanism-the-forum-magazine/.

69 Gutiérrez, *Walls and Mirrors*, 168.

70 See John David Skrentny, *The Ironies of Affirmative Action: Politics, Culture, and Justice in America* (Chicago: University of Chicago Press, 1996); and Graham, *Collision Course*, 137–38.

71 Judis, "Why the Left Will (Eventually) Triumph: An Interview with Ruy Teixeira."

CHAPTER 7

1 Susan Edelman, Selim Algar, and Aaron Feis, "Richard Carranza Held 'White-Supremacy Culture' Training for School Administrators," *New York Post*, May 20, 2019, https://nypost.com/2019/05/20/richard-carranza-held-doe-white-supremacy-culture-training/.

2 Mike Gonzalez, "Carranza's Ideology Insults the People He Claims to Help," *New York Post*, June 17, 2019, https://nypost.com/2019/06/17/carranzas-ideology-insults-the-people-he-claims-to-help/.

3 Delgado and Stefancic, *Critical Race Theory*, 3, 20.

4 Ny Magee, "'Racial Equity' Training Workshops at NYC Public Schools Angering Parents and Teachers," *The Grio*, May 28, 2019, https://thegrio.com/2019/05/28/racial-equity-training-nyc-public-schools/.

5 Iris Marion Young, *Justice and the Politics of Difference* (Princeton, NJ: Princeton University Press, 1990), 122.

6 Delgado and Stefancic, *Critical Race Theory*, 27.

7 Isaac West, "Wedding Cakes, Equality, and Rhetorics of Religious Freedom," *First Amendment Studies* 53, no. 12 (2019).

8 Julian Savulesco and Udo Schuklenk, "Doctors Have No Right to Refuse Medical Assistance in Dying, Abortion or Contraception," *Bioethics*, September 22, 2016, https://onlinelibrary.wiley.com/doi/full/10.1111/bioe.12288.

9 Adam Liptak, "How Conservatives Weaponized the First Amendment," *New York Times*, June 30, 2018, https://www.nytimes.com/2018/06/30/us/politics/first-amendment-conservatives-supreme-court.html.

10 Delgado and Stefancic, *Critical Race Theory*, 34.

11 Louis Michael Seidman, "Can Free Speech Be Progressive?," Georgetown University Law Center, 2018, 1, 11, https://scholarship.law.georgetown.edu/cgi/viewcontent.cgi?article=3056&context=facpub.

12 *Federalist* No. 10, Bill of Rights Institute, https://billofrightsinstitute.org/founding-documents/primary-source-documents/the-federalist-papers/federalist-papers-no-10/#targetText=Federalist%20No.%2010%20(1787), be%20unresponsive%20to%20the%20people.

13 Joshua Mitchell, "The Identity-Politics Death Grip," *City Journal*, Autumn 2017, https://www.city-journal.org/html/identity-politics-death-grip-15500.html.

14 Delgado and Stefancic, *Critical Race Theory*, 29.

15 Art Tavana, "Dave Chappelle Punches Up," *Arc*, September 3, 2019, https://arcdigital.media/dave-chappelle-punches-up-55dfe906efb8.

16 Lyle Denniston, "Has the First Amendment Been 'Weaponized'?," *Constitution Daily*, June 27, 2018, https://constitutioncenter.org/blog/has-the-first-amendment-been-weaponized.

17 People for the American Way Foundation, "Who Is Weaponizing Religious Liberty?," 2016, http://www.pfaw.org/report/who-is-weaponizing-religious-liberty/.

18 Adam Rubenstein, "Steven Pinker: Identity Politics Is 'An Enemy of Reason and Enlightenment Values,'" *Washington Examiner*, February 15, 2018, https://www.washingtonexaminer.com/weekly-standard/steven-pinker-identity-politics-is-an-enemy-of-reason-and-enlightenment-values.

19 Yoram Hazony, "Conservative Democracy: Liberal Principles Have Brought Us to a Dead End," *First Things*, January 2019, https://www.firstthings.com/article/2019/01/conservative-democracy.

20 Patrick J. Deneen, *Why Liberalism Failed* (New Haven, CT: Yale University Press, 2018), 3, 60, 46.

21 Joseph Hogan, "The Problems with Liberalism: Q&A with Patrick Deneen," *The Nation*, May 28, 2018, https://www.thenation.com/article/the-problems-of-liberalism-a-qa-with-patrick-deneen/.

22 William A. Galston, "Populism's Challenge to Democracy," *Wall Street Journal*, March 16, 2018, https://www.wsj.com/articles/populisms-challenge-to-democracy-1521239697.

23 George Packer, "When the Culture War Comes for the Kids," *Atlantic*, October 2019, https://www.theatlantic.com/magazine/archive/2019/10/when-the-culture-war-comes-for-the-kids/596668/.

24 *Plessy v. Ferguson*, 163 U.S. 537 at 559 (1896), Harlan dissenting, https://www.law.cornell.edu/supremecourt/text/163/537#writing-USSC_CR_0163_0537_ZD.

25 110 Cong. Rec. 7420 (1964).

26 Philip Bump, "3 In 10 Strong Trump Supporters Accept or Are Indifferent to White Supremacist Views," *Washington Post*, August 22, 2017, https://www.washingtonpost.com/news/politics/wp/2017/08/22/3-in-10-strong-trump-supporters-accept-or-are-indifferent-to-white-supremacist-views/.

27 Heather Mac Donald, "Trump Isn't the One Dividing Us by Race," *Wall Street Journal*, August 18, 2019, https://www.wsj.com/articles/trump-isnt-the-one-dividing-us-by-race-11566158729.

28 Arthur M. Schlesinger Jr., *The Disuniting of America: Reflections on a Multicultural Society* (New York: Norton, 1998), 23, 13.

29 Bradley Campbell and Jason Manning, "Microaggression and Moral Cultures," *Comparative Sociology* 13, no. 6 (2014): 5, 31–32, https://www.researchgate.net/publication/272408166_Microaggression_and_Moral_Cultures.

30 Campbell and Manning, "Microaggression and Moral Cultures," 9, 10.

31 Campbell and Manning, "Microaggression and Moral Cultures," 22.

32 Delgado and Stefancic, *Critical Race Theory*, 63–64.

33 John Stuart Mill, *Considerations on Representative Government*, in *The Collected Works of John Stuart Mill*, vol. 19, *Essays on Politics and Society* part 2, ed. John M. Robson (Toronto: University of Toronto Press, London: Routledge and Kegan Paul, 1977), https://oll.libertyfund.org/titles/234.

34 Alberto Alesina, Arnaud Devleeschauwer, William Easterly et al., "Fractionalization," NBER Working Paper No. 9411 (2002), 4, 10–11, 14, 8, https://www.nber.org/papers/w9411.

35 Huntington, *Who Are We?*, 145.

CHAPTER 8

1 Michael Gonzalez, "What Clinton Is Sending Elian Back To," *Wall Street Journal*, January 10, 2000, https://www.wsj.com/articles/SB947440605327927474.

2 Huntington, *Who Are We?*, xvii.

3 Holmes, *The Closing of the Liberal Mind*, 13.

4 Burke, "Speech on Conciliation with the Colonies."

5 Burke, "Speech on Conciliation with the Colonies."

6 Archdeacon, *Becoming American*, 12.

7 See Gad Horowitz, "Notes on 'Conservatism, Liberalism, and Socialism in Canada,'" *Canadian Journal of Political Science* 11, no. 2 (1978): 383–99, https://www.jstor.org/stable/pdf/3230784.pdf.

8 Frances Fox Piven and Richard A. Cloward, "The Weight of the Poor: A Strategy to End Poverty," *The Nation*, May 2, 1966, https://www.thenation.com/article/weight-poor-strategy-end-poverty/.

9 George La Noue, "Defining Social and Economic Disadvantage: Are Government Preferential Business Certification Programs Narrowly Tailored?," *University of Maryland Law Journal of Race, Religion, Gender and Class* 12, no. 2 (2012): 274.

10 Congressional Research Service, "Survey of Federal Laws Containing Goals, Set-Asides, Priorities, or Other Preferences Based on Race, Gender, or Ethnicity," R41038 (April 14, 2011), https://www.everycrsreport.com/reports/R41038.html.

11 Mike Gonzalez and Hans von Spakovsky, "Eliminating Identity Politics from the U.S. Census," Heritage Backgrounder, Heritage Foundation report, June 29, 2018, https://www.heritage.org/government-regulation/report/eliminating-identity-politics-the-us-census.

12 Hans von Spakovsky, Elizabeth Slattery, and Roger Clegg, "What Congress Can Do to Stop Racial Discrimination," Heritage Foundation report, April 7, 2014, https://www.heritage.org/civil-rights/report/what-congress-can-do-stop-racial-discrimination. For many of the recommendations I mention here, I am indebted to the authors of this report.

13 Gail L. Heriot, "It's Time for the Executive Branch to Conduct a 'Disparate Impact Inventory': Remarks at the Federalist Society's Sixth Annual Executive Branch Review, April 17, 2018," San Diego Legal Studies Paper No. 18–347, https://papers.ssrn.com/sol3/papers.cfm?abstract_id=3179766.

14 Abigail Thernstrom, "Redistricting, Race, and the Voting Rights Act," *National Affairs* 3 (Spring 2010), https://www.nationalaffairs.com/publications/detail/redistricting-race-and-the-voting-rights-act.

15 See Douglas Amy's "Proportional Representation: Empowering Minorities or Promoting Balkanization?," *Good Society* 5, no. 2 (1995): 22–24, on the work that Lani Guinier and others have undertaken on this front.

16 Alesina et al., "Fractionalization," 8.

17 Sean A. Pager, "Who's In and Who's Out? Confronting the 'Who Question' in Affirmative Action: Can We Learn from India's Answer?," Indiana Legal Studies Research Paper No. 50 (March 12, 2006), https://ssrn.com/abstract=890317.

18 Danny Wicentowski, "St. Louis Decertifies 5 Firms That Claimed Cherokee Ancestry to get Minority Contracts," *Riverfront Times*, July 2, 2019, https://www.riverfronttimes.com/newsblog/2019/07/02/st-louis-decertifies-5-firms-that-claimed-cherokee-ancestry-to-get-minority-contracts.

19 Mora, *Making Hispanics*, 5.

20 Pager, "Who's In and Who's Out?"

21 *Adarand Constructors, Inc. v. Peña*, 515 U.S. 200, at 239 (1995), Scalia concurring.

22 Pager, "Who's In and Who's Out?"

23 National Center for Education Statistics, *Digest of Education Statistics*, Table 214.10, for years 2016–17, https://nces.ed.gov/programs/digest/d18/tables/dt18_214.10.asp; US Department of Education, "The Federal Role in Education," https://www2.ed.gov/about/overview/fed/role.html.

24 National Center for Education Statistics, "Fast Facts: Educational Institutions," https://nces.ed.gov/fastfacts/display.asp?id=84.

25 Jay Schalin, *The Politicization of University Schools of Education: The Long March through the Education Schools*, James G. Martin Center for Academic Renewal, February 2019, 33, 34, https://www.jamesgmartin.center/2019/02/schools-of-education/.

26 Schalin, *The Politicization of University Schools of Education*, 49.

27 *The 1619 Project*, https://www.nytimes.com/interactive/2019/08/14/magazine/1619-america-slavery.html.

28 See Rich Lowry, "Historians Roast the 1619 Project," *National Review*, January 3, 2020, https://www.nationalreview.com/2020/01/1619-project-top-historians-criticize-new-york-times-slavery-feature/; and see the letter to the *New York Times* from five historians critiquing the *1619 Project*, with a response by the *Times* editor in chief, https://www.nytimes.com/2019/12/20/magazine/we-respond-to-the-historians-who-critiqued-the-1619-project.html.

29 See Paul Kengor, "Debunking Howard Zinn's Amerikkka" (on the 2019 book by Mary Grabar, *Debunking Howard Zinn*), in *American Spectator*, September 1, 2019, https://spectator.org/debunking-howard-zinns-amerikkka/.

30 Pat Guild, "The Culture/Learning Style Connection," *Educational Leadership* 51, no. 8 (1994), http://www.ascd.org/publications/educational-leadership/may94/vol51/num08/The-Culture~Learning-Style-Connection.aspx.

31 Cleveland Hayes and Brenda Juarez, "There's No Culturally Responsive Teaching Spoken Here: A Critical Race Perspective," *Democracy and Education Journal* 20, no. 1 (2011), https://democracyeducationjournal.org/home/vol20/iss1/1/.

32 Monica Disare, "Funding for New York City Homeless Students, Universal Literacy in de Blasio's executive Budget," *Chalkbeat*, April 25, 2018, https://www.chalkbeat.org/posts/ny/2018/04/26/funding-for-new-york-city-homeless-students-universal-literacy-in-de-blasios-executive-budget/.

33 Schalin, *The Politicization of University Schools of Education*, 95.

34 See Patrick J. Wolf, "Civics Exam: Schools of Choice Boost Civic Values," *Education Next* 7, no. 3 (2007), https://www.educationnext.org/civics-exam/.

35 Scott Jaschik, "The Governor's Bad List," *Inside Higher Ed*, July 17, 2013, https://www.insidehighered.com/news/2013/07/17/e-mails-reveal-mitch-daniels-governor-tried-ban-howard-zinn-book.

36 William Bennett, Education 20/20 Speaker Series, Hoover Institution, Washington, DC, June 13, 2019, https://www.hoover.org/events/education-2020-speaker-series-william-bennett.

37 Robert Pondiscio, "Classroom Content: A Conservative Conundrum," in *The Not-So-Great Society*, ed. Lindsey Burke and Jonathan Butcher (Washington, DC: Heritage Foundation, 2019), 113.

38 Bennett, Education 20/20 Speaker Series.

39 Milikh, Arthur, "Do America's Universities Undermine the Public Good?," in *The Not-So-Great Society*, ed. Lindsey Burke and Jonathan Butcher (Washington, DC: Heritage Foundation, 2019), 131.

40 Milton Friedman, "The Economy and You: What Lies Ahead" *Stanford Magazine* (Fall/Winter 1977), 7, http://miltonfriedman.hoover.org/friedman_images/Collections/2016c21/Stanford_09_01_1977.pdf.

41 Hawkins et al., *Hidden Tribes*, 138.

Index